Studies in Socialist Pedagogy

D0915824

Studies
in
Socialist Pedagogy

......

Edited by Theodore Mills Norton
and Bertell Ollman

Monthly Review Press
New York and London

Library of Congress Cataloging in Publication Data
Main entry under title:
Studies in socialist pedagogy.
Bibliography: p. 367
1. Socialism and education—Addresses, essays, lectures. 2. Social-
ism—Study and teaching—Addresses, essays, lectures. I. Norton,
Theodore Mills. II. Ollman, Bertell.
LC1030.S73   335'.007   77-91734
ISBN 0-85345-440-X

Monthly Review Press
62 West 14th Street, New York, N.Y. 10011
47 Red Lion Street, London WC1R 4PF

10 9 8 7 6 5 4 3 2 1

Contents

4   Contents

Part IV
Toward Socialist Relations in the Classroom

Part V
Letters from Socialist Teachers

Part VI
Teaching Materials

ACKNOWLEDGMENTS

The editors would like to thank the following publishers and individuals for permission to reprint previously published material.

Antonio Gramsci, "In Search of the Educational Principle," from *Prison Notebooks*. Copyright © 1971 by Quintin Hoare and Geoffrey Nowell-Smith. Reprinted by permission of Lawrence and Wishart, London. *Paulo Freire*, Chapter 2 from *Pedagogy of the Oppressed*. Copyright © 1970 by Paulo Freire. Reprinted by permission of Seabury Press. *Leo Huberman*, "How to Spread the Word," from *Monthly Review*, December 1967. Copyright © 1967 by Monthly Review. Reprinted by permission of Monthly Review, Inc. *John McDermott*, "Campus Missionaries: The Laying on of Culture," from *The Nation*, March 1969. Reprinted by permission of the author. *Ira Shor*, "The Working Class Goes to College," a revised version of an article that originally appeared as "Community Colleges: Slightly Higher Education" in *Liberation*, May/June 1974. Copyright © 1974 by *Liberation* and reprinted by permission. *Michael Meeropol*, "A Radical Teaching a Straight Principles of Economics Course," a revised version of an article published in *Essays Presented to Thornton W. Merriam*. Copyright © 1974 *Review of Radical Economics*. Reprinted by permission of The Union for Radical Political Economics. *Louis Kampf*, "A Course on Spectator Sports" from *College English*, April 1977. Copyright © 1977 by the National Council of Teachers of English. Reprinted by permission. *Ira Shor*, "No More Teacher's Dirty Looks: Conceptual Teaching from the Bottom Up," from *College English*, March 1977. Copyright © 1977 by the National Council of Teachers of English. Reprinted by permission. *David Jhirad and Al Weinrub*, "Action and Reaction: Teaching Physics in Context," from *Science for the People*, September 1972. Reprinted by permission. *Bertell Ollman*, "On Teaching Marxism," from *The Insurgent Sociologist*, Summer 1976. Reprinted by permission. *Martin Sklar*, "Some Remarks on Ollman's 'On Teaching Marxism,' "a shortened version of a paper delivered at a panel meeting of the American Political Science Association Convention, Chicago, September 1976. Reprinted by permission of the author. *Bruce M. Rappaport*, "Toward a Marxist Theory and Practice of Teaching," from *Crime and Social Justice*, Fall–Winter 1974. Reprinted by permission. *Jean Bethke Elshtain*, "The Social Relations of the Classroom: A Moral and Political Perspective," from *Telos*, Spring 1976. Reprinted by permission. *Brent Harold*, "Beyond Student-Centered Teaching," from *College English*, November 1972. Copyright © 1972 by the National Council of Teachers of English. Reprinted by permission.

V. I. Lenin, "The Tasks of the Youth League," from *On Culture and Cultural Revolution* (Moscow: Progress Publishers, 1970), pp. 123–146. *V. I. Lenin*, "On the Significance of Militant Materialism," from *On Culture and Cultural Revolution* (Moscow: Progress Publishers, 1970), pp. 184–197. *Mao Tse-tung*, "Oppose the Party 'Eight-Legged Essay,' " from *On Art and Literature* (Peking: Foreign Languages Press, 1960), pp. 50–74. *Robert Tressell*, "The Great Money Trick," from *The Ragged Trousered Philanthropists* (London: Lawrence and Wishart, Ltd., 1955; and New York: Monthly Review Press, 1978). *Norman Rudich*, "Philistines, Materialists, and Poets: Teaching Marxist Literary Theory in the United States," was written especially for this volume. *Joan B. Landes*, "Teaching Feminist Politics," was written especially for this volume. *Alan Sable*, "Facing Some Contradictions: My Experiences as a White Professor Teaching Minority Students," is published here for the first time.

Contributors

Stanley Aronowitz is Professor of Comparative Culture and Sociology at the University of California–Irvine.

Raya Dunayevskaya is a lecturer and author on Marxist theory and practice.

Jean Elshtain is Associate Professor of Political Science at the University of Massachusetts–Amherst.

Paulo Freire is the Brazilian author of several books on radical teaching.

Antonio Gramsci was a former leader and major theoretician of the Italian Communist Party.

Brent Harold is Associate Professor of English at Wesleyan University.

Leo Huberman was co-founder and editor of *Monthly Review*.

David Jhirad was Professor of Physics at the University of Massachusetts–Boston, and is now staff director of the Union of Concerned Scientists.

Louis Kampf is Professor of English at MIT.

Joan Landes is Assistant Professor in the School of Social Science, Hampshire College.

V. I. Lenin was a leader of the Russian Revolution.

Mao Tse-tung was a leader of the Chinese Revolution.

John McDermott is Professor of American Studies at SUNY–Old Westbury.

Michael Meeropol is Associate Professor of Economics at Western Massachusetts College.

Kai Nielsen teaches in the Department of Philosophy, University of Calgary, Canada.

Theodore Mills Norton is an Instructor in the Department of Political Science, Vassar College.

Bertell Ollman is Associate Professor of Politics at New York University.

Bruce Rappaport was Assistant Professor of Sociology at San Francisco State College and is now an organizer.

Norman Rudich is Professor of French at Wesleyan University.

Allan Sable is Assistant Professor of Sociology at the University of California–Santa Cruz.

Ira Shor was Associate Professor of English at Staten Island Community College and is now on the core faculty of the Union Graduate School.

Martin Sklar was Professor of History at Northern Illinois University and is now associate editor of *In These Times*.

Robert Tressell is the pseudonym for Robert Noonan.

Al Weinrub is Professor of Physics at the University of California–Santa Clara.

William Appleman Williams is Professor of History at Oregon State University.

Introduction
....
Theodore Mills Norton

This anthology, *Studies in Socialist Pedagogy*, is the first multidisciplinary collection of its kind.[1] It is solidly based on the achievements of radicals and Marxists in the sphere of higher education. At the same time, no effort has been made to conceal the inconsistencies, disagreements, and uncertainties of new socialist teachers attempting to grapple with issues of content and pedagogy in institutions not oriented toward socialist objectives. That socialist perspectives have at last been incorporated—to a limited extent, to be sure—into the curriculum must be viewed as a major step forward. That socialist practice must be consciously widened to confront the contradictions contained in this development is an imperative our contributors have already acknowledged.

Much of what we have included in this volume consists of efforts to formulate alternative course content and alternative modes of classroom presentation. What sometimes gets lost in the details of otherwise useful discussions is a strategic conception of the role of higher education in the broader struggle for socialism, and that is what I wish to address here. Although I cannot hope to analyze the university under capitalism,[2] behind my remarks lies a concept of higher education, not as a detached, self-contained "sector" of capitalist society, but as that society viewed from the standpoint of students and teachers caught up in some contradictory processes characteristic of its later history.

Education for Whom?

For the first time in the history of capitalism, the period immediately following the Second World War saw the entry in large numbers, especially in the United States, of children of the working class and of working people into the ranks of those favored by "higher" educational "opportunities." This transformation is reflected in current estimates of enrollment that locate over 11 million people in two- and four-year colleges and 1.5 million in graduate and professional schools. It was doubtless a major condition for the growth of the student movement in the 1960s.[3] (For an examination of some of the structural characteristics of this development, see the article by Ira Shor in Part II of this anthology.)

If this development may be interpreted as reflecting the "needs of the system," it should also be viewed as a positive achievement—and one now under attack—of the working class; and as a definite moment in its evolution toward assuming full control over social production and qualitatively transforming its nature. Called upon to play an expanded role in reproducing capitalist conditions of existence (the knowledge, skills, and attitudes necessary for the production of value)—a role which has increasingly contradicted their humanist pretentions—the universities have been forced to open their doors to an influx of working-class students. And it is these students, some of whom have already entered the faculty ranks, that must be the focus of any socialist strategy for higher education.

Politically, therefore, the strategic goal of the socialist teacher must be to work closely with these students, and their middle-class allies, to protect and extend the gains already made. In liberal language, this means fighting to take the historical tendency to its logical conclusion: the establishment of free, higher education through professional and graduate school for all Americans. In radical language, it means opposing all efforts of the state-capitalist bloc to destroy the material conditions for such education (massive budget cuts, etc.). It means protecting working-class participation in the "sector," whether "public" or "private." And in Marxist language, it means struggling against the capitalist effort to cheapen the cost of the reproduction of labor power, to diminish the *free time* working-class students now have during their post-high school years, and to destroy the cultural level now attained by the working class.

To the extent that socialist teachers understand and act on these strategic political commitments, they must learn to perceive their situation with a type of double vision: in all its particularity, and as a condition and consequence of the total system based on the exploitation of wage labor. The latter is the point of origin and ultimate destination of the working-class student; the former is that (potentially) qualitatively new moment of free time in his or her biography to which I have already referred. For millions of students today, that period of time will be carried along with them, as personal memory and historical experience, to the office door or factory gate—and the historical destiny of the class henceforth encapsulates this period. Its cultural content and political impact—as a dialectical moment in the internal formation of the proletariat—is thus of the greatest importance. The double optic through which the socialist teacher views this phenomenon may be evoked by the notion of "dropping out": a working-class student who today "drops out" of the labor force to attend college will in most cases be taking but an alternative route back into that force. Such a journey is fraught with possibilities of liberation as well as integration. Accordingly, for the socialist teacher to drop out of the battle for survival in the institution, say, to do "real" political work, is precisely to abandon the effort to enhance the liberatory potential of this moment. (See also the article by John McDermott in Part II.)

Education for What?

Education *by* socialists, *with* students from or headed into the working masses, is education *for* socialism. This is true even if the educational institutions in question are under the control of the corporations and the authoritarian state. This educational strategy for socialism should be based on four principles, all of which are to be found in the writings of such socialist teachers as Marx, Lenin, and Gramsci.

Principle 1. As educators and socialists, *we have no new principles to introduce.* This is the great Socratic principle of Marxist education. The working class already knows it is hounded, alienated, and exploited by capitalists and capitalist social relations. Our task is to help it achieve theoretical consciousness of what it already knows and experiences, not to tell it that it knows nothing. If socialism had to wait for working-class students to "internalize" a set of "new ideas," "inculcated" by a handful of socialist pedagogues, then it would have to wait forever. The very division between "inner" and "outer" is a bourgeois antinomy both repro- duced and collapsed in the course of the struggle. If capitalist domination penetrates and restructures the late capitalist individual, including the student and teacher, then it does so as another contradiction—the administered individual is already beginning to think about ways of administering the administrators. People do not need socialists to discover many aspects of their situation. They do this all the time. The task of the socialist teacher is to bring together the evidence already present in the honest records of theory and practice in any "field," to show how that field touches on all the others, and to lend theoretical coherence to the available evidence.

To be sure, the achievement of such coherence is no simple task. The recognition that it must be sought is itself an histor- ical product. During the 1960s the politics of most faculty who sympathized with activist students was limited to a wide variety of support activities on their behalf and at their re- quest. Where the university was the focus of political work, the consensus (heavily influenced by SDS) was that it was the political and social organization of the university, its relations to the local community, the capitalist economy, and the state that had to be attacked. The content and form of university courses did not escape criticism, but in the priorities set up by the antiwar and black liberation struggles, the amount of time and attention left for such activities was minimal. One unfortunate result was that in the classroom a cudgel was often used where a scalpel was required; and only the already convinced—chiefly those brought to consciousness by the struggles mentioned—were willing to entertain socialist perspectives. Even here, as often as not, the absence of a solid analysis of capitalism led to the fading of radical sympathies when their immediate causes disappeared.

All this, however, has now started to change. One result of this radicalization was a notable increase in the number of radical graduate students and young teachers in the 1970s.[4] Disappointed in their hopes for an immediate political solution, many have exchanged writing occasional tracts for more thorough studies of capitalism, laying stress on the special problems of their own disciplines. The appearance within the last four or five years of hundreds of journals and newsletters directed toward left-wing academics is striking evidence of this phenomenon. (See Part VI.) A common and growing concern—of which the present work is a manifestation—of these publications is how to undertake a radical and/or Marxist analysis of their subject matter and to present the fruits of such analyses to students. But while we have tried simultaneously to reflect and forward this process, we are very aware of the real restrictions under which it must operate. The very departmentalization of the university, for example, patently contradicts efforts to undertake a dialectical individuation of aspects of the false totality—capitalism—and continually thwarts attempts of both students and teachers to sustain a coherent critique of the system.

Principle 2. The task of the socialist educator, in concert

with his or her students, is to advance the *critical assimilation of the entire cultural heritage of world history.* When Lenin enunciated this principle, he had in mind primarily the cultural heritage of Russia and Europe. We must take a broader view, encompassing the civilization of all continents, such as Africa, and the hidden heritage of oppressed and exploited groups. This means that in addition to critically absorbing this inheritance we must in many cases seek to unearth it— and to lend full intellectual and political support to colleagues, e.g., those in black and women's studies, who have already launched themselves on this enterprise. Therefore, we must seek to *inform* as well as criticize, *recover* the unknown as well as to clarify the known. Let us recall that the culture industry is notorious not only for *repressing* current information, but for exacerbating "social amnesia," the collective forgetfulness of the struggles of the past.[5] In this light, the socialist educator is one who takes the scientific and humanistic pretensions of the university at and even beyond their face value.

Only in this context can we properly evaluate the bourgeois caricature of the socialist teacher as a political propagandist in the classroom. It is not just that *all* teaching is political, in its emphases and omissions, in interpretations that attach to the very concepts used, or that the socialist cannot even pretend to present his or her position objectively without making his or her commitments clear from the outset; rather, it is because of his or her desire *critically* to appropriate the heritage—instead of serving as a conveyor belt for its "transmission" (the automobile industry allusions are intentional) —that the socialist teacher presents an analysis of such complexity and concern with detail that it can only be countered with the falsifications of those parodied by their parodies. Where the liberal educator proclaims that the university is committed to the search for truth, the socialist adds that the truth is revolutionary. And the truth being what it is—the reality of life under capitalism—the socialist teacher has no interest in lying, hiding the facts, or misleading students in any way. Where there is manifest concern, as in this volume, with the strategy and tactics of teaching, it arises out of the recognition that the truth does not always emerge victorious out of the conflict with halftruths and lies, any more than it automatically forges its own means of expression. Moreover, the conditioning of our efforts to communicate with our students by reified modes of conceptualization and presentation is symptomatic of the fact that we, like they, are dominated individuals. The communicative process is also frequently blocked by the prior immunization of students against dialectical modes of cognition; precisely those forms of critical awareness that would enable them to dispel the mystifications of a society that reproduces slavery in the guise of freedom. Ultimately, there can be no antagonism between the pedagogy and the politics of the socialist teacher. In the first, he or she does everything within his or her power to prepare the student to exercise his or her potential for being human (see the essay by Jean Elshtain in Part IV); in the second, he or she works side by side with this student to create a society worthy of this heightened degree of humanity.

Principle 3. *The educator must be educated.* This "principle" has a vast number of dimensions. First, it does not mean absorbing every detail of an uninformed student rap as the wisdom of the proletariat, but determining from the outset to collaborate with students in order to *learn from them.* The honest mainstream educator, who evokes an extraordinary degree of participation from students by taking seriously their opinions in proportion to the investment they have made in their work (although we must go beyond investment to a conception of joint responsibility for liberation) can still serve as a model for the socialist. The duplicitous teacher, who backhandedly acknowledges his or her students' contribution by incorporating their research into his or her latest book, cannot. We seek, on the contrary, not to exploit our students' efforts, but to give back *to them* what they have given us. In the broadest sense, this means learning everything we can from our students about the actual, historical, and structural social relations of their lives. For it is only by our knowledge about them, which comes from them, that we will be able to articulate more satisfactory pedagogical "techniques."

A wide variety of such approaches are considered in this book; those who have elaborated them are best left to speak for themselves. For the socialist teacher, pedagogical technique must never be equated with technological manipulation of inorganic objects, with the instrumental irrationality of those "systems" approaches to education designed to reproduce the system. It is evident that the educated educator must pursue his or her objectives, not in opposition to students, but with their collaboration. As opposed to the formalistic fetishization of a bundle of "techniques," this implies a willingness to explore a wide range of processes— discussion, lecturing, examining, writing, making films— conceived as social relations among teachers and taught. By social relations, I do not mean the myopic fixation on "group dynamics" characteristic of the process-servers of late capitalism, but an understanding of those modalities that mediate a knowledge of society within the group (class) that both reproduces the system and struggles to break the chains of its collusion with that system.

Accordingly, while the two central sections of this book stress content and mode of presentation, respectively, it is not our intention to drive yet another wedge between form and content. Socialist teaching does not involve a preformed content mechanistically to be stuffed down the throats of the discontented. It is precisely the way in which it strives to grasp the connection between what, in the present circumstances, the student is trying to understand and the means appropriate to understanding it that socialist pedagogy captures the relationship that forever evades the process-fakers and bureaucratic administrators: the unity of theory and practice.

Principle 4. Socialist theory has frequently emphasized a politics of active participation rather than one of passive representation. Such activity has been viewed as the hallmark as well as the only guarantee in practice of the principle of *self-determination*. Thus, in his defense of the Paris Commune of 1871, Marx emphasized its functioning as a *working body* of delegates, which aspect he considered far more important than the various measures it drew up. Similarly, some contributors to this volume have emphasized self-determination in the classroom by encouraging students to transform themselves from passive spectators or consumers of "knowledge" into members of working groups.

I would like to stress two dimensions of an educational praxis tied to the principle of self-determination. First, we must work with students to facilitate their (and our) emergence into a world of collective self-organization (not "self-management") and individual integrity. As for the latter, it must in turn be organically bound up with the group learning of skills and the carrying-out of projects—although this must not involve a unidimensional submergence of the individual in the empirical group—as training today for the vast project of creating a socialist way of life over the long haul. Second, the movement for socialism requires *leaders*, individuals capable of putting their exceptional skills at the service of the class. Some of these leaders, too, will become teachers in a formal sense, new recruits to the ranks of socialist educators. Pedagogy must therefore incorporate the search for leaders and give encouragement, as far as possible, to a new leadership *type*. This is the type of the working-class leader who often leads from the floor rather than the podium, one which is the definite negation of that of the capitalist manager and higher state bureaucrat. To the extent that the university setting permits, we must bend our efforts to search out and encourage the formation of these leadership qualities, not with respect to some imagined immediate gains, but with an eye to liberating humanity from relations between leaders and led.

But if the technocratic educator is often on the lookout for new "leaders for tomorrow," namely, corporate advisers, imperialist tacticians, and other misrepresentatives of the people, whereas the socialist teacher wants to encourage leadership of a new type, something is still wrong with typification. "Concern with the individual" in the late capitalist totality is little more than the nullification of individuality. The massive regime of examinations characteristic of the higher educational system is symptomatic of a deeper illness: individual "traits" which cannot be quantified must be screened out, and anything which does not easily slide into one or another compartment of the approved classification of the Arts and Sciences is immediately viewed as dysfunctional. The socialist teacher caught up in this situation must be extremely careful not to reproduce it in the process of fighting it. For example, rather than flatly rebelling against the system's demand for "standards," the teacher should recognize this for what it is—a request for standardized replacements for those human cogs already worn down by the machinery of society. Merely to rebel against symptoms is to achieve very little. Thus the revolt against stiff grading results in an "inflation of grades," a form of degradation the system can live with as long as it is passed on to the student consumer. The teacher confronted with the problem of standards would do better to try to remember what they might once have been and, even more, to imagine what they might become at a time in which they will no longer confront the individual as alien quantities or qualities.

On the other hand, the teacher must remain skeptical about the hollow humanism which always wants to "retrieve" the faded standards of the Golden Age of the European bourgeoisie and to "apply" them to students who are inevitably found wanting. Such standards, along with the knowledge to which they pertain, must be critically reviewed from the standpoint of the present. It is not the task of the socialist to recreate the glories of an earlier Florence, Paris, Weimar, or Vienna, but to criticize the late capitalist culture which is their negation. Theodor Adorno's remarks on Oswald Spengler are germane to the situation in which teachers and students alike now find themselves:

> Spengler's hunter's eye, which mercilessly scrutinizes the cities of mankind as though they were the wilderness they really are, overlooks one thing—the forces released by decay. . . . The powerless, who at Spengler's command are to be thrown aside and annihilated by history, are the negative embodiment within the negativity of this culture of everything which promises, however feebly, to break the dictatorship of culture and put an end to the horror of prehistory. In their protest lies the only hope that fate and power will not have the last word. What can oppose the decline of the west is not a resurrected culture but the utopia that is silently contained in the image of its decline.[6]

Yet for this silent pledge of utopia to be redeemed, the socialist teacher must have a definite orientation. The ultimate "strategic goal" of socialist pedagogy, a goal that if achieved would mean the transcendence of strategy, is education for citizenship in the socialist community of the future. The movement for socialism cannot be frozen into the concept of one or another of its historical phases; it is never anything less than the quest for the complete resumption of all human capacities and powers alienated under capitalism and the discovery of those that no exploitative totality could ever allow to be expressed, even in alienated form. Indeed, it is important to emphasize the overcoming of alienation as a new birth rather than as merely a renaissance of repressed humanity. If it is not our objective to restore the capitalist past, still less can we hope to revive those working-class capacities which the capitalist present has obliterated. Our struggle is not to reproduce the "independent outlook" of yesterday's craft workers, but to lay the foundations of a society without classes. Socialism is simultaneously the movement for the abolition of the present and the recovery of the future—which only socialism can recover because capitalism has no future. Any conception of strategy which excludes these twin dimensions is both utilitarian and immoral.[7]

The peculiar integrity of the socialist teacher is precisely her or his specificity in the dialectic of change. This specificity is always under attack from two quarters. The drones of reality constantly berate the socialist teacher for "negativity," for "ideological" hostility to the mindless recitation of established "facts." In this view, the problem with socialist teachers is that they are socialists. Simultaneously, the teacher is accused of academicism, of an unwillingness to bring the classroom out into the streets. For the rhetoricians of practice, the problem with socialist teachers is that they are teachers. What the *faux amis* of radical practice wish to forget is that Marx did not set Hegel on his feet in order to cut off his head. When they accuse the socialist teacher of playing with concepts, they overlook the fact that the concepts and constructs fielded in the knowledge factory are already at work in society. It is not that these ideas originate in the academy and then filter down to society, but the reverse. It was not black studies, for example, which created the black liberation movement; and the teacher's responsibility to the latter is to see that its gains in higher education are not subverted or destroyed by the merchandisers and intellectual police of the system. On the other hand, many of the ideas that are traded in the university are reflections of *capitalist* practice. To refuse to reify them into a "higher" reality is already a critical act.[8]

Several contributors to this volume have stressed the value of combining classroom study with the direct experience of participation in organizations for social change or at least amelioration. Yet I find nothing in what they say that implies that the unity of theory and practice should be confused with their immediate identity. The boss's son who begins his rapid ascent to the top with a stint on the shop floor does not thereby become a revolutionary. Criticism of a society which transforms every living fact into a dead abstraction cannot by-pass the process of examining the latter. Revivification in this context often entails its apparent opposite: detached, if committed, consideration of what is no longer capable of independent movement—human life fragmented and redistributed across the categories of a conceptual organization chart.[9]

Yet if green is life's golden tree, then theory is even grayer than Hegel said it was. Becoming a socialist is part of a process; there are few "peak" experiences. In this process it is as important to remove or neutralize barriers, to help people see that the contradictions and rationalizations they confront in everyday life are not natural and boundless but historically generated by a system which exists to be superseded, as it is directly to introduce socialist alternatives. Occasionally, the "negativity" of the socialist teacher is nothing more than an immediate reaction to nonsense endlessly reiterated by uneducated educators. More profoundly and persistently, it is entailed by the requirement to negate, at least in thought, the mechanism which drains everything of qualities and then packages the empty husks of the latter for distribution as eternal "values" on the marketplace of ideas.

For those who have been completely integrated into this machinery, the critical approach of the socialist is not only "negative" but nearly incomprehensible, not least because the "results" of socialist teaching cannot be neatly inventoried. The merchandiser of Western unit-ideas has the immediate satisfaction of counting exactly how many of them have been absorbed by the thoroughly administered student consumer. The intellectual marketplace is the strict inversion of the commodity sphere: the customer is always wrong, except when he or she is "right." Successful adaptation to the perspectives of the parrot's perch automatically purchases the suppliant another inch upward on the greasy pole. The attainment of a genuinely critical consciousness, however, cannot be measured with the counter of instant converts. Unevenly developing, such consciousness cannot be included among the fixed furniture of the mind. If, as I have said, the experience of higher education is a qualitatively new moment in the internal formation of the working class, it is still no more than that: the elimination of this moment would mean another victory for barbarism; its exaggeration would deprive it of the only worthwhile content it could conceivably contain. As socialist teachers, let us never extinguish within ourselves the old injunction to "seize the time"; but let us not forget that in the polar winter of late capitalism the seizing may be the work of a lifetime. It is for all those who have chosen so to labor that we have compiled this volume.

Organization

The section titles in our book are self-explanatory. Articles are placed in one or another part as a result of their main emphasis: many (perhaps most) contain material on the character of the student body and on the content as well as the forms of socialist pedagogy. While some repetition of analysis was unavoidable, our main concern throughout has been to present the most provocative and influential writings, as well as to give some idea of the range of current work in terms of positions taken and disciplines covered. The resulting book is by no means as complete or as balanced as we might wish, but this is due as much to space limitations as to the still-uneven production of works in this area. It is, of course, our fervent hope that our book will help stimulate further inquiry into socialist pedagogy in those disciplines where it has barely begun. Meanwhile, we have included in Part VI a brief bibliography of contributions to the subject to indicate how far it extends beyond the relatively few articles we have been able to bring together in this volume.

If we may end with a word of advice to readers and, particularly, to socialist teachers inclined to set up study groups around these readings (something already tried with some success at New York University): we would encourage them to give due weight to our ordering of the sections, which were designed to clarify and contrast distinctive positions taken on a number of major issues. In particular, please note that there are three more or less direct confrontations, those between Gramsci and Freire (Part I), Ollman and Sklar (Part III), and Rappaport and Elshtain (Part IV), and that most of the letters from socialist teachers in Part V bear upon the Ollman-Sklar debate on how to teach Marxism.

Notes

1. For collections of articles on radical pedagogy in single or closely related disciplines, see *The Review of Radical Political Economics* (Winter 1975); *The Radical Teacher*, December 30, 1969; and *Science for the People* 4 (September 1972). The very useful volume entitled *Counter Course: A Handbook for Course Criticism*, ed. Trevor Pateman (Baltimore, Md.: Penguin, 1972) is, as its subtitle indicates, more concerned with criticism of course content than with pedagogy.
2. On this subject, see Samuel Bowles and Herbert Gintis, *Schooling in Capitalist America: Educational Reform and the Contradictions of American Economic Life* (New York: Basic Books, 1976).

3. Jürgen Habermas, among others, has expressed quite a different point of view. According to him, the student movement in both the United States and the German Federal Republic represented "the first bourgeois revolt against the principles of a bourgeois society that is almost successfully functioning according to its own standards." *Toward a Rational Society: Student Protest, Science, and Politics*, trans. Jeremy J. Shapiro (Boston: Beacon Press, 1970), p. 28.

4. The current massive "retrenchment" in higher education may, however, have begun to undermine the position of radicals, as well as others, at the university level. It is increasingly difficult not only for younger applicants to obtain employment, but for junior faculty members to retain it. Certainly, many radical and socialist teachers are among the ranks of the latter. Moreover, the increasing reliance of some institutions on adjuncts instead of full-time faculty adds to the insecurity of younger radical faculty, politically and intellectually as well as financially.

5. Russell Jacoby, *Social Amnesia: A Critique of Conformist Psychology from Adler to Laing* (Boston: Beacon Press, 1975).

6. Theodor W. Adorno, *Prisms*, trans. Samuel and Shierry Weber (London: Neville Spearman, 1967), p. 72.

7. I owe the precise phrasing of this sentence, the implications of which I have tried to bring out, to a graduate student at the University of Massachusetts, a radical of the emerging generation to which this collection is addressed.

8. For a related approach, see William E. Connolly, *The Terms of Political Discourse* (Lexington, Mass., Toronto, and London: D.C. Heath, 1974).

9. Thus: "He who wishes to know the truth about life in its immediacy must scrutinize its estranged form, the objective powers that determine individual existence even in its most hidden recesses." Theodor W. Adorno, *Minima Moralia: Reflections from Damaged Life* (London: New Left Books, 1974), p. 15.

Part I
......
Classics of Socialist Pedagogy

From
"Tasks of the Youth League"
....
V.I. Lenin

Comrades, today I would like to talk on the fundamental tasks of the Young Communist League and, in this connection, on what the youth organizations in a socialist republic should be like in general.

It is all the more necessary to dwell on this question because in a certain sense it may be said that it is the youth that will be faced with the actual task of creating a communist society. For it is clear that the generation of working people brought up in capitalist society can, at best, accomplish the task of destroying the foundations of the old, the capitalist way of life, which was built on exploitation. At best it will be able to accomplish the tasks of creating a social system that will help the proletariat and the working classes retain power and lay a firm foundation, which can be built on only by a generation that is starting to work under the new conditions, in a situation in which relations based on the exploitation of man by man no longer exist.

And so, in dealing from this angle with the tasks confronting the youth, I must say that the tasks of the youth in general, and of the Young Communist Leagues and all other organizations in particular, might be summed up in a single word: learn.

Of course, this is only a "single word." It does not reply to the principal and most essential questions: what to learn, and how to learn? And the whole point here is that, with the transformation of the old, capitalist society, the upbringing, training, and education of the new generations that will create the communist society cannot be conducted on the old lines. The teaching, training, and education of the youth must proceed from the material that has been left to us by the old society. We can build communism only on the basis of the totality of knowledge, organizations, and institutions, only by using the stock of human forces and means that have been left to us by the old society. Only by radically remolding the teaching, organization, and training of the youth shall we be able to ensure that the efforts of the younger generation will result in the creation of a society that will be unlike the old society, i.e., in the creation of a communist society. That is why we must deal in detail with the question of what we should teach the youth and how the youth should learn if it really wants to justify the name of communist youth, and how it should be trained so as to be able to complete and consummate what we have started.

I must say that the first and most natural reply would seem to be that the Youth League, and the youth in general, who want to advance to communism, should learn communism.

But this reply—"learn communism"—is too general. What do we need in order to learn communism? What must be singled out from the sum of general knowledge so as to acquire a knowledge of communism? Here a number of dangers arise, which very often manifest themselves whenever the task of learning communism is presented incorrectly, or when it is interpreted in too onesided a manner.

Naturally, the first thought that enters one's mind is that learning communism means assimilating the sum of knowledge that is contained in communist manuals, pamphlets, and books. But such a definition of the study of communism would be too crude and inadequate. If the study of communism consisted solely in assimilating what is contained in communist books and pamphlets, we might all too easily obtain communist text jugglers or braggarts, and this would very often do us harm, because such people, after learning by rote what is set forth in communist books and pamphlets, would prove incapable of combining the various branches of knowledge, and would be unable to act in the way communism really demands.

One of the greatest evils and misfortunes left to us by the old, capitalist society is the complete rift between books and practical life; we have had books explaining everything in the best possible manner, yet in most cases these books contained the most pernicious and hypocritical lies, a false description of capitalist society.

That is why it would be most mistaken merely to assimilate book knowledge about communism. No longer do our speeches and articles merely reiterate what used to be said about communism, because our speeches and articles are connected with our daily work in all fields. Without work and without struggle, book knowledge of communism obtained from communist pamphlets and works is absolutely worthless, for it would continue the old separation of theory and practice, the old rift which was the most pernicious feature of the old, bourgeois society.

It would be still more dangerous to set about assimilating only communist slogans. Had we not realized this danger in time, and had we not directed all our efforts to averting this danger, the half million or million young men and women who would have called themselves communists after studying communism in this way would only greatly prejudice the cause of communism.

The question arises: How is all this to be blended for the study of communism? What must we take from the old schools, from the old kind of science? It was the declared aim of the old type of school to produce men with an all-round education, to teach the sciences in general. We know that this was utterly false, since the whole of society was based and maintained on the division of people into classes, into exploiters and oppressed. Since they were thoroughly imbued with the class spirit, the old schools naturally gave knowledge only to the children of the bourgeoisie. Every word was falsified in the interests of the bourgeoisie. In these schools the younger generation of workers and peasants were not so much educated as drilled in the interests of that bourgeoisie. They were trained in such a way as to be useful servants of the bourgeoisie, able to create profits for it without disturbing its peace and leisure. That is why, while rejecting the old type of schools, we have made it our task to take from it only what we require for genuine communist education.

This brings me to the reproaches and accusations which we constantly hear leveled at the old schools, and which often lead to wholly wrong conclusions. It is said that the old school was a school of purely book knowledge, of ceaseless drilling and grinding. That is true, but we must distinguish between what was bad in the old schools and what is useful to us, and we must be able to select from it what is necessary for communism.

The old schools provided purely book knowledge; they compelled their pupils to assimilate a mass of useless, superfluous, and barren knowledge, which cluttered up the brain and turned the younger generation into bureaucrats regimented according to a single pattern. But it would mean falling into a grave error for you to try to draw the conclusion that one can become a communist without assimilating the wealth of knowledge amassed by mankind. It would be mistaken to think it sufficient to learn communist slogans and the conclusions of communist science without acquiring that sum of knowledge of which communism itself is a result. Marxism is an example which shows how communism arose out of the sum of human knowledge.

You have read and heard that communist theory—the science of communism created in the main by Marx, this doctrine of Marxism—has ceased to be the work of a single socialist of the nineteenth century, even though he was a genius, and that it has become the doctrine of millions and tens of millions of proletarians all over the world, who are applying it in their struggle against capitalism. If you were to ask why the teachings of Marx have been able to win the hearts and minds of millions and tens of millions of the most revolutionary class, you would receive only one answer: it was because Marx based his work on the firm foundation of the human knowledge acquired under capitalism. After making a study of the laws governing the development of human society, Marx realized the inevitability of capitalism developing toward communism. What is most important is that he proved this on the sole basis of a most precise, detailed, and profound study of this capitalist society, by fully assimilating all that earlier science had produced. He critically reshaped everything that had been created by human society, without ignoring a single detail. He reconsidered, subjected to criticism, and verified on the working-class movement everything that human thinking had created, and therefrom formulated conclusions which people hemmed in by bourgeois limitations or bound by bourgeois prejudices could not draw.

We must bear this in mind when, for example, we talk about proletarian culture. We shall be unable to solve this problem unless we clearly realize that only a precise knowledge and transformation of the culture created by the entire development of mankind will enable us to create a proletarian culture. The latter is not clutched out of thin air; it is not an invention of those who call themselves experts in proletarian nature. That is all nonsense. Proletarian culture must be the logical development of the store of knowledge mankind has accumulated under the yoke of capitalist, landowner, and bureaucratic society. All these roads have been leading, and will continue to lead, up to proletarian culture, in the same way as political economy, as reshaped by Marx, has shown us what human society must arrive at, shown us the passage to the class struggle, to the beginning of the proletarian revolution.

When we so often hear representatives of the youth, as well as certain advocates of a new system of education, attacking the old schools, claiming that they used the system of cramming, we say to them that we must take what was good in the old schools. We must not borrow the system of encumbering young people's minds with an immense amount of knowledge, nine-tenths of which was useless and one-tenth distorted. This, however, does not mean that we can restrict ourselves to communist conclusions and learn only communist slogans. You will not create communism that way. You can become a communist only when you enrich your mind with a knowledge of all the treasures created by mankind.

We have no need of cramming, but we do need to develop and perfect the mind of every student with a knowledge of fundamental facts. Communism will become an empty word, a mere signboard, and a communist a mere boaster, if all the knowledge he has acquired is not digested in his mind. You should not merely assimilate this knowledge, but assimilate it critically, so as not to cram your mind with useless lumber, but enrich it with all those facts that are indispensable to the well-educated man of today. If a communist took it into his head to boast about his communism because of the cut-and-dried conclusions he had acquired, without putting in a great deal of serious and hard work and without understanding facts he should examine critically, he would be a deplorable communist indeed. Such superficiality would be decidedly fatal. If I know that I know little, I shall strive to learn more; but if a man says that he is a communist and that he need not know anything thoroughly, he will never become anything like a communist.

From
"On the Significance of Militant Militarism"
....
V.I. Lenin

Comrade Trotsky has already said everything necessary, and said it very well, about the general purposes of *Pod Znamenem Marksizma* (Under the Banner of Marxism)[1] in issue no. 1-2 of that journal. I should like to deal with certain questions that more closely define the content and program of the work which its editors have set forth in the introductory statement in this issue.

This statement says that not all those gathered around the journal *Pod Znamenem Marksizma* are communists but that they are all consistent materialists. I think that this alliance of communists and non-communists is absolutely essential and correctly defines the purposes of the journal. One of the biggest and most dangerous mistakes made by communists (as generally by revolutionaries who have successfully accomplished the beginning of a great revolution) is the idea that a revolution can be made by revolutionaries alone. On the contrary, to be successful all serious revolutionary work requires that the idea that revolutionaries are capable of playing the part only of the vanguard of the truly virile and advanced class must be understood and translated into action. A vanguard performs its tasks as vanguard only when it is able to avoid being isolated from the mass of the people it leads and is able really to lead the whole mass forward. Without an alliance with non-communists in the most diverse spheres of activity there can be no question of any successful communist construction. . . .

Engels long ago advised the contemporary leaders of the proletariat to translate the militant atheist literature of the late eighteenth century for mass distribution among the people.[2] We have not done this up to the present, to our shame be it said (this is one of the numerous proofs that it is much easier to seize power in a revolutionary epoch than to know how to use this power properly). Our apathy, inactivity, and incompetence are sometimes excused on all sorts of "lofty" grounds, as, for example, that the old atheist literature of the eighteenth century is antiquated, unscientific, naive, etc. There is nothing worse than such pseudoscientific sophistry, which serves as a screen either for pedantry or for a complete misunderstanding of Marxism. There is, of course, much that is unscientific and naive in the atheist writings of the eighteenth-century revolutionaries. But nobody prevents the publishers of these writings from abridging them and providing them with brief postscripts pointing out the progress made by mankind in the scientific criticism of religions since the end of the eighteenth century, mentioning the latest writings on the subject, and so forth. It would be the biggest and most grievous mistake a Marxist could make to think that the millions of people (especially the peasants and artisans), who have been condemned by all modern society to darkness, ignorance, and superstition, can extricate themselves from this darkness only along the straight line of a purely Marxist education. These masses should be supplied with the most varied atheist propaganda material, they should be made familiar with facts from the most diverse spheres of life, they should be approached in every possible way, so as to interest them, rouse them from their religious torpor, stir them from the most varied angles and by the most varied methods, and so forth.

The keen, vivacious, and talented writings of the old

eighteenth-century atheists wittily and openly attacked the prevailing clericalism and will very often prove a thousand times more suitable for arousing people from their religious torpor than the dull and dry paraphrases of Marxism, almost completely unillustrated by skillfully selected facts, which predominate in our literature and which (it is no use hiding the fact) frequently distort Marxism. We have translations of all the major works of Marx and Engels. There are absolutely no grounds for fearing that the old atheism and the old materialism will remain unsupplemented by the corrections introduced by Marx and Engels. The most important thing— and it is this that is most frequently overlooked by those of our communists who are supposedly Marxists, but who in fact mutilate Marxism—is to know how to awaken in the still undeveloped masses an intelligent attitude toward religious questions and an intelligent criticism of religions.

On the other hand, take a glance at modern scientific critics of religions. These educated bourgeois writers almost invariably "supplement" their own refutations of religious superstitions with arguments which immediately expose them as ideological slaves of the bourgeoisie, as "graduated flunkeys of clericalism." . . .

The well-known German scientist, Arthur Drews, while refuting religious superstitions and fables in his book *Die Christusmythe* (The Christ Myth), and while showing that Christ never existed, at the end of the book declares in favor of religion, albeit a renovated, purified, and more subtle religion, one that would be capable of withstanding "the daily growing naturalist torrent" (4th German edition, 1910, p. 238). Here we have an outspoken and deliberate reactionary, who is openly helping the exploiters to replace the old, decayed religious superstitions by new, more odious, and vile superstitions.

This does not mean that Drews should not be translated. It means that while in a certain measure effecting an alliance with the progressive section of the bourgeoisie, communists and all consistent materialists should unflinchingly expose that section when it is guilty of reaction. It means that to shun an alliance with the representatives of the bourgeoisie of the eighteenth century, i.e., the period when it was revolutionary, would be to betray Marxism and materialism; for an "alliance" with the Drewses, in one form or another and in one degree or another, is essential for our struggle against the predominating religious obscurantists. . . .

In addition to the alliance with consistent materialists who do not belong to the Communist Party, of no less and perhaps even of more importance for the work which militant materialism should perform is an alliance with those modern natural scientists who incline toward materialism and are not afraid to defend and preach it as against the modish philosophical wanderings into idealism and skepticism which are prevalent in so-called educated society.

The article by A. Timiryazev on Einstein's theory of relativity published in *Pod Znamenem Marksizma* no. 1-2 permits us to hope that the journal will succeed in effecting this second alliance too. Greater attention should be paid to it. It should be remembered that the sharp upheaval which modern natural science is undergoing very often gives rise to reactionary philosophical schools and minor schools, trends and minor trends. Unless, therefore, the problems raised by the recent revolution in natural science are followed, and unless natural scientists are enlisted in the work of a philosophical journal, militant materialism can be neither militant nor materialism. Timiryazev was obliged to observe in the first issue of the journal that the theory of Einstein, who, according to Timiryazev, is himself not making any active attack on the foundations of materialism, has already been seized upon by a vast number of bourgeois intellectuals of all countries; it should be noted that this applies not only to Einstein, but to a number, if not to the majority, of the great reformers of natural science since the end of the nineteenth century.

For our attitude toward this phenomenon to be a politically conscious one, it must be realized that no natural science and no materialism can hold its own in the struggle against the onslaught of bourgeois ideas and the restoration of the bourgeois world outlook unless it stands on solid philosophical ground. In order to hold his own in this struggle and carry it to a victorious finish, the natural scientist must be a modern materialist, a conscious adherent of the materialism represented by Marx, i.e., a dialectical materialist. In order to attain this aim, the contributors to *Pod Znamenem Marksizma* must arrange for the systematic study of Hegelian dialectics from a materialist standpoint, i.e., the dialectics which Marx applied practically in his *Capital* and in his historical and political works, and applied so successfully that now every day of the awakening to life and struggle of new classes in the East (Japan, India, and China), the hundreds of millions of human beings who form the greater part of the world population and whose historical passivity and historical torpor have hitherto conditioned the stagnation and decay of many advanced European countries—every day of the awakening to life of new peoples and new classes serves as a fresh confirmation of Marxism.

Of course, this study, this interpretation, this propaganda of Hegelian dialectics is extremely difficult, and the first experiments in this direction will undoubtedly be accompanied by errors. But only he who never does anything never makes mistakes. Taking as our basis Marx's method of applying materialistically conceived Hegelian dialectics, we can and should elaborate this dialectics from all aspects, print in the journal excerpts from Hegel's principal works, interpret them materialistically and comment on them with the help of examples of the way Marx applied dialectics, as well as of examples of dialectics in the sphere of economic and political relations, which recent history, especially modern imperialist war and revolution, provides in unusual abundance. In my opinion, the editors and contributors of *Pod*

Znamenem Marksizma should be a kind of "Society of Materialist Friends of Hegelian Dialectics."

Notes

1. This was a philosophical and socioeconomic journal founded with the purpose of propagating materialism and atheism and fighting against the "graduated flunkeys of clericalism." The journal was published monthly in Moscow from January 1922 to June 1944 (from 1933 to 1935 it appeared once every two months).
2. See F. Engels, *Flüchtlingsliteratur* (Escape from the Refugee Camp), 1859.

From
"Oppose the Party 'Eight-Legged Essay'"
....
Mao Tse-tung

Comrade K'ai-feng has just stated the purpose of today's meeting. What I want to talk about now is how subjectivism and sectarianism use the party "eight-legged essay" as an instrument of propaganda or a form of expression. We oppose subjectivism and sectarianism, but if the party eight-legged essay is not eliminated, the two will still have a hole in which to hide themselves. If we also abolish the party eight-legged essay, we shall checkmate both subjectivism and sectarianism, and these two monsters, once shown in their true colors, can be easily killed, just as a rat crossing the street is chased by all passers-by.

Viewed historically, the party eight-legged essay is a reaction against the May 4th Movement.

During the May 4th Movement, modern-minded people opposed the classical diction in favor of the vernacular, and the traditional dogmas in favor of science and democracy; in all this they were quite right. The movement was then lively, progressive, and revolutionary. The ruling class was indoctrinating students with Confucian teachings and imposing the whole Confucian system as religious dogma upon the people, and all writing was done in the classical style. In short, all things written and taught by the ruling class and its hangers-on were along the lines of the eight-legged essays and dogmas in form as well as in content. These were the old eight-legged essays and the old dogmas. A great achievement of the May 4th Movement was to expose the repulsive ugliness of the old eight-legged essays and the old dogmas and rally the people to fight against them. Another great achievement closely linked with this was the fight against imperialism; nevertheless the struggle against the old eight-legged essays and the old dogmas remains one of its great achievements.

Later on, however, the foreign eight-legged essays and foreign dogmas appeared. Some people in our party, having departed from Marxism, developed these imported goods into subjectivism, sectarianism, and the party eight-legged essay. These are the new eight-legged essays and the new dogmas. They have been so deeply ingrained in the minds of many comrades that great efforts are demanded of us today to remedy the situation. Thus we see that the vigorous, progressive, and revolutionary movement during the May 4th period, the movement which fought against the old feudal eight-legged essays and dogmas was later turned by some people into its very opposite, and that the new eight-legged essays and dogmas emerged. These things are not alive but dead and stiff, not progressive but retrogressive, not revolutionary but an obstacle to the revolution. In other words, the foreign eight-legged essay or party eight-legged essay is a reaction against the very nature of the May 4th Movement.

Subjectivism, sectarianism, and the party eight-legged essay are all anti-Marxist and meet the needs not of the proletariat but of the exploiting classes. They are a reflection of petty-bourgeois ideology in our party. China is a country with a very large petty bourgeoisie, an enormous class which surrounds our party and from which comes a considerable number of our members; these members can hardly be expected to shed their petty-bourgeois tails, long or short, when they join us. The fanaticism and one-sidedness of petty-bourgeois revolutionaries, if not checked and corrected, are liable to engender subjectivism and sectarianism, of which one form of expression is the foreign or party eight-legged essay.

It is not easy to eliminate these things and sweep away all their traces. The job must be done properly, that is, by means of well-reasoned arguments. If our arguments are well-reasoned and to the point, they will be effective. We must first shake up the patient by shouting at him, "You are ill!" and then when he is sweating with fright, tell him gently that he needs treatment.

Let us now analyze the party eight-legged essay and see where its evils lie. We might use poison as the antidote to poison by presenting our case also in "eight legs" and set forth our eight serious indictments.

The first indictment against the party eight-legged essay is its empty, long-winded wordiness. Some comrades love to write long articles, but such articles are exactly like the foot-bandages of a slut, long and smelly. Why must they write articles that are so long and yet so empty? The only possible explanation is that they are determined to discourage the people from reading them. The people will shake their heads at the sight of such empty, long-winded articles. How can they be expected to go on reading them? So the only effect of such articles is to mislead naive people, thereby exerting a bad influence and fostering bad habits.

Since June 22 last year the Soviet Union has been fighting a gigantic war against aggression, yet Stalin's speech on July 3 was no longer than an editorial in our *Liberation Daily*. Had any of our gentlemen written that speech, it would have run to the appalling length of at least scores of thousands of words. We are now fighting a war and should learn how to write short and pithy articles. Although there is as yet no fighting here in Yenan, our troops at the front are daily engaged in battle, and people in the rear are all saying how busy they are. If articles are too long, who will read them? Some comrades at the front also like to write long reports. They take pains to write them and send them here for us to read. Yet who has the hardihood to read them?

If long and empty articles are no good, then how about short and empty ones? No good either. We must ban all empty talk. But our first and foremost task is to throw immediately into the dustbin the slut's long and smelly foot-bandages. Some might ask, "Isn't *Das Kapital* very long? What are we to do with it?" That is very simple: go on reading it. A proverb has it, "Sing different songs on different mountains"; another runs, "Fit the appetite to the dishes and the dress to the figure." Whatever we do must be done according to existing conditions, and writing articles and making speeches are no exception. What we oppose is the long-winded eight-legged essay without substance, but we do not mean that all good writings should be short. Of course we need short articles in wartime, but above all we need articles that have substance. An article without substance is the most unjustifiable and objectionable. The same applies to speeches; we must stop all empty, long-winded tirades.

The second indictment against the party eight-legged essay is its attempt to bluff people by pretentiousness. As some party eight-legged essays are not only long and empty, but also pretentious in order to bluff people, they contain the deadliest poison. Long-winded and empty articles may still be dismissed as merely childish, but pretentious bluffing is worse and, in fact, downright dishonest. Lu Hsun criticized people who sinned in this respect, saying: "Hurling insults and threats is certainly not fighting."[1] What is scientific can bear criticism at any time, for science is truth and fears no refutation. But subjectivist and sectarian stuff in articles and speeches in the style of the party eight-legged essay is mortally afraid of being refuted and, being cowardly, it bluffs people by pretentiousness, believing that it can thus silence people and proclaim itself the victor. Such stuff will not lead to truth but is an obstacle to truth. Truth does not bluff but reveals itself in sincere and honest words and deeds.

Two terms used to appear in the articles and speeches of some comrades: one was "ruthless struggle" and the other "merciless blows." These measures are entirely necessary in coping with the enemy ideology, but it is wrong to apply them to our own comrades. It often happens that enemies and enemy ideas infiltrate into our party, as described in Item 4 of the Conclusion of the *History of the Communist Party of the Soviet Union (Bolsheviks), Short Course.* Against our enemies, we must, of course, resort to ruthless struggle and merciless blows because they are doing the same to us, and any leniency on our part will land us in the very traps laid by these scoundrels. But we should not use these measures against comrades who unwittingly make mistakes; what we should do is to use the method of criticism and self-criticism described in Item 5 of the Conclusion of the same book. In the past, some comrades resorted in such cases to ruthless struggle and merciless blows because in the first place they did not distinguish between friend and foe, and secondly, they were deliberately bluffing. Pretentious bluff is absolutely wrong, no matter with whom one is dealing. As a tactic, bluffing is utterly ineffective against the enemy and can only harm our own comrades. The exploiting classes and the lumpenproletariat normally practice it, but the proletariat has no use for it.

For the proletariat, the sharpest and most effective weapon is a serious and militant scientific attitude. A communist lives not by bluff but by the truth of Marxism-Leninism, by seeking truth from facts, by science. Needless to say, the idea of attaining fame and position by pretentiousness is utterly contemptible. In short, all organizations, in making decisions and giving instructions, and all comrades, in writing articles and making speeches, must base themselves on Marxist-

Leninist truth and seek to serve a useful purpose. This is the only basis on which we can achieve victory in the revolution; any other is worthless.

The third indictment against the party eight-legged essay is that it shoots at random without taking its objective into consideration. A few years ago the following slogan appeared on the city wall of Yenan: "Working men and peasants unite to win the War of Resistance!" The idea of the slogan was quite good, but the character "工" [*Kung,* meaning working] was written as "工," with its perpendicular stroke twisted into a zigzag. How about the character "人" [*Jen,* meaning men]? It became "人," with three slanting strokes added to its right leg. The comrade who wrote them was no doubt a disciple of ancient scholars, but it was rather a mystery why he should have written such characters on the wall of Yenan at the time of the War of Resistance. Perhaps he had vowed that he would not allow the common people to read the slogan; it is difficult to explain it otherwise. Communists who really want to do propaganda must consider their public and have in mind those who will read their articles or listen to their speeches and talks; otherwise they are just making up their minds not to be read or listened to by anyone. Many people often take it for granted that what they write and say is plain to all, but actually that is not so. When they write and speak in the style of the party eight-legged essay, how can people understand them? The saying, to play the harp to a bull, implies a gibe at the audience. If, on the contrary, our main consideration is respect for the audience, then the gibe is turned against the player. Why should he strum away without considering his audience? The party eight-legged essay makes a far worse noise, as raucous as the cry of a raven, and yet it caws insistently at the people. When one shoots an arrow, one must aim at the target; when one plays the harp, one must consider one's audience. Can one then write articles or make speeches without taking the public into account? When any two of us want to strike up a friendship, can we become close friends if we do not know each other's minds and thoughts and feelings? It will never do for our propagandists simply to rattle on without considering, studying, and analyzing their public.

The fourth indictment against the party eight-legged essay is its dry, flat style which reminds one of the *piehsan*.[2] Like our party eight-legged essay, these starving beggars, known in Shanghai as "little *piehsan*," are wizened and repulsive. If an article or a speech merely repeats over and over, again and again a few catchwords like a schoolboy's composition without spirited and vigorous language, isn't it rather like the dreary speech and repulsive appearance of a *piehsan*? In the case of someone who entered primary school at seven, went to middle school in his teens, and graduated from college in his twenties, we should not blame him for the poverty and monotony of his vocabulary because he has never come into contact with the ordinary people. But if we revolutionaries who work with and for the people do not learn the language of the people, we cannot do our work effectively. At present many comrades, even those engaged in propaganda, do not learn that language. Consequently their propaganda is very dull: their articles appeal to few readers and their speeches attract few listeners.

Why should we bother to study language and, what is more, study it intensively? Because one cannot master a language except by hard work. First, we must learn the language of the people. The people's vocabulary is rich, vivid, and expressive of real life. Since many of us have not mastered language, our speeches and articles contain few passages that are lively, effective, and vigorous, and resemble not a person in good health, but the *piehsan*, sickly, emaciated, a mere bundle of withered flesh and sinews. Secondly, we must borrow what we need from foreign languages. We should not use foreign expressions mechanically or indiscriminately, but borrow from foreign languages what is fine and meets our needs. Our current vocabulary has already incorporated many foreign expressions, because the old Chinese vocabulary is inadequate. For instance, we are now at a meeting of *kanpu* [cadres], and the term *kanpu* is derived from a foreign word. We have still to borrow many more foreign things, not only progressive ideas but also new expressions. Thirdly, we must also learn to use what is still alive in the old Chinese language. We have not exerted ourselves enough in studying the old Chinese language and consequently have not made full and proper use of much that is still alive in it. It goes without saying that we are resolutely opposed to the use of expressions or allusions that are already dead, but what is good and useful should be taken over. At present, since some of our propagandists are poisoned by the party eight-legged essay, and refuse to make a careful study of what is useful in popular, foreign, and old Chinese languages, the people do not welcome their uninspiring propaganda; indeed, we have no use for such worthless and incompetent propagandists.

Who are our propagandists? They include not only the teachers, the journalists, and the writers, but all our cadres working in every field. Take the military commanders, for instance. Though they make no public statements, they must talk to the soldiers and have dealings with the local inhabitants. Isn't that a form of propaganda? Whenever a person speaks to others, that is propaganda. And unless one is dumb, one is bound to speak to others. Thus it is imperative that our comrades should study language.

The fifth indictment against the party eight-legged essay is its arrangement of items into A, B, C, D—like sorting out the stock of a Chinese drugstore. Go and take a look at any Chinese drugstore and there you will see cabinets with numerous drawers, each bearing the label of a drug: toncal, foxglove, rhubarb, or saltpeter—indeed, everything that should be there. This method has been taken over by our comrades. In their articles and speeches, their books and reports, first they use the big Chinese numerals, then the small Chinese numerals, then the characters of the series of the ten and the twelve calendar denotations, and then A, B, C, D, a, b, c, d, the Arabic numerals, and whatnot. How lucky that the ancient Chinese and the foreigners have made all these symbols for us so that we can set up a Chinese drugstore with the greatest ease! An article bristling with such numerals and symbols neither formulates problems, nor analyzes them, nor solves them; it argues neither for nor against anything and, for all its verbiage it has no real content and remains a Chinese drugstore. I am not saying that numerals, letters in alphabetical order, and so on are not to be used; all I say is that the approach is wrong. The method imitated from the Chinese drugstore, with which many of our comrades are now infatuated, is the most crude, infantile, and philistine of all methods. It is the method of formalism which classifies things according to their external features instead of their internal relations. If in an article, speech, or report one merely marshals according to external features a conglomeration of internally unrelated concepts, then one is indulging in mental gymnastics, and may lead others to do the same and rest content with the arrangement of surface phenomena instead of pondering over problems or probing the real nature of things.

What is a problem? It is things in contradiction. Where the contradiction is not solved, there is a problem. Once a controversy arises over a problem, you are bound to be for one side and against the other, and you must formulate the problem. To formulate the problem, you must first make a general study of the two main aspects of the problem or contradiction so that you can understand the nature of the contradiction; this is the process of discovering the problem.

Through a general survey or a summary study, problems can be discovered and formulated, but they cannot be solved.

Their solution must be sought through systematic and minute investigation and study, that is, analysis. Analysis is also needed in the formulation of a problem, for otherwise, faced with the bewildering wealth of material, one cannot discern where the crux of the problem, the contradiction, lies. But the analysis needed for the solution of the problem is a systematic and minute analysis. It often happens that a problem has been formulated but cannot yet be solved, because unless we bring to light the internal relations of the factors involved and subject them to systematic and minute analysis, we cannot see clearly the features of the problem, make a synthesis, and then find a good solution. An article or speech, if it is important and is intended to give guidance, should always formulate a problem, analyze it, and then make a synthesis to point out the nature of the problem and suggest the solution; all this certainly cannot be done by any formalist methods. Since infantile, crude, philistine, and idle formalist methods are very fashionable in our party, we must expose them so that everybody will learn to use Marxist methods to study, formulate, analyze, and solve problems; only in this way can we improve our work and ensure the victory of the revolution.

The sixth indictment against the party eight-legged essay is that it shows no sense of responsibility and harms everybody. All the offenses indicated above are due partly to immaturity and partly to lack of a sense of responsibility. Take, for instance, the washing of our faces. We all wash our faces every day, and many of us more than once a day and look carefully in the mirror after washing by way of "investigation and study" in case we have not done justice to our faces. What a sense of responsibility! If our articles and speeches were turned out with the same sense of responsibility, they would not leave much to be desired. If your stuff is not good enough to see the light of day, you had better keep it to yourself. Always bear in mind that it may influence the thoughts and actions of others. If a man does not wash his face for a day or two, it is bad; if he leaves on his face a dirty mark or two, it does not look well; but in neither case is it very serious. It is entirely different with articles or speeches, which are intended solely to influence other people; should our comrades, so serious about their faces, take these things lightly, they would be lacking in a sense of proportion. Many people write articles and make speeches without preliminary study or preparation and, having written them, they do not even bother to go over them in the same way as they would look in the mirror after washing their faces, but send them straight to the press. Often the result can be described as: "A thousand words from the pen in a stream, but ten thousand *li* away from the theme"; such writers may appear to be geniuses, but actually they do harm to many. We must get rid of this bad habit which arises from a lack of a sense of responsibility.

The seventh indictment against the party eight-legged essay is that it poisons the whole party and endangers the revolution. The eighth indictment is that the dissemination of this poison will be a disaster to the nation. These two indictments are self-evident and require no elaboration. In other words, if the party eight-legged essay is not discarded but allowed to go unchecked, it will have the worst possible consequences. In the party eight-legged essay is hidden the poison of subjectivism and sectarianism which, if allowed to spread, will prove disastrous to both the party and the country.

These eight counts constitute our declaration of war on the party eight-legged essay.

As a form, the party eight-legged essay is not only unsuitable for expressing the revolutionary spirit but is apt to stifle it. To develop the revolutionary spirit we must get rid of it and adopt instead a lively and vigorous Marxist-Leninist style. This style has existed for a long time, but it has yet to be enriched and popularized. Once we have destroyed the foreign eight-legged essay and the party eight-legged essay, we shall have a new style which, enriched and popularized, will further advance the revolution.

The party eight-legged essay is not, however, confined to articles and speeches, but is also found in the agenda of our meetings: (1) opening announcements; (2) reports; (3) discussion; (4) concluding remarks; (5) adjournment. Is it not also in the style of the party eight-legged essay to repeat this rigid procedure over and over again at every meeting, large or small, here, there, and everywhere? Reports presented at meetings almost invariably contain the same points: (1) the international situation; (2) the national situation; (3) the situation in the Border Region; and (4) the situation in our department; and the sessions often last from morning till night, at which even those who have nothing to say take the floor as if they owed it to others to do so. In short, there is a complete disregard of the actual conditions as well as a stubborn adherence to the rigid old forms and practices. Is it not time to correct all these things?

Notes

1. This is the title of an essay included in *Northern Dialect with a Southern Accent* (Lu Hsun, *Complete Works,* Chinese ed., Vol. V).
2. Literally "shrunken little wretch," an inclusive name for tramps, loafers, beggars, and sneak-thieves.

From
"In Search of the Educational Principle"
....
Antonio Gramsci

In the old primary school, there used to be two elements in the educational formation of the children. They were taught the rudiments of natural science, and the idea of civic rights and duties. Scientific ideas were intended to insert the child into the *societas rerum*, the world of things, while lessons in rights and duties were intended to insert him into the state and into civil society. The scientific ideas the children learned conflicted with the magical conception of the world and nature which they absorbed from an environment steeped in folklore; while the idea of civic rights and duties conflicted with tendencies toward individualistic and localistic barbarism—another dimension of folklore. The school combated folklore, indeed every residue of traditional conceptions of the world. It taught a more modern outlook based essentially on an awareness of the simple and fundamental fact that there exist objective, intractable natural laws to which man must adapt himself if he is to master them in his turn—and that there exist social and state laws which are the product of human activity, which are established by men and can be altered by men in the interests of their collective development. These laws of the state and of society create human order which historically best enables men to dominate the laws of nature, that is to say, which most facilitates their *work*. For work is the specific mode by which man actively

51

participates in natural life in order to transform and socialize it more and more deeply and extensively.

Thus one can say that the educational principle which was the basis of the old primary school was the idea of work. Human work cannot be realized in all its power of expansion and productivity without an exact and realistic knowledge of natural laws and without a legal order which organically regulates men's life in common. Men must respect this legal order through spontaneous assent, and not merely as an external imposition—it must be a necessity recognized and proposed to themselves as freedom, and not simply the result of coercion. The idea and the fact of work (of theoretical and practical activity) was the educational principle latent in the primary school, since it is by means of work that the social and state order (rights and duties) is introduced and identified within the natural order. The discovery that the relations between the social and natural orders are mediated by work, by man's theoretical and practical activity, creates the first elements of an intuition of the world free from all magic and superstition. It provides a basis for the subsequent development of an historical, dialectical conception of the world, which understands movement and change, which appreciates the sum of effort and sacrifice which the present has cost the past and which the future is costing the present, and which conceives the contemporary world as a synthesis of the past, of all past generations, which projects itself into the future. This was the real basis of the primary school. Whether it yielded all its fruits, and whether the actual teachers were aware of the nature and philosophical content of their task, is another question. This requires an analysis of the degree of civic consciousness of the entire nation, of which the teaching body was merely an expression, and rather a poor expression—certainly not an avant-garde.

It is not entirely true that "instruction" is something quite different from "education." An excessive emphasis on this distinction has been a serious error of idealist educationalists and its effects can already be seen in the school system as they have reorganized it. For instruction to be wholly distinct from education, the pupil would have to be pure passivity, a "mechanical receiver" of abstract notions—which is absurd and is anyway "abstractly" denied by the supporters of pure educativity precisely in their opposition to mere mechanistic instruction. The "certain" becomes "true" in the child's consciousness. But the child's consciousness is not something "individual" (still less individuated); it reflects the sector of civil society in which the child participates, and the social relations which are formed within his family, his neighborhood, his village, etc. The individual consciousness of the overwhelming majority of children reflects social and cultural relations which are different from and antagonistic to those which are represented in the school curricula: thus the "certain" of an advanced culture becomes "true" in the framework of a fossilized and anachronistic culture. There is no unity between school and life, and so there is no automatic unity between instruction and education. In the school, the nexus between instruction and education can only be realized by the living work of the teacher. For this he must be aware of the contrast between the type of culture and society which he represents and the type of culture and society represented by his pupils, and conscious of his obligation to accelerate and regulate the child's formation in conformity with the former and in conflict with the latter. If the teaching body is not adequate and the nexus between instruction and education is dissolved, while the problem of teaching is conjured away by cardboard schemata exalting educativity, the teacher's work will as a result become yet more inadequate. We will have rhetorical schools, quite unserious, because the material solidity of what is "certain" will be missing, and what is "true" will be a truth only of words: that is to say, precisely, rhetoric.

This degeneration is even clearer in the secondary school, in the literature and philosophy syllabus. Previously, the pupils at least acquired a certain "baggage" or "equipment" (according to taste) of concrete facts. Now that the teacher must be specifically a philosopher and aesthete, the pupil does not bother with concrete facts and fills his head with formulae and words which usually mean nothing to him, and which are forgotten at once. It was right to struggle against the old school, but reforming it was not so simple as it seemed. The problem was not one of model curricula but of men, and not just of the men who are actually teachers themselves but of the entire social complex which they express. In reality a mediocre teacher may manage to see to it that his pupils become more *informed*, although he will not succeed in making them better educated; he can devote a scrupulous and bureaucratic conscientiousness to the mechanical part of teaching—and the pupil, if he has an active intelligence, will give an order of his own, with the aid of his social background, to the "baggage" he accumulates. With the new curricula, which coincide with a general lowering of the level of the teaching profession, there will no longer be any "baggage" to put in order. The new curricula should have abolished examinations entirely; for to take an examination now must be fearfully more chancy than before. A date is always a date, whoever the examiner is, and a definition is always a definition. But an aesthetic judgment or a philosophical analysis?

The educational efficacy of the old Italian secondary school, as organized by the Casati Act, was not to be sought (or rejected) in its explicit aim as an "educative" system, but in the fact that its structure and its curriculum were the expression of a traditional mode of intellectual and moral life, of a cultural climate diffused throughout Italian society by ancient tradition. It was the fact that this climate and way of life were in their death-throes, and that the school had become cut off from life, which brought about the crisis in education. A criticism of the curricula and disciplinary structure of the old system means less than nothing if one does not keep this situation in mind. Thus we come back to the truly active participation of the pupil in the school, which can only exist if the school is related to life. The more the new curricula nominally affirm and theorize the pupil's activity and working collaboration with the teacher, the more they are actually designed as if the pupil were purely passive.

In education one is dealing with children in whom one has to inculcate certain habits of diligence, precision, poise (even physical poise), ability to concentrate on specific subjects, which cannot be acquired without the mechanical repetition of disciplined and methodical acts. Would a scholar at the age of forty be able to sit for sixteen hours on end at his worktable if he had not, as a child, compulsorily, through mechanical coercion, acquired the appropriate psychophysical habits? If one wishes to produce great scholars, one still has to start at this point and apply pressure throughout the educational system in order to succeed in creating those thousands or hundreds or even only dozens of scholars of the highest quality which are necessary to every civilization.

In the present school, the profound crisis in the traditional culture and its conception of life and of man has resulted in a progressive degeneration. Schools of the vocational type, i.e., those designed to satisfy immediate, practical interests, are beginning to predominate over the formative school, which is not immediately "interested." The most paradoxical aspect of it all is that this new type of school appears and is advocated as being democratic, while in fact it is destined not merely to perpetuate social differences but to crystallize them in Chinese complexities.

The traditional school was oligarchic because it was intended for the new generation of the ruling class, destined to rule in its turn: but it was not oligarchic in its mode of teaching. It is not the fact that the pupils learn how to rule there, nor the fact that it tends to produce gifted men, which gives a particular type of school its social character. This social character is determined by the fact that each social group has its own type of school, intended to perpetuate a specific traditional function, ruling or subordinate. If one wishes to break this pattern one needs, instead of multiplying and grading different types of vocational school, to create a single type of formative school (primary-secondary) which would take the child up to the threshold of his choice of job, forming him during this time as a person capable of thinking, studying, and ruling—or controlling those who rule.

The multiplication of types of vocational school thus tends to perpetuate traditional social differences; but since, within these differences, it tends to encourage internal diversification, it gives the impression of being democratic in tendency. The laborer can become a skilled worker, for instance, the peasant a surveyor or petty agronomist. But democracy, by definition, cannot mean merely that an unskilled worker can become skilled. It must mean that every "citizen" can "govern" and that society places him, even if only abstractly, in a general condition to achieve this. Political democracy tends toward a coincidence of the rulers and the ruled (in the sense of government with the consent of the governed), ensuring for each nonruler a free training in the skills and general technical preparation necessary to that end. But the type of school which is now developing as the school for the people does not tend even to keep up this illusion. For it is organized ever more fully in such a way as to restrict recruitment to the technically qualified governing stratum, in a social and political context which makes it increasingly difficult for "personal initiative" to acquire such skills and technical-political preparation. Thus we are really going back

to a division into juridically fixed and crystallized estates
rather than moving toward the transcendence of class divisions. The multiplication of vocational schools which special-
ize increasingly from the very beginning of the child's
educational career is one of the most notable manifestations
of this tendency. It is noticeable that the new pedagogy had
concentrated its fire on "dogmatism" in the field of instruction and the learning of concrete facts, i.e., precisely in the
field in which a certain dogmatism is practically indispensable
and can be reabsorbed and dissolved only in the whole cycle
of the educational process (historical grammar could not be
taught in *liceo* classes). On the other hand, it has been forced
to accept the introduction of dogmatism par excellence in
the field of religious thought, with the result that the whole
history of philosophy is now implicitly seen as a succession
of ravings and delusions. In the philosophy course, the new
curriculum impoverishes the teaching and in practice lowers
its level (at least for the overwhelming majority of pupils who
do not receive intellectual help outside the school from their
family or home environment, and who have to form themselves solely by means of the knowledge they receive in the
classroom)—in spite of seeming very rational and fine, fine as
any Utopia. The traditional descriptive philosophy, backed
by a course in the history of philosophy and by the reading
of a certain number of philosophers, in practice seems the
best thing. Descriptive, definitional philosophy may be a dogmatic abstraction, just as grammar and mathematics are, but
it is an educational and didactic necessity. "One equals one"
is an abstraction, but it leads nobody to think that one fly
equals one elephant. The rules of formal logic are abstractions of the same kind, they are like the grammar of normal
thought; but they still need to be studied, since they are not
something innate, but have to be acquired through work and
reflection. The new curriculum presupposes that formal logic
is something you already possess when you think, but does

not explain how it is to be acquired, so that in practice it is assumed to be innate. Formal logic is like grammar: it is assimilated in a "living" way even if the actual learning process has been necessarily schematic and abstract. For the learner is not a passive and mechanical recipient, a gramophone record—even if the liturgical conformity of examinations sometimes makes him appear so. The relation between these educational forms and the child's psychology is always active and creative, just as the relation of the worker to his tools is active and creative. A caliber is likewise a complex of abstractions, but without calibration it is not possible to produce real objects—real objects which are social relations, and which implicitly embody ideas.

Many people have to be persuaded that studying, too, is a job, and a very tiring one, with its own particular apprenticeship—involving muscles and nerves as well as intellect. It is a process of adaptation, a habit acquired with effort, tedium, and even suffering. Wider participation in secondary education brings with it a tendency to ease off the discipline of studies, and to ask for "relaxations." Many even think that the difficulties of learning are artificial, since they are accustomed to think only of manual work as sweat and toil. The question is a complex one. Undoubtedly the child of a traditionally intellectual family acquires this psychophysical adaptation more easily. Before he ever enters the classroom he has numerous advantages over his comrades, and is already in possession of attitudes learned from his family environment: he concentrates more easily, since he is used to "sitting still," etc. Similarly, the son of a city worker suffers less when he goes to work in a factory than does a peasant's child or a young peasant already formed by country life. (Even diet has its importance, etc.) This is why many people think that the difficulty of study conceals some "trick" which handicaps them, that is, when they do not simply believe that they are stupid by nature. They see the "gentleman"—and for many, especially in the country, "gentleman" means intellectual—complete, speedily and with apparent ease, work which costs their sons tears and blood, and they think there is a "trick." In the future, these questions may become extremely acute and it will be necessary to resist the tendency to render easy that which cannot become easy without being distorted. If our aim is to produce a new stratum of intellectuals, including those capable of the highest degree of specialization, from a social group which has not traditionally developed the appropriate attitudes, then we have unprecedented difficulties to overcome.

From
Pedagogy of the Oppressed
....
Paulo Freire

A careful analysis of the teacher-student relationship at any level, inside or outside the school, reveals its fundamentally *narrative* character. This relationship involves a narrating subject (the teacher) and patient, listening objects (the students). The contents, whether values or empirical dimensions of reality, tend in the process of being narrated to become lifeless and petrified. Education is suffering from narration sickness.

The teacher talks about reality as if it were motionless, static, compartmentalized, and predictable. Or else he expounds on a topic completely alien to the existential experience of the students. His task is to "fill" the students with the contents of his narration—contents which are detached from reality, disconnected from the totality that engendered them and could give them significance. Words are emptied of their concreteness and become a hollow, alienated, and alienating verbosity.

The outstanding characteristic of this narrative education, then, is the sonority of words, not their transforming power. "Four times four is sixteen"; "the capital of Pará is Belém." The student records, memorizes, and repeats these phrases without perceiving what four times four really means, or realizing the true significance of "capital" in the affirmation "the capital of Pará is Belém," that is, what Belém means for Pará and what Pará means for Brazil.

Narration (with the teacher as narrator) leads the students to memorize mechanically the narrated content. Worse yet, it turns them into "containers," into "receptacles" to be "filled" by the teacher. The more completely he fills the receptacles, the better a teacher he is. The more meekly the receptacles permit themselves to be filled, the better students they are.

Education thus becomes an act of depositing, in which the students are the depositories and the teacher is the depositor. Instead of communicating, the teacher issues communiqués and makes deposits which the students patiently receive, memorize, and repeat. This is the "banking" concept of education, in which the scope of action allowed to the students extends only as far as receiving, filing, and storing the deposits. They do, it is true, have the opportunity to become collectors or cataloguers of the things they store. But in the last analysis, it is men themselves who are filed away through the lack of creativity, transformation, and knowledge in this (at best) misguided system. For apart from inquiry, apart from the praxis, men cannot be truly human. Knowledge emerges only through invention and reinvention, through the restless, impatient, continuing, hopeful inquiry men pursue in the world, with the world, and with each other.

In the banking concept of education, knowledge is a gift bestowed by those who consider themselves knowledgeable upon those whom they consider to know nothing. Projecting an absolute ignorance onto others, a characteristic of the ideology of oppression, negates education and knowledge as processes of inquiry. The teacher presents himself to his students as their necessary opposite; by considering their ignorance absolute, he justifies his own existence. The students, alienated like the slave in the Hegelian dialectic, accept their ignorance as justifying the teacher's existence—but, unlike the slave, they never discover that they educate the teacher.

The *raison d'être* of libertarian education, on the other hand, lies in its drive toward reconciliation. Education must begin with the solution of the teacher-student contradiction, by reconciling the poles of the contradiction so that both are simultaneously teachers *and* students.

This solution is not (nor can it be) found in the banking concept. On the contrary, banking education maintains and even stimulates the contradiction through the following attitudes and practices, which mirror oppressive society as a whole:

(a) the teacher teaches and the students are taught;
(b) the teacher knows everything and the students know nothing;
(c) the teacher thinks and the students are thought about;
(d) the teacher talks and the students listen—meekly;
(e) the teacher disciplines and the students are disciplined;
(f) the teacher chooses and enforces his choice, and the students comply;
(g) the teacher acts and the students have the illusion of acting through the action of the teacher;
(h) the teacher chooses the program content, and the students (who were not consulted) adapt to it;
(i) the teacher confuses the authority of knowledge with his own professional authority, which he sets in opposition to the freedom of the students;
(j) the teacher is the subject of the learning process, while the students are mere objects.

It is not surprising that the banking concept of education regards men as adaptable, manageable beings. The more students work at storing the deposits entrusted to them, the less they develop the critical consciousness which would result from their intervention in the world as transformers of that world. The more completely they accept the passive role imposed on them, the more they tend simply to adapt to the world as it is and to the fragmented view of reality deposited in them.

The capability of banking education to minimize or annul

the students' creative power and to stimulate their credulity serves the interests of the oppressors, who care neither to have the world revealed nor to see it transformed. The oppressors use their "humanitarianism" to preserve a profitable situation. Thus they react almost instinctively against any experiment in education which stimulates the critical faculties and is not content with a partial view of reality but always seeks out the ties which link one point to another and one problem to another.

Indeed, the interests of the oppressors lie in "changing the consciousness of the oppressed, not the situation which oppresses them";[1] for the more the oppressed can be led to adapt to that situation, the more easily they can be dominated. To achieve this end, the oppressors use the banking concept of education in conjunction with a paternalistic social action apparatus, within which the oppressed receive the euphemistic title of "welfare recipients." They are treated as individual cases, as marginal men who deviate from the general configuration of a "good, organized, and just" society. The oppressed are regarded as the pathology of the healthy society, which must therefore adjust these "incompetent and lazy" folk to its own patterns by changing their mentality. These marginals need to be "integrated," "incorporated" into the healthy society that they have "forsaken."

The truth is, however, that the oppressed are not "marginals," are not men living "outside" society. They have always been "inside"—inside the structure which made them "beings for others." The solution is not to "integrate" them into the structure of oppression, but to transform that structure so that they can become "beings for themselves." Such transformation, of course, would undermine the oppressors' purposes; hence their utilization of the banking concept of education to avoid the threat of student *conscientização*.

The banking approach to adult education, for example, will never propose to students that they critically consider reality.

It will deal instead with such vital questions as whether Roger gave green grass to the goat, and insist upon the importance of learning that, on the contrary, Roger gave green grass to the rabbit. The "humanism" of the banking approach masks the effort to turn men into automatons—the very negation of their ontological vocation to be more fully human.

Those who use the banking approach, knowingly or unknowingly (for there are innumerable well-intentioned bank-clerk teachers who do not realize that they are serving only to dehumanize), fail to perceive that the deposits themselves contain contradictions about reality. But, sooner or later, these contradictions may lead formerly passive students to turn against their domestication and the attempt to domesticate reality. They may discover through existential experience that their present way of life is irreconcilable with their vocation to become fully human. They may perceive through their relations with reality that reality is really a *process*, undergoing constant transformation. If men are searchers and their ontological vocation is humanization, sooner or later they may perceive the contradiction in which banking education seeks to maintain them, and then engage themselves in the struggle for their liberation.

But the humanist, revolutionary educator cannot wait for this possibility to materialize. From the outset, his efforts must coincide with those of the students to engage in critical thinking and the quest for mutual humanization. His efforts must be imbued with a profound trust in men and their creative power. To achieve this, he must be a partner of the students in his relations with them.

The banking concept does not admit to such partnership—and necessarily so. To resolve the teacher-student contradiction, to exchange the role of depositor, prescriber, domesticator, for the role of student among students would be to undermine the power of oppression and serve the cause of liberation.

Implicit in the banking concept is the assumption of a dichotomy between man and the world: man is merely in the world, not *with* the world or with others; man is spectator, not re-creator. In this view, man is not a conscious being . (*corpo consciente*); he is rather the possessor of a consciousness: an empty "mind" passively open to the reception of deposits of reality from the world outside. For example, my desk, my books, my coffee cup, all the objects before me—as bits of the world which surrounds me—would be "inside" me, exactly as I am inside my study right now. This view makes no distinction between being accessible to consciousness and entering consciousness. The distinction, however, is essential: the objects which surround me are simply accessible to my consciousness, not located within it. I am aware of them, but they are not inside me.

It follows logically from the banking notion of consciousness that the educator's role is to regulate the way the world "enters into" the students. His task is to organize a process which already occurs spontaneously, to "fill" the students by making deposits of information which he considers to constitute true knowledge.[2] And since men "receive" the world as passive entities, education should make them more passive still, and adapt them to the world. The educated man is the adapted man, because he is better "fit" for the world. Translated into practice, this concept is well suited to the purposes of the oppressors, whose tranquility rests on how well men fit the world the oppressors have created, and how little they question it.

The more completely the majority adapt to the purposes which the dominant minority prescribe for them (thereby depriving them of the right to their own purposes), the more easily the minority can continue to prescribe. The theory and practice of banking education serve this end quite efficiently. Verbalistic lessons, reading requirements (for example, some professors specify in their reading lists that a book should be read from pages 10 to 15—and do this to "help" their students!), the methods for evaluating "knowledge," the distance between the teacher and the taught, the criteria for promotion: everything in this ready-to-wear approach serves to obviate thinking.

The bank-clerk educator does not realize that there is no true security in his hypertrophied role, that one must seek to live *with* others in solidarity. One cannot impose oneself, nor even merely coexist with one's students. Solidarity requires true communication, and the concept by which such an educator is guided fears and proscribes communication.

Yet only through communication can human life hold meaning. The teacher's thinking is authenticated only by the authenticity of the students' thinking. The teacher cannot think for his students, nor can he impose his thought on them. Authentic thinking, thinking that is concerned about reality, does not take place in ivory tower isolation, but only in communication. If it is true that thought has meaning only when generated by action upon the world, the subordination of students to teachers becomes impossible.

Because banking education begins with a false understanding of men as objects, it cannot promote the development of what Fromm calls "biophily," but instead produces its opposite, "necrophily."

> While life is characterized by growth in a structured, functional manner, the necrophilous person loves all that does not grow, all that is mechanical. The necrophilous person is driven by the desire to transform the organic into the inorganic, to approach life mechanically, as if all living persons were things. . . . Memory, rather than experience; having, rather than being, is what counts. The necrophilous person can relate to an object—a flower or a person—only if he possesses it; hence, a threat to his possession is a threat to himself; if he loses possession he loses contact with the world. . . . He loves control, and in the act of controlling he kills life.[3]

Oppression—overwhelming control—is necrophilic; it is nourished by love of death, not life. The banking concept of education, which serves the interests of oppression, is also necrophilic. Based on a mechanistic, static, naturalistic, spatialized view of consciousness, it transforms students into receiving objects. It attempts to control thinking and action, leads men to adjust to the world, and inhibits their creative power.

When their efforts to act responsibly are frustrated, when they find themselves unable to use their faculties, men suffer. "This suffering due to impotence is rooted in the very fact that the human equilibrium has been disturbed."[4] But the inability to act which causes men's anguish also causes them to reject their impotence, by attempting

> to restore [their] capacity to act. But can [they], and how? One way is to submit and identify with a person or group having power. By this symbolic participation in another person's life, [men have] the illusion of acting, when in reality [they] only submit to and become a part of those who act.[5]

Populist manifestations perhaps best exemplify this type of behavior by the oppressed, who, by identifying with charismatic leaders, come to feel that they themselves are active and effective. The rebellion they express as they emerge in the historical process is motivated by that desire to act effectively. The dominant elites consider the remedy to be more domination and repression, carried out in the name of freedom, order, and social peace (that is, the peace of the elites). Thus they can condemn—logically, from their point of view—"the violence of a strike by workers and [can] call upon the state in the same breath to use violence in putting down the strike."[6]

Education as the exercise of domination stimulates the credulity of students, with the ideological intent (often not perceived by educators) of indoctrinating them to adapt to the world of oppression. This accusation is not made in the naive hope that the dominant elites will thereby simply abandon the practice. Its objective is to call the attention of true humanists to the fact that they cannot use banking educational methods in the pursuit of liberation, for they would only negate that very pursuit. Nor may a revolutionary society inherit these methods from an oppressor society. The revolutionary society which practices banking education is either misguided or mistrusting of men. In either event, it is threatened by the specter of reaction.

Unfortunately, those who espouse the cause of liberation are themselves surrounded and influenced by the climate which generates the banking concept, and often do not perceive its true significance or its dehumanizing power. Paradoxically, then, they utilize this same instrument of alienation in what they consider an effort to liberate. Indeed, some "revolutionaries" brand as "innocents," "dreamers," or even "reactionaries" those who would challenge this educational practice. But one does not liberate men by alienating them. Authentic liberation—the process of humanization—is not another deposit to be made in men. Liberation is a praxis: the action and reflection of men upon their world in order to transform it. Those truly committed to the cause of liberation can accept neither the mechanistic concept of consciousness as an empty vessel to be filled, nor the use of banking methods of domination (propaganda, slogans—deposits) in the name of liberation.

Those truly committed to liberation must reject the banking concept in its entirety, adopting instead a concept of men as conscious beings, and consciousness as consciousness intent upon the world. They must abandon the educational goal of deposit-making and replace it with the posing of the problems of men in their relations with the world. "Problem-posing" education, responding to the essence of consciousness—intentionality—rejects communiqués and embodies communication. It epitomizes the special characteristic of consciousness: being *conscious of*, not only as intent on objects but as turned in upon itself in a Jasperian "split"—consciousness as consciousness of consciousness.

Liberating education consists in acts of cognition, not transferrals of information. It is a learning situation in which the cognizable object (far from being the end of the cognitive act) intermediates the cognitive actors—teacher on the one hand and students on the other. Accordingly, the practice of problem-posing education entails at the outset that the teacher-student contradiction be resolved. Dialogical relations—indispensable to the capacity of cognitive actors to cooperate in perceiving the same cognizable object—are otherwise impossible.

Indeed, problem-posing education, which breaks with the vertical patterns characteristic of banking education, can fulfill its function as the practice of freedom only if it can overcome the above contradiction. Through dialogue, the teacher-of-the-students and the students-of-the-teacher cease to exist and a new term emerges: teacher-student with student-teachers. The teacher is no longer merely the-one-who-teaches, but one who is himself taught in dialogue with the students, who, in turn, while being taught also teach. They become jointly responsible for a process in which all grow. In this process, arguments based on "authority" are no longer valid; in order to function, authority must be *on the side of* freedom, not *against* it. Here, no one teaches another, nor is anyone self-taught. Men teach each other, mediated by the world, by the cognizable objects which in banking education are "owned" by the teacher.

The banking concept (with its tendency to dichotomize everything) distinguishes two stages in the action of the educator. During the first, he cognizes a cognizable object while he prepares his lessons in his study or his laboratory: during the second, he expounds to his students about that object. The students are not called upon to know, but to memorize the contents narrated by the teacher. Nor do the students practice any act of cognition, since the object toward which that act should be directed is the property of the teacher rather than a medium evoking the critical reflection of both teacher and students. Hence in the name of the "preservation of culture and knowledge" we have a system which achieves neither true knowledge nor true culture.

The problem-posing method does not dichotomize the activity of the teacher-student: he is not "cognitive" at one point and "narrative" at another. He is always "cognitive," whether preparing a project or engaging in dialogue with the students. He does not regard cognizable objects as his private property, but as the object of reflection by himself and the students. In this way, the problem-posing educator constantly re-forms his reflections in the reflection of the students. The students—no longer docile listeners—are now critical co-investigators in dialogue with the teacher. The teacher presents the material to the students for their consideration, and reconsiders his earlier considerations as the students express their own. The role of the problem-posing educator is to create, together with the students, the conditions under which knowledge at the level of the *doxa* is superseded by true knowledge, at the level of the *logos*.

Whereas banking education anesthetizes and inhibits creative power, problem-posing education involves a constant unveiling of reality. The former attempts to maintain the *submersion* of consciousness; the latter strives for the *emergence* of consciousness and *critical intervention* in reality.

Students, as they are increasingly posed with problems relating to themselves in the world and with the world, will feel increasingly challenged and obliged to respond to that challenge. Because they apprehend the challenge as interrelated to other problems within a total context, not as a theoretical question, the resulting comprehension tends to be increasingly critical and thus constantly less alienated. Their response to the challenge evokes new challenges, followed by new understandings; and gradually the students come to regard themselves as committed.

Education as the practice of freedom—as opposed to education as the practice of domination—denies that man is abstract, isolated, independent, and unattached to the world; it also denies that the world exists as a reality apart from men. Authentic reflection considers neither abstract man nor the world without men, but men in their relations with the world. In these relations consciousness and world are simultaneous: consciousness neither precedes the world nor follows it. *"La conscience et le monde sont dormés d'un même coup: extérieur par essence à la conscience, le monde est, par essence relatif à elle."*[7]

As men, simultaneously reflecting on themselves and on the world, increase the scope of their perception, they begin to direct their observations toward previously inconspicuous phenomena:

> In perception properly so-called, as an explicit awareness [*Gewahren*], I am turned towards the object, to the paper, for instance. I apprehend it as being this here and now. The apprehension is a singling out, every object having a background in experience. Around and about the paper lie books, pencils, inkwell, and so forth, and these in a certain sense are also "perceived," perceptually there, in the "field of intuition"; but whilst I was turned towards the paper there was no turning in their direction, nor any apprehending of them, not even in a secondary sense. They appeared and yet were not singled out, were not posited on their own account. Every perception of a thing has such a zone of background intuitions or background awareness, if "intuiting" already includes the state of being turned towards, and this also is a "conscious experience," or more briefly a "consciousness of" all indeed that in point of fact lies in the co-perceived objective background.[8]

That which had existed objectively but had not been perceived in its deeper implications (if indeed it was perceived at all) begins to "stand out," assuming the character of a problem and therefore of challenge. Thus, men begin to single out elements from their "background awarenesses" and to reflect upon them. These elements are now objects of men's consideration, and, as such, objects of their action and cognition.

In problem-posing education, men develop their power to perceive critically *the way they exist* in the world *with which* and *in which* they find themselves; they come to see the world not as a static reality, but as a reality in process, in transformation. Although the dialectical relations of men with the world exist independently of how these relations are perceived (or whether or not they are perceived at all), it is also true that the form of action men adopt is to a large extent a function of how they perceive themselves in the world. Hence, the teacher-students and the student-teachers reflect simultaneously on themselves and the world without dichotomizing this reflection from action, and thus establish an authentic form of thought and action.

Once again, the two educational concepts and practices under analysis come into conflict. Banking education (for obvious reasons) attempts, by mythicizing reality, to conceal certain facts which explain the way men exist in the world; problem-posing education regards dialogue as indispensable to the act of cognition which unveils reality. Banking education treats students as objects of assistance; problem-posing education makes them critical thinkers. Banking education inhibits creativity and domesticates (although it cannot completely destroy) the *intentionality* of consciousness by isolating consciousness from the world, thereby denying men their ontological and historical vocation of becoming more fully human. Problem-posing education bases itself on creativity and stimulates true reflection and action upon reality, thereby responding to the vocation of men as beings who are authentic only when engaged in inquiry and creative transformation. In sum: banking theory and practice, as immobilizing and fixating forces, fail to acknowledge men as historical beings; problem-posing theory and practice take man's historicity as their starting point.

Problem-posing education affirms men as beings in the process of becoming—as unfinished, uncompleted beings in and with a likewise unfinished reality. Indeed, in contrast to other animals who are unfinished, but not historical, men know themselves to be unfinished; they are aware of their incompletion. In this incompletion and this awareness lie the very roots of education as an exclusively human manifestation. The unfinished character of men and the transformational character of reality necessitate that education be an ongoing activity.

Education is thus constantly remade in the praxis. In order to *be*, it must *become*. Its "duration" (in the Bergsonian meaning of the word) is found in the interplay of the opposites *permanence* and *change*. The banking method emphasizes permanence and becomes reactionary; problem-posing education—which accepts neither a "well-behaved" present nor a predetermined future—roots itself in the dynamic present and becomes revolutionary.

Problem-posing education is revolutionary futurity. Hence it is prophetic (and, as such, hopeful). Hence, it corresponds to the historical nature of man. Hence, it affirms men as beings who transcend themselves, who move forward and look ahead, for whom immobility represents a fatal threat, for whom looking at the past must only be a means of understanding more clearly what and who they are so that they can more wisely build the future. Hence, it identifies with the movement which engages men as beings aware of their incompletion—an historical movement which has its point of departure, its subjects and its objectives.

The point of departure of the movement lies in men themselves. But since men do not exist apart from the world, apart from reality, the movement must begin with the men-world relationship. Accordingly, the point of departure must always be with men in the "here and now," which constitutes the situation within which they are submerged, from which they emerge, and in which they intervene. Only by starting from this situation—which determines their perception of it—can they begin to move. To do this authentically they must perceive their state not as fated and unalterable, but merely as limiting—and therefore challenging.

Whereas the banking method directly or indirectly reinforces men's fatalistic perception of their situation, the problem-posing method presents this very situation to them as a problem. As the situation becomes the object of their cognition, the naive or magical perception which produced their fatalism gives way to perception which is able to perceive itself even as it perceives reality, and can thus be critically objective about that reality.

A deepened consciousness of their situation leads men to apprehend that situation as an historical reality susceptible of transformation. Resignation gives way to the drive for transformation and inquiry, over which men feel themselves to be in control. If men, as historical beings necessarily engaged with other men in a movement of inquiry, did not control that movement, it would be (and is) a violation of men's humanity. Any situation in which some men prevent others from engaging in the process of inquiry is one of violence. The means used are not important; to alienate men from their own decision-making is to change them into objects.

This movement of inquiry must be directed toward humanization—man's historical vocation. The pursuit of full humanity, however, cannot be carried out in isolation or individualism, but only in fellowship and solidarity; therefore it cannot unfold in the antagonistic relations between oppressors and oppressed. No one can be authentically human while he prevents others from being so. Attempting *to be more* human, individualistically, leads to *having more*, egotistically: a form of dehumanization. Not that it is not fundamental *to have* in order *to be* human. Precisely because it *is* necessary, some men's *having* must not be allowed to constitute an obstacle to others' *having*, must not consolidate the power of the former to crush the latter.

Problem-posing education, as a humanist and liberating praxis, posits as fundamental that men subjected to domination must fight for their emancipation. To that end, it enables teachers and students to become subjects of the educational process by overcoming authoritarianism and an alienating intellectualism; it also enables men to overcome their false perception of reality. The world—no longer something to be described with deceptive words—becomes the object of that transforming action by men which results in their humanization.

Problem-posing education does not and cannot serve the interests of the oppressor. No oppressive order could permit the oppressed to begin to question: Why? While only a revolutionary society can carry out this education in systematic terms, the revolutionary leaders need not take full power before they can employ the method. In the revolutionary process, the leaders cannot utilize the banking method as an interim measure, justified on grounds of expediency, with the intention of *later* behaving in a genuinely revolutionary fashion. They must be revolutionary—that is to say, dialogical—from the outset.

Notes

1. Simone de Beauvoir, *La Pensée de Droite, Aujourd'hui* (Paris); ST, *El Pensamiento político de la Derecha* (Buenos Aires, 1963), p. 34.
2. This concept corresponds to what Sartre calls the "digestive" or "nutritive" concept of education, in which knowledge is "fed" by the teacher to the students to "fill them out." See Jean-Paul Sartre, "Une idée fondamentale de la phénoménologie de Husserl; L'intentionalité," *Situations I* (Paris, 1947).

3. Eric Fromm, *The Heart of Man* (New York, 1966), p. 41.
4. Ibid., p. 31.
5. Ibid.
6. Reinhold Niebuhr, *Moral Man and Immoral Society* (New York, 1960), p. 130.
7. Sartre, "Une idée fondamentale," p. 32.
8. Edmund Husserl, *Ideas—General Introduction to Pure Phenomenology* (London, 1969), pp. 105-06.

Part II
······
Who Are We Teaching?

How to Spread the Word
....
Leo Huberman

In the late 1930s I sat in on a course of education for trade unionists. That these workers had a desire to learn was evident by their enrollment in a class held in the evenings, after they had done a day's work. That the teacher knew his subject was manifest from the brilliance of his lecture. That the combination of students' desire and teacher's grasp of the material did not result in learning was obvious from the fact that before the hour was over, several members of the class were asleep; it was apparent, too, from the decline in enrollment—the next class was attended by only half the students, and the third time the class met, less than a quarter who had signed up were in attendance.

This, by and large, has been the experience in trade union education in the United States. Union officials, badgered by the pleas of the education director to appropriate the small sum needed for trade union classes, finally yield, reluctantly. The classes are held, and they fizzle. The union officials then declare triumphantly, "See, the workers don't want to learn." The teacher, saddened by his experience, agrees. But the conclusion is totally wrong: it isn't that the workers do not want to learn—that is seldom the case. The cause of the failure is that *the teacher does not know how to teach.*

This experience is not unique to trade union classes. It

happens with radical groups, too. And it happens in under-developed countries where revolutionary ardor fills new classrooms with enthusiastic workers and peasants—and poor teaching, just as quickly, empties those classrooms.

This need not happen. Workers and peasants, no matter how impoverished their previous educational background, will stay the course, and they will learn, if the teaching they get is good teaching.

What is good teaching? What did that teacher in the trade union class do wrong? He had talked for about ten minutes when a hand went up and a student asked a question. It was a thoughtful question. The teacher should have felt flattered—he had said something which had stimulated one of his listeners to think. He should have felt like hugging the questioner—instead, he was annoyed. The smooth flow of his carefully planned lecture had been interrupted and he put off the questioner with "I'll come to that later."

His mistake was in being concerned only with subject matter; he should have been concerned with students. He was a lecturer, not a teacher. The lecturer teaches subject matter; the teacher teaches people. The difference is crucial.

Obviously, where classes are very large and the lecturer stands before so many faces that he cannot possibly know them as individual human beings, good teaching by my definition is not feasible. Here the lecturer does his job well if he masters his material and presents it in as lively a manner as possible. But that trade union class had only seventeen students, and in a class that size (up to a limit of twenty-five) it is easy for the teacher to get to know his students as individual human beings with varying backgrounds, and good teaching is possible.

It is possible because the teacher can base his lesson on the background and experience of the students and, by skillful questioning, get them to participate in the learning process. The subject matter is no longer an end in itself but a vehicle for making the students think, for giving them tools for understanding the world and their position in it. From the lecture hall, students emerge with a body of information; from a good classroom discussion in which they have participated actively because the subject matter is keyed to their experience, students emerge with an analytical approach to problems, with a comprehension of underlying forces. The subject of the first lesson in that trade union course was an introduction to the capitalist system. As I said above, the teacher gave a brilliant lecture beginning with feudalism, the change to capitalism, the words of Karl Marx, exploitation of the working class, the whole bit. But he wasn't *teaching*, he was *telling*. He was telling the working class in words what it had experienced in life, instead of drawing from that experience the analysis he wanted the students to make.

Here below is a summary outline of the way the same subject was taught to a group of trade unionists in a workers' summer school. It should be noted that in this class and those that followed, no one went to sleep, the lively discussion was enjoyed by both teacher and students, the students were enthusiastic about the school, and tests showed that they had, in fact, learned what was taught them.

No tape recording of the class session is available so it should be understood that the questions and answers are only a fragment of the whole, listed merely to show the approach, to give the flavor of the discussion, to clarify the technique.

Questions	*Answers*
Where do you work?	• Students give the names of the companies where they are employed. (This question serves the additional purpose of helping the teacher to get to

know his students and the students to know each other in their first meeting.)

Why do you work?

- Have to work in order to live.
- Can't eat without working.
- Just gotta get that dough each week to pay the rent.

Does the man who owns the factory work alongside you?

- (Laughter) That'll be the day.
- I've never seen him.
- My plant is owned by a big corporation.

Have you ever seen the stockholders of the corporation working in the plant?

- No, they don't work there.
- Of course not.

But you all agree you *had* to work in order to live; now you tell me there are some people who live without working. How come?

- They don't have to work because they own the factory.
- They get profits from the business.

Then there are two groups of people in our society. One group, to which you belong, lives by . . . ?
And the other group to which your employer belongs lives by . . .?

- Working.

- Owning.

(*Teacher writes on blackboard*)
2 groups
Workers—live by working
Employers—live by owning

Have you always had work?

- Yes.
- I was laid off for five months once.
- My factory was closed during the Depression for over a year.

Mary says her plant was closed down for over a year. But she works in a textile mill. Didn't people need the shirts her mill turned out? And Henry's refrigerator plant, he tells us, was shut down for five months. Didn't people want refrigerators any more?

- Sure, people needed shirts but they couldn't pay for them because they didn't have any money, so the boss had to shut the mill down.
- When Henry's boss couldn't sell his refrigerators, he closed the plant.
- If I were him I'd have done the same thing. He's gotta make a profit or he must go out of business.

You mean to say that even though people needed shirts and wanted refrigerators, unless the owner made a profit, he closed up?

- Yes, he's in business to make money.
- If he doesn't make money, he shuts down the plant.
- It doesn't matter if he's a good buy or a bad guy, unless he makes a profit, he has to close up.

What you are saying, then, is that in our system of production, goods will be produced only if there is a profit?

- That's right.
- Unless there's a profit, there's no production.

Was that always true?

- Guess so.
- No, there was a time when people made what they needed for themselves, when they needed it.

Why don't they make shirts, and refrigerators, and washing machines, and autos for themselves now?

- Don't have the money.
- You need factories and raw materials and expensive equipment to make the things people want nowadays.

Let's sum up what we have discussed so far. You say that in our system of production there are 2 groups
(*teacher points to blackboard*)
Workers—live by working
Employers—live by owning

The employers live by owning (*teacher writes on blackboard*)
The employers own:

the factories
equipment, machinery
raw materials

the means of
production

The employers own what is necessary to produce goods in our society. This system of production is called
(*teacher writes on blackboard*)

CAPITALISM
Object—not to produce goods as needed
but
to make a profit

Now let's continue. The owners of the means of production, the employers, are also called capitalists. Which of the two groups, workers or capitalists, have more power? Why?

- The bosses have the most power because they have more money.
- The capitalists have the most power because if they don't give you a job, you can't pay your bills.
- The capitalists have the most power because if you don't work you starve, if they don't work they've got enough money to live on.

What gives them more power?

- They own the means of production.

Which group has the most power with the government? Let me answer that question by reading a quotation from a book written a long time ago: "The facts of the situation amount to this: that a comparatively small number of men control the raw material of this country; that a comparatively small number of men control the water power . . . that the same number of

men largely control the railroads; that by agreements
handed around among
themselves they control
prices, and that same group
of men control the larger
credits of the country. . . .
*The masters of the govern-
ment of the United States
are the combined capitalists
and manufacturers of the
United States.*"

The man who wrote that
was in a position to know.
He was President of the
United States when he
wrote it. His name was
Woodrow Wilson.

In our next lesson, we will
discuss what the working
class can do to protect itself
from the power of the capitalist class.

It is apparent from this lesson that a discussion does not
mean merely aimless talk leading here, there, and everywhere.
The good teacher must know his subject as well as the lecturer; he must have the same mastery of his material but, in
addition, he must give thought to the best way of presenting
it in terms of the experience of his students. He must have a
lesson plan. This does not mean such strict adherence to his
plan that he won't be quick to pick up and pursue this or
that interesting point arising from the students' responses—
but it does mean that he must not be sidetracked indef-

initely. His lesson must have a beginning, a middle, and an end. He must know before the discussion begins the basic points he is going to make and he must make them.

A key point to remember is that the discussion must never be allowed to become a dialogue between teacher and a student with the other students feeling that they need not listen until a question is directed specifically to them. The students must listen carefully to other student responses as well as to teacher questions. There are techniques for establishing this continual participation. "Do you agree with what John just said, Philip? No? Then what's your answer to the question?"

In this connection, the good teacher never makes the mistake of calling upon students in order. When the first question is directed to Student A, the next to Student B, and the next to Student C, there is no need for Student Z to pay any attention because he knows precisely when he will be invited to participate; until that moment arrives the discussion can become irrelevant to him.

There is an even more important reason for not calling upon students in a set order. The good teacher is concerned less with subject matter than with the people he is teaching. He wants them to learn to think. If he is alert and has done his job well, all the students will have participated in the discussion before it is over and he will then be aware of their background and capabilities. He will *know* his students, and consequently he can direct questions to them in accordance with their varying ability. The easy questions will go to the less able students—it is important for them to get a feeling of accomplishment—and the more difficult, more subtle questions will be directed to the brighter students—they must be extended to the utmost or they will lose interest.

The good teacher never teaches a lesson without using the blackboard, and he should insist that the basic points he writes on the blackboard should be recorded by the students in a notebook, along with other notes they choose to take themselves. There is a sound reason for the blackboard and the notebook: some people learn by hearing; some people learn by seeing; some people learn only by using their muscles; and almost everybody learns best by a combination of all three. Thus, the discussion itself will be suited to those who learn by hearing; the basic points on the blackboard will help those who learn by seeing; and writing in the notebook will drive the points home for those who must use their muscles to learn. The notebook, with the fundamentals of each lesson therein recorded, will be of use to the student for review purposes and, for the brightest ones, it can become a tool for teaching others when the need arises. And the need already exists for more classes for workers, newcomers to the radical movement, and peasants in the underdeveloped countries.

Campus Missionaries:
The Laying on of Culture
....
John McDermott

About a year ago I accepted an invitation to speak "against the war," at, let's call it, the University of Dexter. It is located in the city of that name, one of the major manufacturing towns of the Midwestern industrial belt. Since Dexter is somewhat off the main circuit for antiwar speech-making, I read up on the university and the town, and what I found made me look forward to my visit.

The university tended to draw most of its students from the town itself. They came heavily from working-class families and were often the first in their families to attend college. Frequently English was not the only language spoken at home. More significant was the fact that the city itself had at one time considerable fame for working-class militancy. One of the great early strikes of the Depression was fought in Dexter, and the issue was not settled in the workers' favor until that had fought the National Guard to a draw in pitched street battles. Before that the city had been a center of Socialist Party activity, and still earlier, a stronghold of IWW sentiment. Thus I looked forward to my visit as an opportunity to talk to the kind of students seldom reached by Movement speakers.

It wasn't. Attendance at the well-publicized meeting was spotty; those who came tended to be about evenly divided between faculty and graduate students, almost all of whom were from outside the state. And there were no students at the party to which I was taken later in the evening, though they had helped plan the meeting, for student segregation is the campus rule at Dexter, no less within the Movement than outside it. Perhaps it was that or perhaps my disappointment at the absence of "normal" students at the evening's meeting; anyhow, I deliberately forced the party to become a meeting. It had taken no great powers of observation to note that the antiwar movement at Dexter, and, by extension, its left, was largely a preserve of the faculty and some fellow-traveling graduate students, and I was interested to discover why that was so. In particular, I wanted to explore the role these teachers had adopted in relation to their "normal" students and to examine with them the contradiction between that professional role and their wider political aspirations. I have taught in several universities, I've suffered the same contradiction and was unable to overcome it.

The more prominent feature of the discussion which followed, and of all the subsequent ones I've started on the same subject in similar situations, was that the faculty, all of them, still aspired to teach in elite schools. Dexter, after all, is what is popularly known as a "cow" college. A state school, it gets those students who, for lack of skill or money or interest, don't go to the main state university and couldn't "make" the liberal arts colleges in the area, even if they wanted to. Its students are very much vocationally oriented and still tied to their families. Most of them live at home.

Dexter is frequently under nuisance attack by some right-wing faction or other. It pays rather badly and is not in an attractive metropolitan area. Its library is inferior, it provides little research money, and the teaching loads are heavy. The administration is fusty and conservative, as is much of the faculty.

My faculty friends, obviously talented men and women, had not reconciled themselves to this exile. They deprecated the region, the town, the university and, especially, the students, even the graduate students. Loyalty and affection they reserved for the graduate schools from which they had come, and they reflected this feeling in their teaching and counseling by relating only to that one student in a hundred who might go on to one of those prestigious graduate schools. Those were the students who shared with them the culture of books and civility—and scorn for Dexter; who might by their success at a "good" graduate school justify the faculty's exile in Dexter. Of course they didn't put it that way, and neither did I when I taught in similar places. They saw themselves as embattled missionaries to the culturally philistine. They worked hard and creatively with the students who merited hope. As for the others, these men and women, in spite of their expressed scorn, nourished a vision, hesitantly expressed, of a society in which no student would be oppressed by cultural bondage to ignorance, vocationalism, anti-intellectualism, or provincialism. In fact, that attitude and hope gave rise to, and was expressed in, their left-wing politics.

The guests at the party were woefully ignorant of the backgrounds of their "normal" students. They were vaguely aware that most of them came from working-class families, though what that might mean aside from greater resistance to formal education they had no idea. Nor did they have any knowledge of Dexter's militant labor tradition. This was sad, for it penalized the faculty in a number of ways. To cite an apparently trivial instance, most of the faculty present were concerned about attacks made on the university by the right-wingers in town. Respect for free speech and expression had an important place in their scale of values, and they tried to convey it to their classes, using all the familiar academic examples, from HUAC witch hunting and Joe McCarthy, to Stuart Mill, Milton, and Sophocles.

Yet that they might relate the principle of free expression to the problems of Wobbly agitators in the 1910s or CIO organizers in the 1930s (or white-collar workers in the 1970s) —in short, relate it to the actual cultural history (or future) of their own students—never occurred to them. Instead, they were put off when the students responded to the alien and seemingly irrelevant world of HUAC and Milton and academic freedom with either passive unconcern or active hostility.

I believe this example successfully characterizes how the great majority of faculty behave in schools like Dexter, including, especially, the left wing of the faculty. Socialized like all their fellows into a rigid professional role by their university, graduate school, and early professional experiences, they have neither the information nor the inclination to break out of that role and relate openly and positively to the majority of their students who cannot accept the culture of the university world as their own.

University professors as a group seem exceptionally uncritical of the limited value—and values—of a university education and the acculturation it represents. In their view, students who are really open to their classroom and other cultural experiences at the university will, as a rule, turn out to be more sophisticated, more interested in good literature, more sensitive morally than those who are less open or who have not had the benefit of college. These students will also be free of the more provincial ties of home, hometown, region, and class. In short, most academics take it as an article of faith that students benefit by exchanging their own culture for that of the university. It is by far the most common campus prejudice.

And it would be harmless enough if it were limited in its sanction to those students who allow their university education to "take," who do well at university work and will go on to graduate school and then to a place within the university world or, perhaps, into some other related profession. University attitudes and values are appropriate to that world.

But what about the others, the cultural rednecks, the "normal" students at a place like Dexter? Do they really profit from acquiring the attitudes, values, lifestyles, and so forth of the peculiar culture whose institutional base is the university? One way of attacking this question is to ask to what extent those values, attitudes, and lifestyles may be usefully transferred to other institutional settings—to little towns and big cities, to industrial or agricultural life, to life in a corporation or in government.

That was about as far as we went at that party a year ago. We agreed that we were part of a university system which was actively engaged at its Dexters in destroying whatever indigenous culture might remain among the American working class. We recognized that, consciously or not, we had assumed an invidious clerical relationship to our student laity. Like medieval priests or missionaries to the heathen, we dispensed a culture to all our students, despite the fact that a scant few could participate in it. For the others, the language of that culture, like Latin to the colloquial, was grasped largely in rote phrases, its symbols and doctrines recognized but only dimly understood. To the extent that this majority of students acquired the external trappings of the university, they seemed both culturally pacified and made culturally passive. Pacified because they were accultured away from their own historical values and traditions; passive because they could at best be spectators of a culture whose home remained an alien institution.

In the year that has passed since my visit to Dexter my views of the relationship of general culture to political culture have very much developed under the influence of Edward Thompson's *The Making of the English Working Class*. I find particularly persuasive and suggestive Thompson's demonstration of how certain aspects of the general culture of the English working class, over a period of time and under the stress of events, came to support a specifically political culture—that is, to enlarge its capacity to define its social interests and to struggle successfully in their behalf. I shall cite several instances of this, for I want later to use them to illuminate the problem at Dexter from a new and, I think, hopeful standpoint.

Thompson shows that the movement into the factories in England of the late eighteenth and nineteenth centuries was made up of two distinct streams. One was the movement of poor, dispossessed rural persons to the city and the factory in search of opportunity; the other of highly skilled, often literate craftsmen being pushed down the social and economic ladder by the new forces of industrialism and technology. The former, abruptly torn from their rural poverty, had some reason to view the change as an improvement. The cultural shock of the transition, the traditional passivity to authority, the stimulus of urban life, and the novelty of cash wages might easily have disguised for a time the exploitative nature of their place in the new factory system. The urban craftsmen, however, having a sense of their own skill and worth, with still lively guild traditions, and a strong sense of declining status and economic position, were most unlikely to think of the factory experience as a road to opportunity. They knew it for the oppression it really was. It was the meeting of these two groups that proved so creative for the future of the working-class movement. The skilled printers, weavers, and mechanics recognized that their lot was cast with the unskilled rural migrants, and they became a creative element among the larger mass. Their literacy, their talent for organization, their family and folk memories that working people had once lived secure in their homes, livelihoods, and craftsmanship, were transferred over the years to the mass of working people. But they were transferred with a radical difference. By contributing them to the cause of the entire working class, what might otherwise have been merely a narrow defense of guild interests was instead universalized into a struggle for the rights of all Englishmen, a struggle for the rights of man.

Thompson also shows how important for the new working-class movement was the experience so many workers had in the dissenting churches. Men and women who, over the years, had learned to contend with the problems of maintaining a minister's salary, keeping up the church and parsonage, administering an active religious and social program, and organizing regional church activities were able to apply these skills to nascent working-class organizations. Of particular importance was their long experience of persecution at the hands of the Church of England. Both ministers and congregations had learned how to preserve their churches and beliefs in the face of official hostility and repression. Thus when Pitt, Burke, and their successors attempted to destroy the new working people's organizations, these were able to go underground, preserving their organizations, maintaining their programs and extending their networks throughout the country.

Still another general cultural factor cited by Thompson as a primary support for the growing working-class movement was the belief among the English lower classes that they were "freeborn Englishmen." The phrase had no precise meaning, but it was habitually called into play to criticize or resist any arbitrary act against the populace and its organizations, any claim to special place by the upper classes, any innovation in government control over the speech, writing, travels, or associations of the common people. It was a useful and eminently flexible weapon in the hands of the working-class movement against the power of the capitalists and the wiles of Edmund Burke.

What makes Thompson's work of more than antiquarian interest is the suggestive analogy it offers to situations such as that at Dexter. There is a double movement into such universities today, somewhat as there was a double movement into the factories of England two centuries ago. On the one hand, a flood of lower-class young people is moving into these universities, seeking entrée into the old independent professional middle class which university attendance supposedly affords. It is necessary to add "supposedly," for passage through a nonelite university no longer qualifies one for that kind of life. The jobs for which the Dexters and the junior colleges prepare students are elementary and secondary teaching, the lower levels of social work, white collar jobs, petty management—that is, employments which were once semiprofessional, but which now are being rapidly industrialized by bureaucracy, managerial science, and the IBM machine. Thus the lower-class students who go to Dexter only appear to escape from the world of industry; they are really taking the first vocational step into a new kind of industrial life.

The second movement into such institutions as Dexter is of a gifted minority of educated persons, who identify with the values, accomplishments, and prestige of elite professions, but are forced by the economics of academic employment to take positions they consider beneath their skills, their sense of worth and accomplishment, their lively memories of the recent past.

But here the analogy with Thompson's English working class begins to break down, for these latter specifically and pointedly refuse to make common cause with the lower-class students with whom they share daily existence. This gifted left minority does not help the students to develop an effective and vital popular political culture. On the contrary, it often occupies the vanguard of a university culture which, as I suggested above and now wish to argue more fully, pacifies lower-class students.

The most obvious political characterization of university culture is that it lives by, and presents to its students, the values and attitudes appropriate to its own upper-middle-class lifestyle—a style that is part of the older, now declining, professional middle classes. As indicated above, a university education did once promise membership in the professional classes. This meant that university graduates could ordinarily expect a life of considerable social and economic independence, some measure of personal influence in local business and political communities, significant autonomy and initiative in carrying out their daily work, and thus the possibility of enjoying the pride that follows from personal accomplishment and craftsmanship.

Could it be clearer that no such life awaits the graduates of the nation's Dexters? Today a degree from a second- or third-line institution is a passport to a lifestyle of high consumption and of reasonable job security. But it will probably be an industrial lifestyle, characterized by social and economic dependence on a large institution, by little or no political or social influence, and by participation in rationalized work processes wherein one must try merely to "get by" and not step on anybody's toes. Consider, therefore, how the professionally oriented values of the university's culture might function in such an industrial environment. High on the scale of university values, now and in the past, stands the virtue of tolerance—not only personal tolerance in the face of new or differing ideas, attitudes, and values but the belief that tolerance itself is of greater personal and social value than the substance of almost any set of creeds. Such a value was useful in the professional worlds of the past, for it would normally help diminish conflict in a middle class made up of highly autonomous individuals. And in elite circles even today it diminishes the weight assigned to ideological differences and helps to harmonize the social and political relations of our pluralistic, semiautonomous industrial, educational, government, and other managers. It carries the advantage, too, that it opens managers to the merits of technological and organizational novelty in a political economy strongly oriented to such innovations.

But how does this belief function for the young men and women of Dexter, who will normally occupy the lower and middle levels of great institutional bureaucracies, and who may have reason to resist those very same innovations: speedup, compulsory overtime, more and more alienating work processes, forced transfer to another city or region, institutional propaganda, Muzak, and the other normal tyrannies of personnel managers? Is it a value that helps them to initiate or continue those collective struggles which are necessary to defend or enhance their interests; or does it rob them of the moral and ideological assurance which must support the beliefs of people who challenge the social legitimacy and retributive power of authority?

A second political aspect of university culture is its almost uniform hostility to the institutions of local and community life. Many churches, fraternities, veterans' associations, councils, and boards upon which local and community life in America is built are havens of the narrowest sorts of provincialism, racism, intellectual baiting, babbittry, and jingoism. For these reasons, and for reasons having to do with the demands of the national economy for college-trained persons, the tendency of university experience is to propel the young away from local and community life and toward national life and its institutions. A result of the university's liberalism, cosmopolitanism, and technologism, this tendency is supported by the national culture, by the students themselves, and by their parents.

But it should be combated by those, like my friends at Dexter, who are interested in building mass resistance to the prevailing currents of American life. A young person from Dexter, unless extraordinarily gifted or fortunate, has almost no means of gaining influence in national politics. And to the extent that university culture directs great masses of lower-

and lower-middle-class young people into the institutions of national rather than local and community life, it assists in disenfranchising them from political influence. Of course, the conventional representatives of university culture argue that the decline of local politics and local institutions is inevitable, given the institutional needs of twentieth-century industry and government, the gradual nationalization of American life, and the march of technology, i.e., liberalism, cosmopolitanism, and technologism. But we should begin to question whether this inevitability amounts to more than advantageous prejudice. For the kind of society which these university spokesmen describe as inevitable appears to be coincidentally one in which the PhD takes its place with property and birth as a means to political influence and social status.

Similarly, the ignorance, racism, and the like which characterize so much of local life should not put us off. Given the preoccupation of the left, over the past epoch, with national rather than local concerns and institutions, it is not surprising that local America has become a playpen of unchallenged right-wing attitudes, persons, and organizations. Of course, one could not expect, even under the best conditions, that the lifestyle of local America will rival the faculty club in gentility, civility, humanist learning, and other caricatures of university life. But that is not its test, any more than the theological elegance of the dissenting churches was the test of their usefulness to a struggling movement of ordinary Englishmen. Those who are today concerned about a different kind of economic barbarism and a similar kind of worldwide crusade should draw the appropriate lessons.

A third political aspect of university culture is its latent hostility to two of the more valuable and humane realities in current popular culture. One cannot move around this country without being impressed by its egalitarianism, that is, the depth and vitality of the ordinary American's feeling that he or she is as good as the next person. And the other reality so important in our popular culture is the well-nigh universal belief among our people that they possess an extraordinary range and variety of substantive rights. Like the belief in the "freeborn Englishmen," the belief in substantive rights is often vague and contradictory. Nevertheless, the history of popular political movements is the history of ordinary people acting in behalf of what they believe to be their substantive rights.

It would be too much to say that the university's culture is uniformly hostile to these popular realities, for the situation is ambiguous. However, it is not difficult to identify important hostile tendencies. Thus in contrast to the normal American acceptance of the principle of equality, the professoriat strongly values formalized difference of age, academic rank, scholarly reputation and, it may even be, accomplishment. The effect of this sort of deference is somewhat difficult to gauge and it may be tendentious on my part to believe that it influences student attitudes on legitimacy, authority, and equality. Perhaps the issue is instead that university men and women, by failing to provide a living example of egalitarian relationships, merely fail to make common cause with the American people in their resistance to the hierarchic tendencies implicit in the social and economic system.

A more secure case can be made against the disposition in the university world to identify right not with substantive but with procedural matters. Peter Gay expressed this position in the Summer 1968 issue of *Partisan Review*: ". . . democracy is essentially procedural and what matters is not so much (important though it may be) what a given policy is as how it is arrived at." Persons as fortunately placed as Professor Gay, whose substantive rights are well established in easily available procedures, have an understandable tendency to overlook the fact that, for example, tenure, sabbaticals, choice of hours, and freedom of expression on the job are virtually unknown outside the academic world. Obviously there are other important and thorny issues here as well. Without going into them at any length, note that the test of Professor Gay's remark is its fidelity to historical fact. From that point of view, it tends to obscure the fact that the great libertarian and democratic turning point in postwar American political history, a turning point with great promise still, came not from the narrow defense of procedural rights by academic and other liberals against Joe McCarthy in the 1950s but from the assertion of substantive rights in the 1960s by mass movements of students, blacks, professors, and ordinary Americans.

The students at Dexter, and a great number of their countrymen, rightly view the liberal and academic preference for procedural right as a defense of privileges which they themselves are denied. Many view the principle of academic freedom, for example, as they view some of the laws of property. It is a tricky device which enables professors to do things, like criticize the dean or the country, for which ordinary people can be fired; just as the law of property is a tricky device which enables installment houses and loan companies to do things for which ordinary people can be sent to jail. The goal is not to do away with academic freedom, or any other hard-won libertarian procedure. A better approach would be to shape a university culture which would help to extend Professor Gay's tenure, sabbaticals, and freedom of expression on the job to everyone, on campus and off.

The existence of hostile tendencies toward egalitarianism and the primacy of substantive rights is very much related to still a fourth political aspect of university culture. Even though the university is the home and source of much of the libertarian ideology within our culture, it is often the source of authoritarian ideology as well. I have two cases in mind. The first has to do with the extensive commitment to technologism found among many faculty members. A considerable body of university opinion believes with Zbigniew Brzezinski that the promises of modern technology demand for their social realization a society characterized by "equal opportunity for all but ... special opportunity for the singularly talented few." The evasiveness of the formula should not be allowed to obscure the authoritarian social and political processes which are envisioned and justified by it—processes today best exemplified in the area of national security, where the equal voting opportunities of all are nullified by the special bureaucratic opportunities open to a singularly talented few. The second of the university's authoritarian ideologies I call "clericism." To borrow from Brzezinski's formula, it is the claim to "equal cultural rights for all, but special cultural authority for a singularly scholarly few." I refer to the still widespread (but declining) academic belief that, whatever else culture may include, it also includes the Western Heritage, the Western Tradition, the Literary Tradition, the traditions of reason and civility, etc., and that these are most fully embodied in the profession of academe and the written treasures of which academe is priestly custodian and inspired interpreter.

This principle underlies faculty sovereignty over curricular matters, justifies any and every required course, and oppresses first-year graduate students. It received its most prosaic formulation in the observation by Columbia's vice dean of the graduate facilities that "whether students vote 'yes' or 'no' on an issue is like telling me they like strawberries." Clericism and technologism have their good points; no one wishes seriously to derogate either the social or the moral value of good scholarship or competent technology. But as principles under which to organize cultural or political life they are distinctly hostile to the interests of great numbers of nonelite students, the social classes from which they are drawn, and especially the social classes they will consti-

tute when they leave the university. For clericism and technologism, like the doctrines of apostolic succession and of
property which they tend to replace, transpose major areas of
social concern from the purview of all to the treasure house
of the few. Culture, no less than politics, is a critical factor
in the nature of social organization; in the distribution of
power, reward, and status; in the infliction of powerlessness,
oppression, and despair. This is becoming increasingly understood with regard to politics, where ten years of war, urban
decay, and increasing social chaos seem to have been the fruit
of the same decade's obeisance to technology's claims. But I
am not persuaded that clericist depredations on culture are
similarly recognized.

As I think was made clear at the start of this essay, the
faculty at Dexter did not feel called upon to know the
specific cultural history and experiences of the students they
taught. Neither they nor anyone in the academic profession
consider it their task to use their own superior symbolic gifts
and wider historical perspective to identify the specific historical culture of their students, to clarify its ambiguities, to
criticize it, purging it of its moral (not geographical) provincialism, and thus to assist the students in developing a culture
which is at once personally ennobling and politically self-
conscious. On the contrary, at Dexter and elsewhere the
faculty assume that it is their duty to replace the students'
actual culture with an alien culture. Missionaries from these
graduate schools, like clergy from colonial empires everywhere and in every time, feel confident that what they bring
is good for the natives and will improve them in the long run.
In culture, as elsewhere, this is manifestly not so.

Consider the matter of historical traditions. No acculturation worth the name should be permitted to block the
transmission of Dexter's militant working-class traditions.
Even granting, as is probably the case, that only a small

minority of the Dexter students are children of Depression workers or the earlier Wobblies, to assist, even if only negatively, in destroying these traditions is to minimize for most of the students the opportunity to discover the reasons for their attitudes on a score of moral and social questions, the reality of their social lives, and the possibility of rebuilding a more human culture in Dexter for their own advantage. White intelligentsia recognize this danger when they peer across cultural lines at blacks or Vietnamese; why are they so blinded by the class lines of their own society? It should come as no surprise, therefore, that the anti-intellectualism of the students is often as deep and as bitter as the hatred exhibited by other colonial peoples toward foreigners and their works.

A university culture which related positively and creatively to the traditions and history of the working classes, blue collar and white collar, would find allies not only among the hippies and the leftists of Smith and Williams but from the "squares" of Dexter as well.

What is particularly disturbing about cultural pacification in the university is that it is not entirely an accidental phenomenon. At least since Herbert Croly's *Promise of American Life* (1909), America's dominant historians have been strongly nationalist, more interested in discovering and celebrating the American essence or character, the national mainstream, consensus, or moral epic, or the peculiar quality of our national integration, than in emphasizing its divisions, especially those based on class. It has often crossed my mind that when liberal historians two decades hence write the chronicle of the Southern freedom movement of the early 1960s or of the anti-Vietnamese War movement of today, they will find imaginative and persuasive reasons to show that the first was really part of the New Frontier and the second of the Great Society. It was thus that their predecessors have managed to reduce the richness and variety of popular revolt in the 1930s to the bureaucratic dimensions of a Washington-based "New Deal."

Fortunately, some of the younger historians, such as Staughton Lynd and Jesse Lemisch, have begun to undermine the epic poetry of the Crolyites by reviving interest in the history of popular insurgency in America. Thus they have created the possibility that at least at some universities young people will be reacquainted with the real diversity and conflict of their past. More than that, and without exaggerating its importance or extent, this new scholarship provides a point of departure for a fundamentally different university culture than the one I have been describing.

Faced with the vast social diversity of America and in opposition to the variety and strength of its Populist traditions, the thrust of university culture is to pacify its working-class "natives" and thus, I believe, to help preclude any fundamental change in national politics and priorities. Because of the surge of rebellion on campus since last spring, it is likely that this is understood better now among faculty than it was at the time I visited Dexter. But many university men and women, comparing the university's cultural values to those of industry, the mass media, and the military, or to the restless hositility of lower- and working-class America, remain partisans and priests of academe, convinced that for all its faults it is, at least minimally, a humane alternative to its rivals.

The analogy I made earlier to the work of Edward Thompson points in a more hopeful and, I think, more realistic direction. A survey of recent campus rebellions would show that it is no longer only the Harvards and the Berkeleys which suffer serious student unrest; some of the most interesting and militant activity occurs at the nonelite schools. In addition, scores of young men and women continue to be exiled by their elite graduate schools into a lifetime of work in the nonelite universities. The narrowest interests of these teachers and their most lofty professional and political aspirations lie in the same direction. It is to take up the task, in common with their students, of rebuilding the vitality of a popular resistance culture, that is, of a culture which will "enhance the capacity of ordinary Americans to identify their social interests and to struggle successfully in their behalf."

This is not a task which individuals can successfully undertake in isolation, nor one whose champions will be free of serious reprisal at the hands of university and political authorities. Nevertheless, there are already a handful of campuses where the work has begun, in critical universities, liberation courses, seminars in local and working-class history, student-taught courses for faculty, and research projects on local and campus decision-making. It remains for others to add to these hopeful beginnings.

The Working Class Goes to College
••••
Ira Shor

> "Boxing makes you sweat and smell. Stay in school. Be a thinker, not a stinker."—Advice from the Champ, in the movie *Rocky*
>
> "... the American Dream turned belly up, bobbed to the surface of cupidity unlimited, went bang in the noonday sun."
> —Kurt Vonnegut, *God Bless You, Mr. Rosewater*

A new piece of the American Dream has been pushed across the table to the working class. Workers in large numbers have finally been getting their crack at college. From the late 1950s to the early 1970s, two-year campuses sprouted up as fast as McDonald burger bins, opening at the rate of one every ten days in the last decade. Who do these new colleges serve, and how? Who built them for what purposes?

The two-year schools now enrolling some 4 million workers have played a significant role in America's developing consumer-military economy. Postwar affluence has floated domestically on automation, credit buying, waste production and consumption, and the expansion of the service and public sectors of the work force. Internationally, the American economy has been exporting capital and manipulating the intercontinental flow of materials. This kind of advanced capitalism has an advancing problem with the absorption of surplus labor and goods. Unemployed workers and unsold goods and services put social and economic heat on society. Large parts of both these surpluses have been absorbed by taking workers out of the labor pool and into higher education, and by building colleges that consume without producing anything material. Junior colleges, as a form of waste production and consumption, swallow unemployed and devour goods (paper, furniture, brick, cement, plumbing, glass, office machinery, athletic supplies, etc.) and services (computer grading and registration, banking, laundry, food delivery, gas, electricity, telephone, etc.). Technological advances have meant that less and less American labor is producing more; for capitalism to survive, more and more labor has to be retired from production into other spheres. In this cybernetic nexus, the junior college takes its place as a materially nonproductive phenomenon. From mass higher education for workers, the system surely gets something from nothing. Only welfare and the military challenge education in nonproductive consumption.

Like the military, the junior college serves to extend by two to three years the high school regimentation of young adult workers. Part of the discipline takes place off-campus, as the two-year student body is exploited by business as a large, poorly paid underclass of temporary and part-time labor. At the working-class college where I teach, some three-quarters of the students hold low-wage part-time jobs. They work crazily staggered hours, often far from home and school. The national chains of supermarkets, discount stores, hamburger joints, and service stations depend heavily on this manipulable, unprotected source of labor. Young worker-students float from Korvette's to Burger King to the A&P, always expendable, with a crowd of job-seeking fellow-students lined up at the door waiting for the first opening.

Junior college attendance serves to keep students dependent on employers because they can't accept full-time work and still go to school. They are able to earn money only before, after, or in-between classes.

In addition to the higher profit margins business reaps from using part-time labor, college for the working class also serves business' need to have the work force trained in the new technologies. Besides monitoring the unemployed for the state, and devouring excess goods and services for the economy, community colleges offer the technical training which the private sector demands and the public sector pays for. Business needs trained workers, but refuses to pay the cost of educating its own employees. By building public community colleges with tax funds, the state has socialized business' training costs. First, workers are taxed so that the state can construct its higher education training centers; then, workers are asked to pay tuition for an economically necessary, business-oriented education. In serving the needs of business, mass higher education has become another big business. It is structured hierarchically, like the giant corporations, gets organized by unions, and is run primarily by privileged white men.

Not only do the hard economic needs of the system find some solution in the two-year college network, but ideological needs are serviced here as well. The American Dream needed to be updated as a culturally integrating force. Worker alienation has been rising dramatically, as social services disintegrate, jobs become harder to find, work becomes more and more meaningless, and inflation races for the moon. The lean American Dream fattened itself on manna from higher education. Hundreds of new community colleges opened as jobs began closing, offering on campus new skills, opportunities, and vistas to American workers.

In times past, white European colonialists found the American Dream in political liberty and cheap land. Later, in the nineteenth century, the Dream's legendary emblem became "Go West, young man." With the closing of the frontier at the turn of this century, the dream changed into a small-business vision, the family farm or the small family enterprise in town. As monopoly capital rationalizes all corners of economic life, family businesses have been disappearing along with family farms. Today, instead of the illusion of "working for yourself," a new ideal is promoted by the state and the economy. The *career* is the modern form of the Dream. The new road upward through the career is through the elaborate school system, which now includes college for working people. In the 1940s and 1950s it was customary for workers to begin their careers right out of high school. Now, college has become almost mandatory. Working people toy with all kinds of fantasies of wealth—through the lotteries, gambling, and so on—but higher education has emerged as the most publicized route to status and success.

To make possible the mass entry of workers into college, a national infrastructure of community colleges had to be built, thousands of new teachers had to be recruited, and the new Dream of the career had to be marketed. After having been tracked away from college throughout American history, the working class now was sold the idea that big things would come with higher education. Through national television, radio, and magazines, and through high school counseling services, workers heard of the new opportunities for training, jobs, and advancement. Workers were told how much more college graduates earned. But even as workers picked up on this theme, they could only go to school if a whole new system of colleges was built especially for them. The old network of public and private elite colleges had costs, residency, and academic requirements beyond worker resources. Hence, a massive building program was launched, leading to the inauguration of nearly a thousand new non-residential, low-tuition community colleges, near worker homes. By the mid-1960s, the mass higher education strategy had established beachheads in worker consciousness and in the neighborhoods. Because this new network was for the *working class*, it emerged physically, operationally, and scholastically very different from the plush and reposeful Ivy League. The new campuses were functional and institutional: giant parking lots filled with jalopies and souped-up specials, cinderblock buildings and prefabs, computer registration, large classes, fiberglass furniture, courses jammed into a tight schedule to maximize use of time and space, teaching machines, and the inevitable fluorescent-formica cafeteria with its gray tuna fish and greasy fries. Such was the egalitarian face America turned to its workers. And the workers literally stormed in by the millions, forced by the economy to acquire college credentials, and driven on by their own healthy desires for upgraded skills, advanced learning, and new opportunities.

Junior colleges often opened their doors first in local high schools, before state funding capitalized them into their own plant-like campuses. Initially, many of the workers' old high schools began giving day and evening classes close enough to home for workers to attend before or after work. The prescribed curricula were heavily vocational and regionally oriented, flexibly designed to meet the needs of local government and business. Financed by worker taxes, the community colleges used career curricula to adapt to local conditions. Skills needed by nearby industry and government became one-year certificate or two-year associate degree programs. In addition, a transfer-track was built in for the most aspiring and scholastically gifted workers, who could go on to higher degrees at other colleges.

Many community colleges not only began in high schools, but often employed former high school teachers as the foundational instruction corps. In the dawn of its expansion, the two-year network had to reach down to the lower grades for both its material base and its labor. High schools served the state as a primitively accumulated source of facilities and teacher cadre for a new mass line in higher education. Secondary teachers had the option to work part time in the new junior colleges, moonlighting for extra income. Many worked evenings and in summers to get the MAs and PhDs needed to win full-time jobs in the colleges, along with which came higher pay and prestige. Community college teaching is the least prestigious in academe, but in terms of daily labor, time off, wages, and class ambience, it is distinctly a step up from high school. The new American Dream quickly went into action: for the new college teachers and the worker-students, the junior college presented social mobility.

Burned out of the family farm and family business, the phoenix of the Dream rose from ashes to legitimize the system once again. Workers who could no longer believe in "moving to the country" or in "working for yourself" were presented with a credible alternative: higher education. The challenge came personally and immediately: improve yourself to get ahead. Opportunity is close at hand: your junior college is nearby, you can live cheaply at home, fees and tuition are low, your friends go there. The curriculum was legible, refreshing, and even a break from the old routine: you could become an orthopedic assistant, medical technologist, X-ray technician, dental hygienist, child-care assistant, or legal secretary; you can study media electronics, mechanical, civil, or electrical engineering, environmental science, auto dynamics, computer technology, or nursing. Vocations that were once taught in high schools or on-the-job were upgraded into credentialing programs and renamed as "para-professions," a linguistic hocus-pocus appropriate to the marketing of the new careers.

The American system announced that reports of its death were premature. Higher education, like military spending, advanced to center stage as one critical pivot for the postwar renaissance. The state was tapping its most durable integrating mechanism and mythology by posing college as the new route to wealth. And if you couldn't make it the new way, the system protected its flank by convincing you that it was your own fault. On the farm or in a small business, it was your own poor management that ruined your chances for success. In the junior college, intricate tracking and cooling-out techniques (described intimately by Burton Clark as far back as 1959) monitored your progress, or lack of it. Computerized transcripts and apologetic counselors served notice: it is your own dullness, your thickness with books that caused your failure, or destined you for the lesser programs, the lesser careers. For the millions of workers who made it through and for the millions who were dropped out, the system could take credit for being generous (for spending your own money to educate you for the needs of business), blameless (for flunking you out or for graduating you into jobs once performed by noncollege labor), and progressive (for democratizing higher education opportunities). Higher education for workers has matured in America as a complex of disguises and mutually penetrating contradictions: millions of workers have gotten better skills and the best academic education ever offered workers in this country; millions of workers have been taken into college to hide unemployment, and then graduated into a job market that has no work equal to their intellect or skills, from campus facilities and programs decidedly inferior to the colleges lavishly funded for the elite. Because workers themselves wanted college educations—and open access to higher education is a legitimate demand, even if the system turns it into an undemocratic process—the growth of the junior college network has strengthened the image of America as an open society.

While economic needs facilitated the state's development of worker-colleges, the old group of elite private and public universities remains, to ensure that minimal social needs for high-level researchers, scientists, and managers are met. Below these sanctuaries is the new boiling pot of academe. Prior to the mass arrival of worker-students, the elite preserve had articulated comfortable standards, canons, methods, a common language, and reading lists. The tracking of workers into college first preciptated a (still ongoing) pedagogical crisis in the academy, and then a fiscal crisis in the public sector. Addressing curricular problems, publishers turn out book after book and journals churn out paper after paper on how to teach the "new learners." Only some of all these efforts have helped. Working-class language, culture, and experience are antagonistic to the genteel ambience of academe. A struggle between bourgeois pedagogy and proletarian students has long been underway. The conflict of values and styles is stark, often painful, sometimes productive, occasionally comic. In the disruption of institutional decorum, there is a real chance for radical teachers to develop a working-class pedagogy.

This new college struggle—between the state's higher education tracking for workers, and the workers' attempt to grow through college—suggests that the first two years of college are being risked in preference to another more threatening kind of class warfare. (It's easier for the state to face and monitor workers in classrooms than in the streets.) This recruitment of college as yet another means of social control is causing dislocations throughout academe. As the newest and highest point of struggle, community college life takes the lead in posing politicized questions to the entire teaching profession. Issues such as literacy teaching, open access, equal opportunity for women and minorities, compensatory programs, lack of parity in tax support for elite and worker colleges, have hegemonized recent debates in educational circles.

The American academy never used to weed out, detain, and track working people, so it has little experience in dealing with the problems. Pedagogically, one impulse has been to imitate Harvard, but that doesn't work. The high schools are imitated also, but these new colleges are supposed to be more than high school. The process goes on, clumsily, incoherently, as both the former secondary and the elite teachers trained in universities don't know what's effective from any point of view. Also, workers looking for the Dream sense the confusion and the con, the insult to their intelligence and their aspirations, so they resist "their" colleges. They've seen it all before, and carry over from high school more and more cynicism, hostility, and suspicion of education. Their forms of resistance are both passive and active. Nonattendance and nonperformance are the limits of their pacifism. Vandalism, fights, con games on teachers, drug-taking, theft, and legitimate intellectual challenges comprise their active sabotage.

They have been swept up into the long-range trend in American society to lengthen education for everyone. The upper classes always received whatever duration of schooling was necessary for them to rule. Workers had to fight for each level of schooling, and had in mind quality education for themselves and their children. When they saw what they would get in the classrooms, they often had impulses to fight their way out. But, the legal requirements and the economic need for schooling have made the compulsory kindergarten-to-college odyssey an epic battleground of the classes. Formerly, the only level of school separate from class war was the level just beyond the mass participation of workers. Now, higher education has a whole network of worker-colleges, and working people even get into some universities, so America's academy is no longer immune. Wherever surplus labor arrives as freshmen and freshwomen, the solidity of college life and teaching methods is disrupted.

A further contradiction in the state's higher education strategy is that the two-year college indirectly aids the women's movement. The new two-year schools have made it easier for more women (as well as minorities) to enter college. For working-class women, who previously would have been tied to the home, to part-time work as a supplement to the family income, or to office jobs with low pay and no career ladder, the local junior colleges may prove more liberating than for the men. College systems at all levels have felt the effect of the women's movement through affirmative action battles and demands for women's programs. What is especially noteworthy is that the feminist opening to the left has a base in worker-colleges as well as elite ones, unlike the new left of the 1960s, which rose and declined on upper-class campuses. At the college I teach in, the feminism in society-at-large is sinking more roots among working-class women students. The new women students are also generally more motivated and successful in my college than their working-class male counterparts. One reason, besides the impact of feminism on the women, is that high-achieving working-class men are pushed by society and by their families into colleges more elite than a two-year school. The women, tracked to babies and kitchens, or to low-level white collar and service jobs, receive less encouragement to struggle through college. The same story of unequal opportunity applies to minorities, who, like working women, have the most to lose from cutbacks in community colleges.

Perhaps the most basic contradiction built into the form of the community college is the humanities-vocational split. Before community colleges massively absorbed workers, the range of education available for maturing working people was confined to vocational/academic high schools, post-secondary technical institutes, union apprentice academies, government job programs, and much on-the-job training. The bottom sectors of the working class drifted into the military, into crime, or wandered from one unskilled job to another. Middle sectors found spots in the police, fire, and sanitation departments, or got into a union through a friend or relative, or took an industrial job that started them at the bottom of the ladder. The "cream" of the working class had two upper tracks set aside for it in both the lower grades and in the high schools. One track identified middle-level personnel (public school teachers, accountants, mid-range gray and white collar supervisors), while the other track selected a few young worker-students for accelerated classes and special schools that led to university education. The university-bound fraction became homogenized with the children of the elite when it arrived at the best colleges, there to be processed and bottled into a literary/scientific aristocracy, the highest level managers and thinkers in any institution.

With the expanded system of two-year schools for workers, the community college emerges as a fragile marriage of vocational training to liberal arts. In the history of American higher education, few colleges shared a single mission of doing both. Workers who pass through the bipolar campus programs are still tracked into lower-level managerial and technical work. But, to sell higher education to the working class as a positive advance, the two-year schools had to emerge as real *colleges*, that is, one pedagogical step above the old forms of technical training. So, the community college was compelled to offer to workers what the former levels of education lacked: a comprehensive liberal arts component. Otherwise, the new mass higher education would be ideologically weak in its offer of progress, of something new and better for workers. Without the luxury of liberal arts, something the elite virtually monopolized before 1960, the two-year college could not be effectively merchandised as a *college*, as a new road to the American Dream. Hence, the community college made a concession to the working class by offering potentially dangerous courses in literature, sociology, history, psychology, political science, philosophy, and art. It required competence in the traditionally repressive basic skills: reading, writing, and arithmetic. In technical

and business courses, it borrowed, upgraded, and institutionalized the kinds of depoliticized skills-training that used
to be done elsewhere.

While literacy and technical skills are essential for the job
market, humanities are not. So, liberal arts are viewed skep-
tically and contradictorily by worker-students. Many want to
be complete human beings, and know that liberal arts facilitate self-growth. Many are so economically pressed that they
just want to get in and out of college fast, into a job that
helps them pay their bills. It's not clear at all that studying
poetry or that Western civilization courses will help pay the
rent or make them more competitive in the tight labor
market. The ambivalence of workers toward the humanities
component is matched by the ambivalence of humanities
teachers toward the students. Liberal arts can be fun and
liberating and enlightening, but they also can be mystifying,
boring, insulting to workers, and oppressive. There is a complex delicacy involved here, because technical training
doesn't claim to be anything more than what it is, while
humanities have to justify the mystique of opening up new
worlds of experience. History courses which overwhelm students with isolated facts or which teach how great changes
depend on great men reinforce social stasis, sexism, and
worker alienation from school. Literature courses which only
glorify great authors foreign to working-class culture will be
met with many blank and hostile faces. Sociology and
psychology courses which abstract reality into statistics or
into types will be experienced by workers much like their
connection to the Internal Revenue Service—a bunch of irrelevant paperwork you're forced to do to survive. These few
examples are authentic characterizations of how some of
my own worker-students experience their liberal arts education. There have been notable exceptions—openings into
radical pedagogy that are genuinely valuable.

Radical teachers who are designing democratic, rigorous,

and entertaining courses have a serious role to play in the community colleges. The task in liberal arts especially is to present workers with the submerged history of social movements, with the means to see *their own* reality in dynamic and dialectical ways, with the feeling that they have things to do in reforming society, and with the skills needed to bring art into the mainstream of life. Positive goals for radical pedagogy include the need to detoxify the worst ideology drilled into workers and all levels of society—sexism, racism, and authoritarianism. Some of these kinds of courses are available in community colleges, but the overall curriculum is still dominated by the old orthodoxy.

The impact of the economy goes beyond creating worker ambivalence to liberal arts. With more jobs in America being destroyed than created, working people will have to stay in school longer, for lack of work off-campus, and to meet the growing "credentialism" of employers, the escalation of credentials demanded for a job without a coordinate escalation in pay or responsibility. The longer workers stay in college, the more potentially liberating liberal arts they will wind up taking. As the economy extends the duration of schooling for workers and keeps them out of the labor market for prolonged periods of time, the greater is the chance workers will have to break out of their socialized acceptance of their role in the American scheme of things. By delaying the arrival of young workers into fixed adult jobhood, the state solves some of its surplus labor problems, but it sows the seeds of a long-range development: the emergence of a people's intelligentsia, a radical working-class pedagogy, and the massive distribution of higher education with higher aspirations in an economy that can't deliver the goods. Community colleges are more adult and open than the high schools, so they are less effective agencies of social control, which suggests that they can give to workers a chance to think over their lives and gain critical awareness. These potentials should prove to be the most important contributions community colleges can make to American society. Surely, the two-year college network won't be enshrined for the technical training it develops for business needs. The skills workers want and need do not get rewarded in a contracting economy. According to the HEW study of *Work in America*, some 85 percent of junior college graduates take jobs that previously were performed by workers with lesser credentials, while 25 percent of the worker-graduates never get to work in the fields they were trained for. Further, when working-class students finally land a job, in or out of their degree field, they often need more training, on the job, just as in the old days. The same economic system that mandates college training refuses to guarantee that the training will lead anywhere. Yet, in their two or three year college sojourn, worker-students are peaceably unemployed or underemployed—quietly consuming without producing.

A cloudy future contributes to their alienation from schoolwork. More and more, they see the big lie in the new Dream—the lack of connection between hard work now and a good job later. This malaise in the American Dream machine joins other centrifugal forces leading to social disintegration. Working people bottled up at the bottom take their revenge in crime, sabotage, strikes, low productivity, absenteeism at work and in school. They are less willing to make the sacrifices needed to fight a foreign war or to support the rigors of family life. In terms of their studies in college, they fade in and out, sometimes working seriously and sometimes not. They do, however, seem to treat their "budget" colleges a lot more seriously than the colleges treat them. Large classes, impersonal counselors and administrators, poor food in cafeterias, uncomfortable lounges, crowded libraries, and militarized registration for courses all signal to them that they are higher education's third-class citizens. Dehumanizing colleges step on working people's dreams, but bad news on campus is really not news at all. Working people have already sipped a bitter tea from school and other institutions before they reach college. Their cumulative experience leaves them in a condition of injured pride and unpurged anger. This transaction delivers an unpaid bill on campus and off, with vandalism, alcoholism and drugs characterizing the pathology of everyday life. Community colleges can't simultaneously promote and destroy worker aspirations without putting more heat on the system. Yet, they were built as a way of taking pressure *off* the system. The next act of this national contradiction is still being written.

The students in this drama live in a world of noise and speed. They commute from home to school to work and then back to home or to school again. Their time is so harassed that serious study is hard. Family life is crowded and unsupportive or unconducive to intellectual work. Elite students living in academic enclaves are surrounded by people doing similar things. Working-class students living at home have to fit college work into all the other demands of being wage-earners, parents, or being young adults sharing rooms with other siblings. Unable to afford their own apartments, young workers lack the independent space they need to grow into sexually and intellectually spacious adults.

In the face of these problems, they pride themselves on their toughness. They don't whine, ask for pity, or feel sorry for themselves. Their desire for independence and their need to show the world that they can "hack it" keep them from asking for help. Every institution in their lives has tried to make them obedient, but they are left rebellious. They can marshal enormous energy when something becomes important to them, like getting a camera or a car, or going to a concert or on a trip. They value friendliness, but they trade a lot in violence to win respect or to feel power, as a restorative to their crushed egos. Years of socialization in and out of the schools has left them with the ability to think creatively and critically.

Radical teachers, with their students, have to confront the above-cited realities and distortions inflicted by the mass media. The minds of the students have been invaded and occupied by the armies of television, radio, glamor magazines, pulp movies, sensationalist tabloids, and rock music. The language of these media encourages passive spectatorism in the audience; it is riddled with violence and sexism; it promotes unlikely fantasies of liberation, of "striking it rich," or of finding at last the "girl of your dreams" or "Mr. Wonderful." The media's "news" mixes Madame Tussaud with Ripley's "Believe It or Not," spotlighting the bizarre corners of life, or glamorizing the rich and powerful. Working people's major access to issues or to world affairs, outside of the prescribed school curriculum, is the mass media news source, which on TV and radio is a lightning ten-second flash of headlines and three-sentence reports. Saturated by so much meaningless noise and language, the mass audience is surrounded by a world of debased communication. Such trivialized experiences with thought and information habituate working people not to think at length or deeply about ideas or reality. They don't listen carefully—to the news, to their teachers, parents, bosses, cops, or to each other—unless there is something special going on, like a spectacle involving crime, sports, money, sex, or instruction on how to do something they need (like getting a job, financial aid, or cheap car insurance). The sensory flood from media joins the rush of daily life to make their minds work too fast to do close reading of texts and critical scrutiny of ideas. Their mental potentials remain undeveloped, but also undestroyed.

A pedagogy designed *for* working people must sail the sea of mass experience. Only then can it engage all their waiting brainpower. Working people can develop literacy and conceptual skills when they finally get into a class where they want to learn. In this task, radical teachers can take nothing for granted. New teaching methods rooted in working-class life will have to be developed. The teacher's display of respect and warmth for worker-students will be helpful, but it won't be enough. An atmosphere of trust will have to be supplemented by the tough task of implementing a concrete pedagogy that works where the old methods failed. The inventiveness of educators like Paulo Freire demonstrates just how big a departure from tradition is needed.

Even when we put together an elaborate working-class pedagogy, we can't expect it to work right away or all the time. The workers arriving in college come to class with a self-protective suspicion of school. They are wary of teachers, even radical ones, and may choose not to cooperate with or even notice that radical teaching is offered to them. Teachers invest so much energy in their courses that they are easily hurt and discouraged when students refuse to participate. It's worth remembering that life in America has taught workers that you have to make it on your own. Class solidarity is low; students can mistrust each other as much as they mistrust teachers; they have trouble believing that people who are not relatives or close friends will take risks for each other. One survival skill of workers is to be cagey, in school or anyplace else. They want to sit tight and check things out for a good while, before they are ready to take any risks. From their point of view, unfamiliar radical classrooms are going to be as threatening as they are potentially liberating. They are smarter than we, or they themselves, can imagine. Yet they have not been taught to examine or to value their own experience as a source of knowledge. Knowledge is what teachers do, or what's kept inside books and libraries. Weak in conceptual skills, they are full of criticisms of bosses, parents, cops, teachers, the government, the schools, the corporations, etc., but they are convinced that they live in the best country in the world.

My own experience of being lifted out of the working class, and of years of teaching in the working class, have shown me

how hard it is to gain possession of cultural skills. Reading
closely, writing clearly, philosophizing, and verbalizing are
the means by which you can penetrate history, get a feel for
ideology, see some of the nearly invisible forces pushing
society forward, and gain some control of your own life. The
chance to do all these things is available now at a wider
variety of colleges and to a broader sector of working people
than when I was a freshman fifteen years ago.

While college opportunities for workers remain diverse, the
open door has been closing. Cutbacks in the public sector
budget have allowed only a 2 percent growth in enrollment in
the two-year schools for 1976. The year before, these same
campuses registered a 16 percent increase in students. As part
of the forced freeze on admissions, 375,000 veterans enrolled
under the GI bill alone disappeared. New York's City University drove away some 30,000 nonelite students by ending
free tuition and open admissions. Simultaneously, private
colleges have taken the offensive and are out-competing
public ones for tax subsidies. An egalitarian period in higher
education is in retreat.

For over a decade the monumental expansion of the nation's junior colleges neatly served the economy's need for a
nonproduction growth sector in higher education. An expanding war economy fueled college growth. In turn, college
growth fueled the economy by absorbing surplus goods and
labor, while creating demand for new services and retraining
workers at public expense. Now the intricate "career palace"
of two-year colleges has turned into a house of cards. Part of
the problem is that workers have had to leave college as
recession and inflation eat into the discretionary income
many of them would use to go to school. In addition, the
colleges themselves are asserting formidable deterrents:
higher tuition, stiffer admission and retention standards, less
financial aid, reduced compensatory education programs, and
an elite "back-to-basics" movement waving the flag of re-
nascent conservatism.

What's gone wrong is that education and all other social services are casualties of the hard times. Private enterprise has been experiencing a falling rate of profit which, over a period of time, creates a shortage of capital for new investment, thus slowing growth and leading to even smaller profit margins. To reverse this process, business seeks investment capital by cutting the burgeoning public sector budget and by freezing the wage gains of workers. New capital is being directed into energy and food development, and into making America's industrial plant competitive with the newer capital-intensive economies of Europe and Japan. To facilitate these private sector needs, banks withhold loans for public operations and governing bodies retrench the budgets of all non-defense agencies. In the competition for national wealth, worker organizations are not strong enough to insist on their right of open access to quality higher education. Upwardly mobile workers with college credentials are already posing the discipline and wage problems business fears. Narrowed access to higher education will close off the workers' road to the higher skills which legitimize higher wage demands. The strategy is to depress worker aspirations, to increase work discipline and decrease salaries.

The phrase "over-aspiring workers" is gaining currency in education circles. Nonelite students are accused of lowering the "standards" of the academy, and of expecting too much from the job market. To deal with the new economic crisis, two state strategies for education are emerging, besides the broad cutback in budgets and full-time enrollments. Both plans will effect curriculum conversions at all levels of worker education. The first strategy is to push career education in the lower grades. Working-class school children from first grade on will be tracked into "career clusters," like "allied health employment" or "clerical science skills." By the time students reach high school they will be ready to begin part-time work for low wages in local government or business. The lure to teenagers will be the spending money they will earn and the time away from their oppressive school buildings. Such an arrangement would once again make adolescents a massive source of cheap labor, while also tracking them away from college. For adults, a new mass line in higher education is already booming. Colleges at all levels, including the Ivy League, are getting into the "adult education" market. "Adult" or "continuing education" represents a replacement of full-time study with part-time schoolwork. College as a full-time career ladder is receding from workers while college as a part-time evening or weekend program is advancing. Because more adults will receive smaller doses of college, this new form of higher education for workers has the built-in contradiction of bringing even more working people into school. What portends even greater problems for the system is that the new "adult education" has to emphasize "self-growth" or "self-development" more than the promise of economic advancement. The withholding of degree opportunities from worker-students will temporarily slow down the massive output of worker-graduates, but cheap and accessible college learning based on an ideology of self-growth will propel more working adults into creative and critical development. This conversion strategy for mass higher education is supple because it gives workers something as it takes away something else. As a short-term solution to take heat off the economy, it offers working people more and less at the same time. Simultaneously reactionary and progressive, the "adult education" plan is a finger in the dike, against which more waves of educated workers will be pounding in the years to come.

The story of the working class in college shows how vulnerable workers are to the needs of the economy. It also shows how vulnerable the economy is to crises and to even unorganized resistance by workers. Business and government keep working to stabilize American society, yet it remains in constant need of adjustment. Initiative in this flow of forces still eludes working people. Business and government act within the parameters of labor reaction. This kind of tug and pull drives American society backward and forward at the same time. Workers finally enter college in an historic opening up of the academy, but they are offered a debased and manipulative campus to call their own. Once inside, they "take the ball and run"—to places they were supposed to go and to places never intended for them. Millions have passed through and millions more want in. Other generations of labor could only long for the opportunities for higher education open to this generation. Their mass experience of college will continue to affect the temper and direction of American life. The roots higher education has sunk in worker experience will be one limit on the state's need to cut down the very tree it planted.

Part III
......
Toward the Dialectical Presentation of Content

A Radical Teaching a Straight Principles of Economics Course
....
Michael Meeropol

For many of us in the Union for Radical Political Economists (URPE), the most important thing we do as radical
economists is to teach what our departments call "principles
of economics" courses. These courses serve the function,
especially in nonelite schools, of mystifying the ordinary
citizen into "understanding" why certain things are the way
they are in the United States. I put "understanding" in
quotes because in fact the obscurity and formalism of the
courses instead serve to convince students that it is all too
complicated for their "feeble" brains. Either way, the course
usually serves to obscure the conflicts and negative features
of the system under which we live. As teaching radical
economists, we can act to counter this deception. It may
seem a drop in the bucket when stacked against sixteen
years of mis-education, but we must recognize that every
seed of doubt, of real questioning, of *true education* (namely,
the inculcation of critical thinking and the stimulation of
intellectual curiosity) is worth planting. We are not alone as

This is a revised version of remarks presented at a panel discussion on
teaching introductory economics at the regional conference of the
Union for Radical Political Economics, New England, December 8,
1973. Many thanks are due to copanelists Grace Horowitz, Bill
Lazonick, and Gerald Szama, and to Sam Rosenberg and Heidi Hart-
mann for subsequent comments.

individuals; there are other teachers like us in these students' pasts and futures. Afterward, we must hope that when structural tensions in the system produce a similar short-run spasm to that which occurred in the 1960s, the seeds we plant will take root and flower. Until events and trends move many, we must painstakingly continue to try and move people by ones and twos. Countering the apologetics and falsehoods of neoclassical economics *right from the start* in the principles course is the way I maintain my intellectual integrity and act as a principled radical. At the same time, and I also think this is important, we should not shirk from teaching neoclassically oriented principles courses. In an ideal educational system, students should not be burdened with this garbage, but until that point it is elitist and foolishly purist to refuse to have anything to do with such courses. We should not isolate ourselves in principles of political economy courses and allow the rest of the students to take principles of apologetic economics. Students have already internalized much of the pro-capitalist ideology of these courses, and a year of uncritical instruction will increase the brainwashing. Teaching these courses is our best way of critiquing them.

This piece represents a summary of how I parallel the neoclassical apologetics in the textbook I use with an alternative right from the beginning. I teach at a nonelite four-year private college where the majority of students are taking the principles course as part of the required business core curriculum. *Contemporary Economics* by Milton Spencer is the only text used. All of the examples quoted are from this, but most of the material is also in other major texts.

Countering the Text

There is a certain value to being in disagreement with a textbook used in a college course. Such disagreement forces the students to think for themselves. They cannot merely avoid confronting your ideas by "yes-ing" you because of the book's alternative approaches; and conversely, they cannot "yes" the book without challenging you. I think we should encourage students to do this, especially if we are convinced we are right. We must present the traditional textbook views as well as our own in an honest manner.

The most important point to raise right at the start of the course is that there is a serious and consistent challenge being mounted to the orthodoxy represented by the textbook. The first point of difference is over defining the scope and method of economics. Economics is defined by the text I use as "a social science concerned chiefly with the way society chooses to employ its limited resources, which have alternative uses, to produce goods and services for present and future consumption."[1]

I immediately counterpose to this conception of economics (which I label "pure economics"[2]) a broader concept—political economy. I introduce this by noting the key word "society" and suggesting that all elements that go to explain society's decisions must be investigated. Whereas the text's economic analysis takes the institutional framework (tradition, command, or the market) as given and the policies of the government also as given, *political economy* seeks to make government actions and other institutional data endogenous to the analysis.

The "scientific" method—reasoning from abstract principles to build up theories—is also (very sketchily) described at the start of the text. I supplement this with a schematic analysis of the role of abstraction in this method in order to conceptualize the difference between economics and political economy. If the whole of reality is represented as a square on the blackboard, abstraction is the method of isolating certain parts of reality (a small circle within that square), so that they can be studied carefully and all their interactions understood. If we have abstracted correctly, we will learn meaning-

ful things about the whole of reality, but abstracting correctly is a very difficult and uncertain process. I stress that
much of the debating within the economics profession is over
which kinds of abstractions are valid and which are not.[3]
Economics isolates some small circle of reality within the
large square, while political economy isolates a larger piece of
reality which *includes* that isolated by "pure" economics.
Thus, political behavior, social attitudes, etc., are to be
explained, not just to be noted. I add that this makes for
more difficult and less precise analysis, but in my opinion it
is essential if students wish to avoid the feeling that economic
theory is totally unconnected with reality. On the other
hand, the so-called pure economic analysis has the virtue of
being simpler to understand, as far as it goes.

The Factors of Production

In general, when texts introduce the factors of production
they seek to make them eternal "forces" that must exist in
all economies. This fits in with the desire to isolate economic
reality from political and social reality. Labor is defined as
human effort directed toward production. Land refers to
natural resources, including the powers of the soil. Capital
is carefully defined as "a produced means of further production."[4] The organizing or leadership factor is called entrepreneurship. The parallel analysis using the political economy
approach seeks to put flesh and blood on these factors of
production and to introduce the element of power in the
relationship between the people who interact at the point of
production. I begin to introduce this by asking: "What about
money?" The book says:

> The term "capital" is frequently employed by businessmen to mean
> money—that is, the funds invested in a business or the money avail-
> able to purchase capital goods. But since money itself is not a pro-
> ductive resource, it is not the same as a factor of production.[5]

Now most students will wonder about this, and generally the most perceptive questions have been of the order of: "But without money, no production will occur." After defending the book by noting that money produces nothing by itself—it is the fuel and tractor that do the actual pulling of the plow, etc.—the students and I generally come to the understanding that the textbook's analysis of factors of production reduces them to the most general "forces" that aid production. In that light, money is indeed not an immediate factor of production as defined by the book. The political economy approach, because it specifies the institutional framework, recognizes the importance of money. Within the institutions that frame how "society chooses to employ its limited resources . . . (etc.)," money represents the *power* of the entrepreneur in his[6] role as an organizer of the other factors of production. Factors of production are applied at the point of production by people, either directly by laboring or indirectly by permitting the use of machinery or land that they control. The possessor of money has the power to command the people who supply these factors of production. The reason the students think money should be a factor of production is because *under our system* capital in its money form directs the economic system. In fact, I tell them, your views reflect why we refer to our system as *capital-ism*. The "pure" economics approach sees capital as one among equals of the eternal forces of production that must be present in *all* economic systems.

True, when it comes to defining capitalism, the textbook presents a definition that the political economist will accept:

Capitalism is a system of economic organization characterized by private ownership of the means of production and distribution (such as land, factories, railroads, etc.) and their operation for profit under predominantly competitive conditions.[7]

However, the implications to be drawn from this definition are quite different when considered from the pure economics

and political economy viewpoints. If this definition is coupled with a view of capital as one factor of production among
equals, it suggests that capitalism is the system of *free* access
to ownership of capital—truly free enterprise. From the political economy point of view I note that private ownership of
the means of production is not the same as *personal* private
property like a toothbrush, an automobile, or even a private
home. There is no question but that there is free access to
this type of property. However, what is crucial in capitalism
is *wealth-producing property*. At this point I raise an important question which seems like a digression but really is not:
Does the ownership of private property mean the existence
of power over others?

The classroom discussions of this issue take a while to work
themselves out. Some students don't see any connection.
Some emphasize things like the ability of the landlord to tell
the tenant not to have pets, children, noisy parties, etc.
Others counter with the view that the state, via eminent
domain and the taxation laws, can "confiscate" property.
The point I try to make is that if the owners of wealth-
producing property are to successfully produce wealth with it
they must command labor and other factors of production.
Otherwise, they must rely only on themselves and their
immediate families. The only way the owners of private
wealth-producing property can command other factors of
production is if there are a large number of people *without*
such property who must work for someone in order to survive. It is the fact that the ownership of the means of production is in the hands of a few that confers on them power over
others. When people come to work for these owners, they
place their labor power under the direction of their bosses.
The larger the bloc of property owned, the more influence
the owners have over larger and larger numbers of people.
Finally, of course, if they own really large blocs of property,
they can influence the state to intervene in the economy to
their advantage.

Returning, then, to the initial point about free access to capital, I note that the political economy approach argues that for a system like this to survive, access to capital must be limited to relatively few people. Otherwise, a dangerous labor shortage might arise and the system could not perpetuate itself. Similarly, were the access to capital in large blocs not so limited, the ability to control the state would be less clear.

Introducing the State

In most "pure economics" analysis there is a short discussion of the role of government, even in a pure market society. The books note that under *laissez-faire* conditons the government should limit itself to the preservation of law and order. I ask what the most important aspect of this law and order is. My answer: the enforceability of contracts. A market economy, if it is going to function, needs to have owners secure in their property, and buyers and sellers (in product or labor and other factor markets) secure in their already agreed-upon bargains. I remind students that if a homeowner decides to stop paying the bank the monthly mortgage check, the bank forecloses and can physically remove that individual from the property. If the individual resists, the state has the power and the duty to meet that force with force. If the individual stands on his/her porch with a shotgun, the state can and will use deadly force—even kill the offending contract-breaker. The security of the market economy, as in any other economy, rests on the ability of the state to use force, even shooting to kill, to keep individuals playing according to the rules. The next step in the argument is to remind people that the protection of private property is a primary law-and-order responsibility of the state. This is very important because the state may have conflicting pressures brought to bear upon it. The political economy approach will note that, on balance in our society, the protection of property must

prevail over other personal rights when these rights affect
someone else's property. Civil rights legislation is an obvious
counter-example to this, and the issue can really be left up
in the air for the students to make up their own minds
whether our legal system favors property rights over human
rights, and whether or not it should.

The Circular Flow

The distinction between political economy and "pure
economics" is finally clarified when the discussion of the circular flow of economic life is introduced. As presented in
most economics texts, it is labelled as a simplified picture of
the overall structure of a capitalist system. It creates a household sector, where all the owners of production are, and a
business sector, empty until one householder takes his/her
entrepreneurship quantum and becomes a businessperson.
I reproduce Figure 1 on the blackboard and then fill in
the household sector with the four factors of production.
The chief criticism of the analysis is that one must contem-
plate a business sector empty until an individual "fills" it by
exercising her/his entrepreneurial capabilities. Since money
has not really entered the picture, we just assume this person
is able to combine the factors of production and produce a
product. If enough is sold over the top flow in the diagram,
there will be enough to pay the factors of production,
including the original entrepreneur. The original money to
lure the factors of production other than entrepreneurship
to the empty business sector is assumed to come from the
capital market. Yet here reality arises to suggest an alternative. Based on the motto "Unto everyone that hath shall be
given" (which I generally counterpose to Milton Friedman's
"there is no free lunch" aphorisms), I remind students that
not just anyone can borrow money. In fact, in our society
success in the business sector depends on starting off with

a large bloc of capital. Thus, I counterpose Figure 2 to Figure 1.

The distinction is between propertied and nonpropertied households. The former own wealth-producing property which *is* their capital, whether it be as machinery, land, or liquid assets that can be used to command other factors of production. The latter must supply their labor, and supply some liquid capital in the form of savings. The rationale behind this analysis is based on the asymmetrical patterns of social mobility demonstrated by a capitalist society. The question is then whether this circular flow diagram is a better abstract picture of the United States than the one from the

Figure 1
Circular Flow[8]

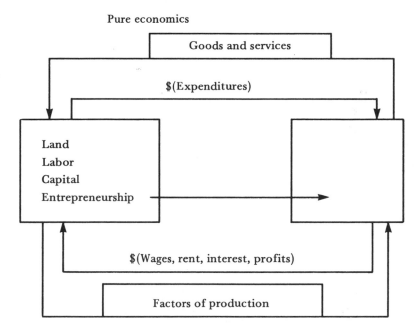

textbook. Empirical issues such as the ease of setting up small businesses, the success of small businesses (a very high proportion of all such enterprises fail within a year of their inception), the domination of the economy by large established corporations, and the domination of these corporations by less than 1 percent of the population, can be brought to bear throughout the semester to help the students in their roles as referees between these two approaches.

Most textbooks have a chapter on "Marx and the planned economy of the Soviet Union." When Marx is introduced, the affinity of Marxism with the political economy circular flow diagram can be mentioned, and therefore the debate between

Figure 2
Circular Flow

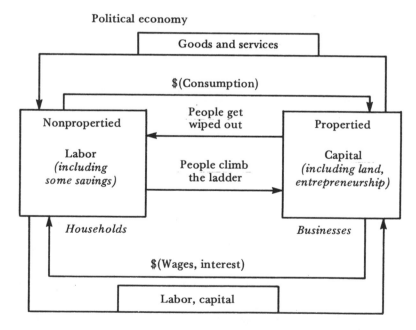

Marxism and modern economics is introduced as an on-going one that has validity for today's economics.

This paralleling can continue to whatever level of sophistication one chooses to take the course. Figures 3 and 4 represent the introduction of national-income accounting. The key distinction is that the political economy approach reserves investment decisions for the propertied class and postulates a higher marginal propensity to consume for the nonpropertied class (generally assumed to be a lower income group). One of the elements of divergence between the two approaches is the ease with which the political economy approach deals with the corporate sector. The corporation itself in the "pure economic" analysis is the "person" who is the entrepreneur, yet this legal "person" is not in the household sector. The advantage of the corporate form (limited liability), which reduces the investment risk, is an advantage conferred by the government, something totally absent from the "pure economics" diagram. However, in the political economy diagram, even with the government absent, large blocs of capital and people are already ensconced in the business sector. Thus, the source of the corporate privilege is unimportant; the fact of the corporation's existence is already recognized.

Further complexities can be added: (1) We can introduce government and speak about redistributing income, tax reforms, etc. Using the political economy approach of Figure 4, we can discuss, for instance, the income distribution effects of an increase in corporation income taxes. (2) Using Figure 2 we can discuss the alienation of the blue collar worker as arising from not having control over the workplace. Difficulties of social mobility and the persistence of inequality can also be explained by harking back to this diagram. (3) Even the pseudoprogressive tax system that Milton Friedman finds so irrational can be explained as an attempt to do two things at the same time: appear to redistribute income while at the

Figure 3
Savings and Investment in the Circular Flow: Pure Economics

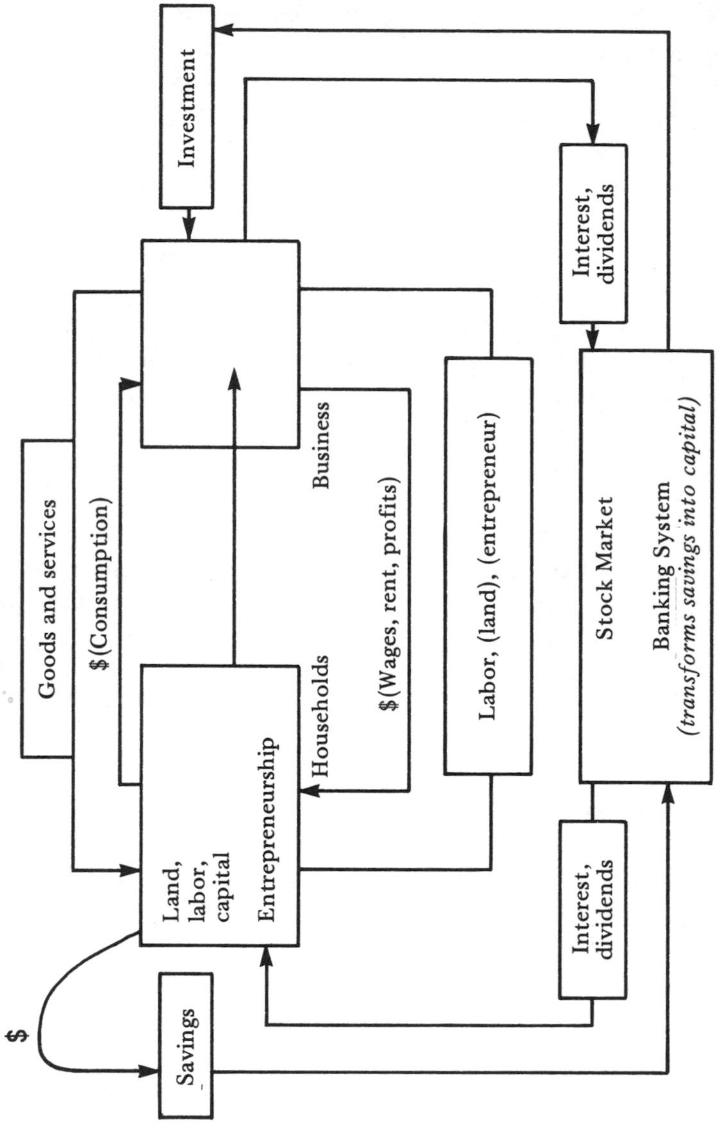

Figure 4
Savings and Investment in the Circular Flow: Political Economy

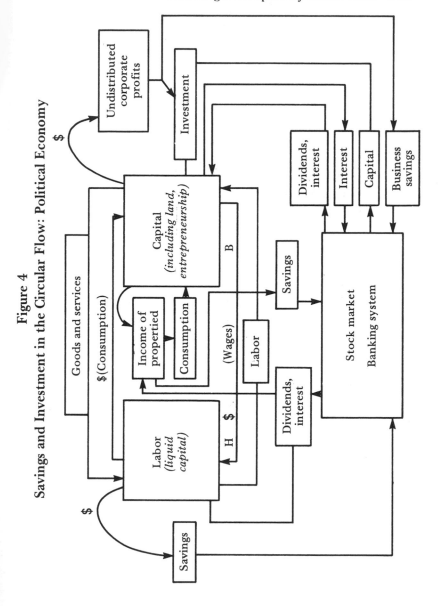

same time *not actually* doing so. This maintains the political legitimacy of *capitalism* as a "fair" system without undermining the economic inequality that it thrives on. (4) As a final example, building on the role of the state in the economy when it is first introduced, we can note that maintaining law and order from the point of view of United States corporations internationally is what Third World nations and radicals call imperialism.

Thus, the initial ideas suggested when I introduce alternatives to the text at the beginning become the basis for radical perspectives throughout the course, as well as in upper division courses. Such a foundation permits all the radical extra readings we assign to be fully appreciated by the students. They will understand what the challenges to neoclassical economics are all about. During the radicalization of the late 1960s, due to the previous repression and the then almost total isolation of radical thought from the intellectual currents of America, much New Left development took place in an intellectual vacuum. The more people like us teach "alternative" approaches to economics, sociology, psychology, history, political science, anthropology, philosophy, and about the social responsibilities of scientists and engineers, the less likely it is that such an intellectual vacuum will develop again. The seeds of doubt we plant, the alternative ways of understanding the United States we present, the hopes for a better future we affirm, can be a part of any future "making of connections." This is the most we can hope for at present;[9] it is the least we can strive for if we wish to indeed be part of the solution.

Notes

1. Milton Spencer, *Contemporary Economics* (New York: Worth Publishers, 1971), p. 2.

2. This term is used only for convenience. In fact, such economics is hardly pure, and has its own (unspoken) political elements. I don't use the more obvious term "bourgeois economics" because in presenting "both sides" I want to use neutral language.

3. The Cambridge controversy over what constitutes "capital" is perhaps a prime example of this. See G.C. Harcourt, *Some Cambridge Controversies in the Theory of Capital* (Cambridge: Cambridge University Press, 1972).

4. Spencer, *Contemporary Economics*, p. 18.

5. Ibid.

6. I don't use sex-neutral pronouns here because, as with all areas of power, men predominate.

7. Spencer, *Contemporary Economics*, p. 31.

8. These figures are based on ibid., p. 40.

9. It has been suggested that this sentence is too pessimistic and that political activity is possible even at very sleepy schools. As one who is currently trying to build a political movement to force a reopening of the Rosenberg-Sobell case, I cannot disagree. However, as *radical economists* I'm afraid in most schools we are stuck with being teachers. That's my realistic appraisal; I don't believe it is necessarily pessimistic.

A Course on Spectator Sports
....
Louis Kampf

Though I make my living as a teacher of literature, I have taught a course on mass spectator sports for the last two years. I intend to teach the course again. My reasons for doing so are serious, and derive from my political concerns as a socialist. I want to educate myself, to begin with, about an important area of culture: polls show, after all, that most people read little more than the sports section in their newspapers; I, for one, eagerly scan the latest sports results before I turn to the front of the paper. I also want the opportunity to talk to students I ordinarily don't get to talk to—those who may not have the slightest interest in literature or high culture, but are passionate about sports.

Mass sports—both spectator and participatory—play an important role in our culture and in the political economy. Playing in a softball league may be one of the few ways of getting away from the miseries of the office, the factory, school, or one's family. How many boys from low-income families clutch to the reality of the American Dream in the form of the multimillion dollar contracts signed by the likes of Catfish Hunter, Joe Namath, and Walt Frazier? And why the millions of fans? Rooting for one's favorite team is among the few ways left for anyone to show group loyalty. But that yearning for group loyalty also allows entrepreneurs to exploit the culture of masses of people. In the current stage of capitalist development, sports is one area of the service sector still capable of expansion. Several years ago, *Fortune* reported that Japanese capitalists are now stressing "quality of life investments." The qualities referred to are illustrated by the more than ten thousand bowling alleys built in Japan in 1970. In the United States there is now a booming business in tennis equipment. To create the boom, working-class prejudices against tennis had to be broken down; furthermore, spectator etiquette had to be transformed from a norm of restrained clapping for a well-executed shot to one of raucous applause for one's favorite player or team. How were such transformations engineered? Teaching this course, I hoped, would lead me to some answers for such questions.

I also meant to learn something about myself. I'm a professional—an intellectual with a proper degree of skepticism. Yet sports has a nagging hold on me. It played a significant role in shaping my consciousness as I grew up. I can't shake its effects, and still find myself rooting for some team or other, though I know the whole spectator sports business is a ripoff.

I was also concerned with the role of sports in the history of industrial capitalism. We have difficulty explaining how class consciousness develops, or fails to develop, or is displaced by false consciousness. Modern mass spectator sports and large-scale organized recreational activities came into existence in the West—especially in England and the United States—as the Industrial Revolution hit its full stride during the nineteenth century. Sports and recreation were consciously used to keep working people off the streets, out of trouble, and wrapped up with anything but their most vital political concerns. Mass sports became subjectively the most important life activity for millions as the elements of autonomy, creativity, and play became increasingly separated from work—as work became tedious labor. Sports also became an important instrument of sex-role differentiation and male supremacy. I wanted to learn more about such interrelationships.

Finally, I wondered how my practice as radical activist and organizer, both on and off the campus, might relate to sports. If I were involved in a community project, how would I relate to the sports activities in that community? How might I write about sports in a community newspaper? Should I try to organize a campaign supporting girls' attempts to get into the Little League?

The Course

I made it very clear that anyone who did not take the course seriously would be asked to leave. Many students have told me that I should have been more strict about enforcing this rule. The procedure is unpleasant, but the students have to know that the course is not a gag or a gut—though it may be fun.

The course's chief requirement was that each student participate in a group research project to be presented to the rest of the class. I gave the class a list of suggested research topics. The students made additions to the list. The class then divided itself into groups according to preference for a particular topic. The groups met regularly. Each group was also in charge of teaching one or more readings. The research topics chosen over the two terms the course has been taught were: sex roles and sports; sports heroes; why hockey is more popular than basketball in Boston; betting in various cultures; a class analysis of bettors at a nearby racetrack; sports as big business; self-competitive sports; regional and national differences in the popularity of certain sports.

Finding appropriate readings for the course was difficult. Little of value has been written about sports. Naturally, sports magazines, newspapers, popular sports biographies and autobiographies, and children's books are worth studying because millions read them. We do not really know what they do to people's heads, so there are serious questions to be asked. However, many students resented being asked to read more than a small amount of trash. The students and I read the sports section in the papers as well as some magazines, and wrote comments about them in journals we kept for that purpose. I read the students' journals once a week, and handed out copies of my own journal to everyone in class.

As a guide for class discussion, I gave the students a list of questions to ask themselves. Here are some of them: What is a sports fan? Why am I one? What are the motives for sports?—pleasure? challenge? escape? fame? Why win? Does competition need to be antagonistic? What do I experience when playing or watching?—joy? love? hate? curiosity? detachment? anger? anything else? Does my social background have anything to do with the sports I enjoy?

The Readings and Class Discussion

1. Arthur Miller: *Death of a Salesman*

The play broadly draws the apparent parallel between success in football and in business. The parallel turns out to be an illusion which allows the salesman to continue believing in the American Dream. In discussing the play, the students quite naturally, and without my prompting, raised most of the social, political, and psychological issues I wanted the course to focus on. Most of the students saw themselves in the play, and wondered how their own interest in sports was related to their notions of success and their relationships to their parents. However, discussion of the play was not nearly so lively the second time the course was given. Most of the students, it turned out, had read and discussed the play in high school. Apparently this dampened their interest.

2. I had to give a long lecture on the history of sports in the United States, since there is no reading I can assign on the

subject that is both reasonably short and accurate. Some of the topics I tried to cover were: the development of mass recreation and entertainment in general; how development of these, as well as of mass sports, was a function of urbanization, which process broke up traditional village and town entertainments; the relation of ideologies about work and recreation to industrial capitalism's changing labor needs; the rise of professional recreationists as a response to urban unrest; the class structure of sports activities (which social class played and/or watched what sports); investment patterns in sports (the role, for example, of early trolley companies in building sports facilities at the edge of town, a trolley-ride away). I concluded the survey with the formation of the National Baseball League in 1876. It became the model for all leagues in Europe and the Americas. Gamblers put the league together. It was an act of capitalist rationalization: if the gamblers were going to take bets on baseball games, they had to be sure the games were actually going to be played. Having a league with more or less permanently stationed teams also made fan loyalty possible. Rationalization of enterprise and fan loyalty to the team—here we have the beginning of the modern sports era. The combination made large-scale investments possible; consequently, it also opened the possibility for the extensive manipulation of people's consciousness.

3. David Mandell: *The Nazi Olympics*

This is a pedestrian and thin history of the modern Olympics. I had hoped that the book would begin a discussion of nationalism and sports. Alas, the book bombed. The students could not get themselves to take it seriously, and therefore found it difficult to relate the historical events to themselves. The fiction of *Death of a Salesman* had seemed more real to them.

Given this failure, I eliminated Mandell's book the second

time I taught the course. Instead, the students read two short essays: Gerald Ford, "In Defense of the Competitive Urge"—a compendium of most of the common inanities about sports building national character, preparing us to fight the enemy, teaching us how to do well in business, and being vital in maintaining law and order; and Marie Hart, "Sport: Women Sit in the Back of the Bus"—an intelligent analysis of sexism in sports, and the relationship of the urge to win to the machismo so prevalent in public and private life. The two essays made a useful contrast, and led to a rich discussion of the relationship of sexism and sports to political and social life.

4. Louis Kampf: "What's Happened to Baseball?"

I could not find an appropriate reading about baseball, so I wrote this brief essay for the occasion. In it I discussed baseball's changes in organization and audience since the early 1940s, when I first began to follow and play the game. I especially emphasized the disappearance of minor, semipro, and local leagues, of the Negro leagues, and of large-scale participation by adults in sandlot ball. The discussion was reasonable, but not fervent. The students took baseball for granted—an old uncle—and therefore could not expend much energy on it. Most interesting was the discussion of the relationship of various ethnic and racial groups to this exclusively (but not quite) American game, nearly incomprehensible to most Europeans.

The second time I taught the course I decided to take a chance with Roger Kahn's *The Boys of Summer*. It didn't work. Most of the students could not identify with Kahn's nostalgia for the Brooklyn Dodgers of the 1950s; they found his autobiographical digressions irrelevant, even impertinent; worst of all, Kahn's attempt at literary sophistication kept them from focusing on the social issues which are the heart of the book.

5. Jerry Kramer, ed.: *Lombardi: Winning Is the Only Thing*
This is a collection of evaluations of Vince Lombardi by some of the players he coached. Several of them are surprisingly honest and perceptive. Since Lombardi was a sentimental fascist who loved children, pregnant women, and General MacArthur, the book led students to dwell on the authoritarian aspects of organized sports.

The next year I substituted Kramer's *Instant Replay,* his diary of a season played under Lombardi in Green Bay. The book touches on most of the issues one needs to discuss about football: violence, spectator fanaticism, sexism, racism, football as a business venture and a means of social mobility, etc. Kramer is an intelligent propagandist for football and the social system, and therefore a very useful witness. I did have occasional difficulties in keeping the discussion from bogging down in the details of football strategy.

6. Gary Shaw: *Meat on the Hoof*
This is one player's very moving account of growing up with football in Texas. Shaw describes how the game infantilized him, destroyed his capacity for nonauthoritarian human relationships and love, and corrupted his perceptions of the social and political world around him (a nervous breakdown led to an attempt to restructure his life). He then discusses alternatives to the way players and spectators now experience football. The book gripped most of the students. Some couldn't quite believe Shaw's gruesome account of football training. Primarily, it led them to think about what sports is doing to their own world of feeling and sexuality, and how such matters of the emotions relate to the politics of their country.

7. Old boxing movies
One student's father had been a prizefighter. He now ran a bar in New Bedford, Massachusetts, which showed boxing movies from the 1920s and 1930s. The student screened

some of them for the class. New Bedford has a large Portuguese immigrant population which has taken to boxing as Irish, Jewish, and Italian immigrants did in the past. The class, therefore, had a context within which it was able to discuss how boxing had changed, since New Bedford's boxing scene is a relic of a lost world. Most of the discussion focused on ethnic and class loyalties. The dominant feeling in class was that boxing heroes gave ethnic and racial minorities a false sense of power.

The next time I taught the course I tried to get some students to do a research project on the New Bedford boxing scene. Unfortunately, there were no volunteers.

8. Jackie Stewart: *Faster*

The second time I taught the course, I wanted the class to discuss auto racing. This book is one year's diary of the Grand Prix circuit by the greatest Formula I driver of the last decade. Stewart is brashly honest about his expensive tastes, his love of money, and his desire to do business and rub shoulders with the powerful and wealthy. During the season which he describes, several of his friends were killed in racing accidents. Now the several varieties of auto racing constitute the United States' most popular spectator sport. Success is based on skill, mechanical ingenuity, and the availability of money rather than on physical power. Death or serious injury is a real possibility. Spectator loyalty is fierce; occasionally even nasty. Yet little happened in class discussion. I wound up trying to convince the students that auto racing was worthy of their attention. I'm not sure what went wrong, though I suspect it had something to do with the social origins of the students—a matter to which I'll return further on.

9. "The Only Game in Town"

This was an article in *Sports Illustrated* about the cultural hold ice hockey had on a small Canadian town. Hockey had become the town's model for most aspects of everyday life.

It gave people their sense of identity, and was used to fudge over social and political conflict. Class discussion tended to become fixated on hockey violence, which was then very much in the news. However, the service a sport can render to a town's power structure and for received morality did not go without attention. One group of students looked into the financing of hockey rinks in Massachusetts and discovered that several corporations were using state funds to make sizable profits for themselves.

10. David Wolf: *Foul*

The book is about Connie Hawkins, once the most spectacular basketball player around. Hawkins, who grew up in Bedford-Stuyvesant, one of Brooklyn's black ghettos, had been falsely accused of taking a bribe in high school to shave points. Vindication came slowly, and most of Hawkins' prime years were wasted clowning around with the Harlem Globetrotters. While describing these events Wolf gets into the nature of college recruiting, racism in major sports, the culture of schoolyard basketball, and the social function of style. The students were gripped by the book. The discussion occasionally tended to get away from basketball and to concentrate on racism in the United States. Once again, the issue of how athletic prowess can give a minority a false sense of power came up.

11. The reports

They were a mixed bag—some very useful, others less so. The students agreed that they got a great deal out of working in groups. Generally they felt good about having done a piece of work they were interested in, and reporting on it to their fellow students. I learned a good deal from a number of them. Most of the reports made clear that the students had learned to look at sports as a social, political, and economic phenomenon.

12. Course summary
We spent several hours summarizing the content of the course and considering how it might be improved. I introduced some themes which I thought had emerged time and again during the course, and which expressed tensions within the culture of industrial capitalism:

(1) Sports is part of the country's economic base; it is also part of its cultural superstructure. Awareness of this dual function creates emotional difficulties for many people.

(2) In an industrial capitalist society sports is supposed to be a form of personal escape from the prison of work, yet people—and especially performing athletes—are constantly reminded that winning at sports is a patriotic duty and a training school for one's life, which will be competitive.

(3) Play apparently allows the individual freedom and autonomy, yet it is used to teach children that they must obey rules.

(4) Team sports stress the primacy of the group, yet one is rewarded for individual accomplishment—a giant ego is a prerequisite for stardom in sports.

13. Additional readings
The only additional books I put on reserve were:
Foster Rhea Dulles: *America Learns to Play*
Dulles, a conservative diplomatic historian, wrote this long history of recreation in the United States as a lark. Being a conservative, he really believes that sports ought to be an important instrument of social control. As a result, he is quite clear and accurate about the social function of modern mass sports.

Paul Hoch: *Rip-Off the Big Game*
Hoch's Marxist analysis of contemporary spectator sports is essentially accurate, though occasionally vulgar and glib. I could not use it as a primary text because Hoch assumes that

the reader is on his side politically. Most of my students were not.

As I mentioned earlier, little worth reading has been written about sports. Some useful theoretical work, heavily influenced by Marcuse, has been published in French, German, and Italian journals. However, they assume a solid knowledge of Marxism—something I could hardly expect of my students. As for the literature in professional sociological and psychological journals, it is dominated by quantitative studies which avoid most of the central issues I tried to raise.

What have I learned? A great deal, though not as much as I would have liked. In preparing for the course it was fascinating to read some of the materials in the New York Public Library's section on play and recreation. The recreation movement was (and is) even more nationalistic, authoritarian, sexist, and antiworking class than I had anticipated. I learned how very aware the ruling class was in the nineteenth century that it had to try and control the culture of the working class. Toward this end, business groups pulled no punches in enlisting the church, the schools, the police, and the new profession of recreationists to do their share in bringing about the sports explosion in the United States. I did not learn much about the role of sports in political organizing. One needs the example of practice, and few community groups have had the time or energy to experiment with sports programs. As for the radical community newspapers in my area, cultural matters hardly ever seem to get into their pages. I asked the class to try and develop alternate models for community sports, but they were not interested in utopian fantasies. Finally, I learned how deeply sexism and gay-baiting is built into our culture of sports—machismo reigns supreme.

As for the students, nothing I've ever taught has made them so aware that their cultural life does not take place in a realm separate from practical life. I think most of them learned that what one does and thinks about in one's leisure time is an index to what one does at work, in school, or at home. Having understood this much, they also began to see that their leisure activity and their culture were being appropriated and manipulated so that their loyalties and energies would be confined within safe boundaries.

One difficulty I experienced in class discussion was that it is very easy to get bogged down in arguments about the aesthetics of sports and the psychology of the individual athlete. After all, the point of the course was to get away from formalist and psychologist approaches to sports. I continually had to stress that the object—and subject—of our study was the spectator.

Another difficulty was that nearly all of my students were white, male, and middle class. This might be one reason why they did not take to auto racing, since its audience is primarily working class. The second time the course was given there were two blacks and three women. Their presence made discussions about racism and sexism much more guarded. (A large number of women tried to get into the course the second time, but registration had been closed. I assume that the renewed interest about women in sports was responsible for this interest.)

I intend to keep teaching and changing this course. I hope others who share my perspective will have the inclination and time to teach similar or related courses. I would like to hear from them.

Philistines, Materialists, and Poets: Teaching Marxist Literary Theory in the United States

....

Norman Rudich

Most American students are deficient in the philosophical background indispensable for an understanding of the Marxist theory of literature. Philosophy is not taught in our high schools, nor is it required in college. The history of philosophy is usually limited to an introductory survey. Majors and seriously interested students are taught that language analysis, modern logic, and a variety of positivistic epistemologies have discredited the metaphysical systems of the past. This has not prevented Existentialism, philosophical Freudianism, and Pragmatism from gaining currency and a certain popularity in American academic thought. Thus are American students deprived of an irreplaceable intellectual training: of ease in recognizing, forming, and defining basic concepts, of the method and habit of systematic and critical thought, of the ability and even the desire to raise fundamental and universal issues of human life, of the power to relate, generalize, and synthesize the diversity of their knowledge, of the capacity to think for themselves, to understand their own lives and problems as something more than individual case histories. But, after all, why would policymakers for American education today want students to think for themselves?

After the expulsion of Marxism from American education in the 1950s, students heard about it tangentially in school as one of those anachronistic, metaphysical systems, long ago refuted and useful only in "knowing your enemy." Of course, for such wisdom you do not have to study philosophy: anti-Marxism is ubiquitous, it is the mother's milk of American education. But the problem is not so much anti-Marxism as it is antiphilosophy, and, beyond that, the anti-intellectualism of the American ideology pragmatically nurtured by our seasoned image-makers. I do not feel unduly impeded by the class prejudices, political conservatism, or religious preconceptions of my students. In fact, seriously committed and thoughtful religious students frequently arrive better equipped than pragmatic liberals to understand, debate, and take reasoned positions on the Marxist approaches to literature. Nor do I have any complaints about the intellectual capacities of my students, who are usually intelligent and motivated.

The trouble begins as soon as I introduce the term materialism, and of necessity, the congeries of terms and notions such as idealism, dialectical, subjective, objective, praxis, etc. which delimit and extend that key concept for the purposes of explaining literary phenomena. There is immediate interest, lively discussion, intellectual excitement. Students love philosophy and if I don't prevent it, our course in literature turns into a vast, vapory, and amateurish course in philosophy and its history. The problem of background cannot be solved in the classroom. The students have to solve it largely on their own as best they can by spending more time than they originally expected reading the *Theses on Feuerbach, The German Ideology, Anti-Dühring,* and other philosophical writings of the founders, supplemented by more recent resumés and commentaries.

The next discovery is that most American students find it difficult to reason in dialectical-materialist terms. Materialism is un-American. It connotes to most young people money grubbing, lust for possessions, smug middle-class comfort, etc. Some slightly more sophisticated versions equate biological determinism and behaviorism with materialism. Since it is tacitly assumed that social behavior is no more than the sum of individual behaviors, the interplay of stimulus and response takes on the appearance of a universal, materialistic explanation of social behaviors. To this I counterpose the famous passage from Marx's preface to *A Contribution to a Critique of Political Economy,* in which forces and relations of production are presented as the material basis on which are erected historically conditioned political and legal institutions to which correspond various philosophical, religious, aesthetic, etc. superstructures or "forms of consciousness." Dialectic is useful in pedagogy. By bringing in the notions of labor, property, class, mode of production, social development, and political change as the living sources of consciousness, we take an important step forward in distinguishing dialectical materialism from the mechanical stimulus and response model of experimental psychology. We have introduced a new way of relating the individual to the society in which the various "forms of consciousness," including the aesthetic, are generated.

At this point, in the minds of the students, materialism becomes economic determinism. This marks an advance from the biopsychological individual of behaviorism in the sense that *homo economicus,* who produces, exchanges, and consumes, necessarily implies the existence of social relations, i.e., the ways a worker, a shopkeeper, and a tycoon of industry maximize their gains and minimize their losses are not reducible to a single model. But it is important to extend and deepen the critique of *homo economicus* because many students think that he (or she) is a Marxist invention. It is good to dispose of him by showing his bourgeois origins, narrowness of perspective on human motivations, philistine pragmatism, etc. Again, this critique opens the way to new ideas, e.g., the differences between material and spiritual production, the opposition between *homo economicus* and the humanistic view of the fully developed, many sided human personality. Finally, it is useful to point out that Engels, several times in later years, had to defend Marxism against both friends and enemies who reduced it to a one-sided, economic causal system. He also recognized Marx's and his own responsibility in contributing to that error, while explaining that, in the process of developing and defending the new point of view against its detractors, they were brought to exaggerate the economic aspect to the detriment of ideology.

However, the real test is not philosophy in general, but aesthetics in particular. If there is one area in which materialism seems most out of place, inapplicable, contrary to the nature of the subject, it is the arts. (And I have it comparatively easy since I teach literature; it is incomparably harder, for example, in the history of music.) Aesthetics is the natural habitat of idealist thought, whether we approach it from the point of view of the subject matter or from that of the student-critic. It is easy to explain to students why the inventor; the explorer, the scientist, the statesman, etc. are readily conceivable as social beings responding to particular problems of theory and application arising at a definite time and place. But the artist is someone special, different, endowed with a personality, with a vision that makes his or her inner life more interesting than that of ordinary mortals, because it is the matrix of artistic creation. Art for artist is the acme of self-expression, the domain of the unique, of pure subjectivity, of play, of the release of irrational or subconscious impulses, of self-realization, of being rather than meaning, of form for its own sake—in brief, of absolute individuality. Art is a biological need, a psychological drive, a pure—and that means unconditioned—expression of the age. The work of art expresses the artist. It is his or her vision of the world, or at least as much of it as can be communicated. Its connections with that world, especially if it is seen as based on material production, relations of production, property, class struggle, and revolution, are distant, to say the least, and certainly not essential to its comprehension or appreciation. That must be so, or how explain the multiplicity of interpretations, reactions, attitudes, and feelings which art draws from each individual reader? How decide which interpretation is the best or even better than most? What does dialectical materialism have to do with the infernal and paradisiac visions of Dante, the perfect sensuousness of Keats's feeling for living things, the metaphysical fantasmagorias of Kafka? And even when artists address themselves to the realities of their time, of what interest are they as such, once they have been transformed into the "stuff that dreams are made of"? Moreover, when art and politics are mixed, the result is propaganda, which is an abasement of its universal human mission, an encroachment on the free expression of the artist for purposes foreign to art. These are deeply held convictions among many students.

Now all this is not simply false. In fact, it has some important truths in it, truths which must be disinterred from the romantic wrappings which make them theoretically unusable. To rehabilitate these notions through a dialectical and materialist interpretation is the task of the course. It must be done conceptually, through reasoned argument, and practically, in showing its use in literary criticism of particular works.

The selection of readings for the body of the course combines past and present great literature which either has been studied by good Marxist critics or which I have worked on sufficiently to propose my own Marxist interpretation. We read the *Orestia*, along with George Thompson's *Aeschylus and Athens*; *Hamlet* and *King Lear* with Arnold Kettle's *Shakespeare in a Changing World*; a Balzac novel with Georg Lukács' *Studies in European Realism*. Several recent anthologies have enabled me to introduce more theoretical readings into the course.[1] Theory is valuable and useful but it should be directed toward practical criticism. The aim of the course is to demonstrate that a Marxist reading of literature enriches comprehension and aesthetic experience. This can only be achieved by analyzing literary texts with the aid of theory. There is no such thing as a naive, or, as the French put it, innocent reading of literature. I try to make students conscious that they are bringing to these works their prejudices, backgrounds, expectations, and preconceptions; in brief, their diverse ideologies which sometimes enlighten and sometimes blind them to the meanings and qualities of literary works. They should be encouraged, however, to develop their own interpretations of literary works before launching into the study of the critics. This makes them better critics of critics and that, too, is an important dimension of the course. But the real test comes when the teacher puts his or her own scholarly and critical work on the line. To quarrel with George Thompson through Rudich just does not have the same excitement as the direct clash of ideas which is one of the privileges of the classroom situation. That is why I shall illustrate my teaching method by summarizing the interpretation of Coleridge's "Kubla Kahn" which I have presented many times to my classes and which I eventually published as an article.[2]

"Kubla Kahn" is one of the most enigmatic poems of English literature. It is frequently cited as an example of "pure poetry," inspired word music devoid of definable meaning, an explosion of the unconscious creative powers of the poet. It has lent itself readily to Freudian, mythic, and religious interpretations. These receive plausibility from the fact that Coleridge claimed that the poem came to him as an opium dream which he wrote out effortlessly in a single stretch until a debt-collector, "the man from Porlock," barged in, broke the spell, and prevented the completion of the poem. A number of scholars have given good reasons to doubt the story, but I do not think its truth or falsehood is decisive for its interpretation.

I begin by an explication of the poem rather than setting out the biographical, historical, political, and ideological data surrounding its composition. A close examination of the language of poetry and the complex forms which extend and circumscribe its meanings can alone raise questions whose answers are the basis of interpretation. The historical or sociological approach which establishes a one-directional causality between external events and poetic meaning is theoretically and practically inadequate in criticism because it fails to explain why the poet chose *these* rather than *those* realia out of the myriad possibilities at hand; in brief, it is an undialectical view of the creative process. Criticism should move from the poet to the world in order to understand how and why a particular reality received shape in the poem.

At first reading the students are puzzled as to how to apply all this methodological wisdom to a poem about Xanadu, Mount Abora, and the milk of Paradise, which despite the best will in the world and the liveliest imagination, persistently escape connection with modes of production and class struggle.

Kubla Kahn

In Xanadu did Kubla Kahn
A stately pleasure-dome decree:
Where Alph, the sacred river, ran
Through caverns measureless to man
    Down to a sunless sea.
So twice five miles of fertile ground
With walls and towers were girdled round:
And there were gardens bright with sinuous rills
Where blossomed many an incense-bearing tree;
And here were forests ancient as the hills,
Enfolding sunny spots of greenery.

But oh! that deep romantic chasm which slanted
Down the green hill athwart a cedarn cover!
A savage place! as holy and enchanted
As e'er beneath a waning moon was haunted

By woman wailing for her demon-lover!
And from this chasm, with ceaseless turmoil seething,
As if this earth in fast thick pants were breathing,
A mighty fountain momently was forced:
Amid whose swift half-intermitted burst
Huge fragments vaulted like rebounding hail,
Or chaffy grain beneath the thresher's flail:
And mid these dancing rocks at once and ever
It flung up momently the sacred river.
Five miles meandering with a mazy motion
Through wood and dale the sacred river ran,
Then reached the caverns measureless to man,
And sank in tumult to a lifeless ocean:
And 'mid this tumult Kubla heard from far
Ancestral voices prophesying war!

    The shadow of the dome of pleasure
    Floated midway on the waves;
    Where was heard the mingled measure
    From the fountain and the caves.
It was a miracle of rare device,
A sunny pleasure-dome with caves of ice!

    A damsel with a dulcimer
    In a vision once I saw:
    It was an Abyssinian maid,
    And on her dulcimer she played,
    Singing of Mount Abora.
    Could I revive within me
    Her symphony and song,
    To such a deep delight 'twould win me
That with music loud and long,
I would build that dome in air,
That sunny dome! those caves of ice!
And all who heard should see them there,
And all should cry, Beware! Beware!
His flashing eyes, his floating hair!
Weave a circle round him thrice,
And close your eyes with holy dread,
For he on honey-dew hath fed,
And drunk the milk of Paradise.

It is best to make the first stage an open discussion, with the students contributing their insights as they come. It usually turns out that, unencumbered as they are by the tradition of scholarly interpretations—the only preconceptions they express being their own—a certain number of common sense facts about the poem are discovered and retained by the class. The poem is divided into two parts, the first concerning Kubla Kahn, the building of his pleasure dome, the fountain and caves; and the second, having to do with the poet, his feelings, dreams, and reactions to the emperor's project. Some students are very sharp in spotting symbols, metaphors, and their interconnections, and it is wise to let them discuss and argue the virtues of their own interpretations. Nevertheless, the point is to guide them slowly toward the interpretation which the teacher intends to propose as a way of taking the discussion into a qualitatively new stage. Using what I can of the previous discussion, I give my own reading, which I can only sum up here.

Kubla, who reigned over one of the greatest empires the world has ever known, devotes himself to the building of a great work of civilization, a place of beauty, repose, and pleasure. He gives orders that fortifications be built in an exotic place near a river believed to be sacred, at the point where it cascades into fathomless caves. Within the walls and towers there are juxtaposed natural forests and man made gardens. Thus do the opening lines of the poem associate the ideas, directly or symbolically expressed, of imperial decree, geometric reasoning, and death. As we advance in the poem, it will also be seen that these are male attributes.

Nowhere does the decree mention, and nowhere is it indicated, that Kubla is aware that within or hard by his artificial paradise is the horrendous fountain which is the source of the sacred river. The chasm from which it springs is identified with the female, orgasmic fury, and the pangs of birth. Thus by opposition we may confirm the symbolic attribution of death to the caves, and by extension to the kind of reason of the imperial decree. This is once more confirmed at the end of the stanza when Kubla hears "ancestral voices prophesying war." The following change of tone is also a change of persona. The poet, part in wonderment, part in irony, comments on the emperor's work. The contradictions of male-female, caves-fountain, death-birth, sacred-holy, ice-sun mingle in the shadow of the pleasure dome. But this superficial mingling is no synthesis. He says, "It was a miracle of rare device," i.e., an artificial balance of irreconcilable forces which cannot long endure. The use of the past tense tells us that all the great works of Kubla have returned to dust.

Finally Coleridge comes on stage as "I." He describes a vision of a woman singing about the sources of the Nile, another sacred river, which is, according to legend, the true location of the Garden of Eden. She is a creature of his imagination, in other words, the female principle or muse of poetic inspiration who stands in contrast to the woman of the fountain, a symbol of the unbridled, irrational forces of nature. If he could recall her song, i.e., recover his lost poetic inspiration, he would build a spiritual paradise (Christian and not pagan), which would frighten and inspire all humankind. The poet, not the emperor, is the creator of the true Utopia. The effort of the state to build a perfect model of human happiness ends in failure. Poetic, not political, vision can lead humankind to the reconciliations of those opposing forces that define their alienation in this world. This much can actually be worked out from an examination of the poem itself.

The nature of the discussion now changes in a number of ways. Faced with a coherent interpretation of the poem, the students raise questions and objections, suggest other possibilities, and, above all, demand other than internal evidence as confirmation of my reading. Again, as well as I can, I resist bringing in the personal, social, and political dimensions until it is established that the poem itself demands them, that it is not an arbitrary or dogmatic methodological rule concocted by Karl Marx and Co. because it serves the purpose of the revolution. Philosophically and pedagogically the point is crucial because it involves the proposition, in various ways denied by modern bourgeois schools, that poetic language genuinely refers to "the real world." "The real world" to most means "the external world" or "nature," as distinguished from the "inner world" of the mind. This metaphysical and therefore irreparable separation of subject and object both contains and is contained by the individualist preconception of cultural creation which attains its fullest flowering in aesthetics. The first thesis on Feuerbach makes the philosophical point clearly enough: "The chief defect of all hitherto existing materialism—that of Feuerbach included—is that the thing, reality, sensuousness, is conceived only in the form of the *object* or of *contemplation,* but not as *human sensuous activity, practice,* not subjectively."[3] The pedagogical significance of these ideas emerges when they are applied in poetic theory: poetry is not an imitation of nature but of action; poetic language does not refer to the "external world" as separated from the human subject but to the real, human, sensuous activity in the world, i.e., to the dialectical unity of subject and object which is objectively their mode of being in praxis. That is why myth, fantasy, and dreamwork can effectively refer to the reality of human action in which all the powers of the mind are needed in order to appropriate the world sensuously as experience and ideologically as comprehension. Poetry exhibits in theoretical and sensuous form, i.e., imaginatively through mimetic language, the concrete and dynamic unity and interplay of subject and object which constitutes action.

From student evaluations, it is clear that what they like best about my approach is that it does not sacrifice the sexual, philosophical, and religious aspects to a straight political reading. For some it is a discovery that a Marxist interpretation of literature does not mean the reduction of poetry to politics. What they quarrel with is my claim that it is the political theme, the identification of Kubla with the state and Coleridge with the poet, that gives the maximum coherence to the poem. Kubla is also male, rationalist, pagan. Those themes and their opposites also inform and structure poetic meaning. It will be noted that the debate about dominant themes is really dealing with opposed notions of the content of the poem. The students take for granted the validity of certain kinds of poetic content, i.e., sexual, philosophical, religious, and are even ready to accept the political, but not as the major organizing idea. Few see the ideological options involved in their reflexive polarization of politics and poetry.

But the decisive arguments that once more force forward the movement of ideas derive from the other aspect of the poem. The students soon recognize that they have in Coleridge a formidable ally in their defense of the individualist and romantic aesthetic outlined earlier in this paper. Coleridge's poet rejects the state and all its works. He is in inspired contact with natural and divine energies which place him beyond and above society, history, and politics. His visionary and expressive powers, which appear to ordinary people as a kind of madness, are unique. Coleridge, and only Coleridge, could have written this poem. Even if there are external influences, literary, personal, and social, they are transformed in the creative process into live metaphors of eternal value for the aesthetic enrichment of each reader.

It is at this point that the "background material" which, in fact, is Coleridge's life in England at the end of the eighteenth century, can be brought in with greatest effectiveness. By invoking evidence from the sociopolitical realities of England in the 1790s and Coleridge's responses to them, the double aim is to support my reading of the poem and to rebut the romantic myth of the gratuitous poet. As journalist and political thinker, as well as poet, Coleridge was a man of his times who felt deeply the great issues raised by the French Revolution. He opposed Pitt's policy of alliance with the feudal monarchies of Europe, including the Russian tsars who were plotting a Bourbon restoration in France. This took some courage at a time when arbitrary arrest for sedition was not uncommon. He denounced the social injustices of English society, war profiteers, and venal journalism, edited his own newspaper, the *Watchman,* while seriously considering a career in public life. With friends and associates he worked out a theory of an ideal society, a "pantisocracy," which they planned to establish in Pennsylvania, on the banks of the Susquehanna. It was a project he was the last to abandon. His letters, articles, and poetry reveal, throughout his early career, that he was a politically conscious and active person.

It can be shown through a study of these writings, of the evolution of his political ideas from radical supporter of the French Revolution to indignant enemy of Napoleon, of his letters to friends and family in 1798, around the time he wrote "Kubla Kahn," that this poem marks his break with his political past and a turning toward religious, moral, and personal issues which correspond to the conservatism and Tory twaddle of his later years. This break can be dated as definitive in January 1798 when Napoleon's invasion of Switzerland revealed to Coleridge once and for all that the French Revolution and all the ideas of the Enlightenment which it epitomized were the work of the Evil One. The following months are punctuated with retractions, self-deprecations, and promises to reform, e.g., "France: An Ode" and, especially, his long letter to his conservative brother, written in April, just two or three months before the probable date of the composition of "Kubla Kahn."

It is not precise to say that Napoleon represents Kubla, although Coleridge did accuse him of trying to establish a Tartar Empire in Europe. It is the state in general, Pitts's and Washington's, as well as Bonaparte's, that he rejects as inherently corrupt and as God's punishment for the sins of man. Whether Coleridge dreamt this poem hallucinogenically or invented an ingenious literary hoax, the result is the same. "Kubla Kahn" is a mythopoetic reenactment of his political disillusionment at the failure of the French Revolution to bring liberty, equality, and fraternity to the peoples of the world. It led to government by tyrants and merchants which made mockery of the high hopes and aspirations of all idealistic people of good will. Kubla symbolizes the failure of *homo politicus*. His poem calls for the reign of *homo poeticus*.

The discussion is again transformed. As expected, some students are convinced, some hesitant, and some skeptical about this reading of the poem, but the issues raised by the supporting historical, political, and biographical arguments introduce new problems of a broad theoretical interest which cannot be posed within the previously established frameworks. Coleridge becomes a case in point for the whole romantic theory of poetic creation and for poetics in general. If a poem like "Kubla Kahn" can be seen as a response to a historical situation, if Coleridge's view of the poet, which is therein distilled, can be refuted by demonstrating that it is, at least in part, an escape from politics, then all our categories of aesthetic thought have to be reexamined.

For if language, even the most subjective, lyrical, and vatic, is a sociohistoric product, does this not reduce the poet to a chronicler, historian, or journalist, possessing perhaps more emotional intensity than most such chroniclers, but basically a recorder like them of the times he or she lives in? What differentiates poetry from other modes of discourse? What is its specific value beyond the charms and seductions of style,

picturesque metaphor, rhythm, ornament, and symbolic complexity? If Coleridge wanted to denounce the state and praise
the poet, why didn't he write an essay? What does "Kubla
Kahn" add to *Biographia Literaria,* or to the *Statesman's
Manual?* The students want to know whether or not we are in
danger once more of reducing poetry to something else and
they mean *politics.* They want above all to preserve the idea
of the poetic individuality against the ubiquitous encroach-
ments of social claims.

Here I can only summarize the steps of the argument which
brings in more fully than before the dialectics of the materialist interpretation. With a responsive class most points can be
elicited from the students through directed discussion. Language is a sociohistoric product; poetry is a personal appre-
hension, adaptation, and elaboration of the communal
language; poetry, therefore, displays one person's individual
appropriation of social consciousness. This is a critical, selective, and synthesizing process in which the poet enriches the
social consciousness with his or her experience and personality, thus revealing new possibilities of meaning formerly
hidden in his or her linguistic heritage. Poets are producers of
new language, new social consciousness, precisely because
they discover and create out of their experience and activity,
personal meanings which they make available to the culture
that produced them. By writing a poem instead of an analytical explanation, the poet recapitulates mimetically the qualities of direct and personal experience, his or her life in the
process of being lived, which is the basis of consciousness and
insight. Mimetic representation has its own laws, its own dialectic which should not be confused with mere copying of
external reality or states of mind. The imitation of an action
carries with it expression, interpretation, evaluation, and
generalization of its significance. In poetry these are in the
state of fusion; criticism separates them for purposes of
analysis.

Political disillusionment drove Coleridge to rethink not only political, but all human relationships—historical, moral, cultural, sexual—on a metaphysical plane, to seek as he put it "the *causa causarum* of things." Myth is a mode of poetic generalization which allows him to contrast the emperor and the poet rather than Napoleon and Coleridge. Ideologically, the condemnation of the state and the comprehension of the revolutionary imperial phenomena of Napoleonic Europe are completely distinct. When I give some examples from the American New Left of the metaphysical transposition of political realities—"Paradise Now," "Down with Alienation," or the French, "L'Imagination au Pouvoir!"—the discussion enters a new and final phase.

For it is not sufficient to show the materialism of the method sociologically, the way that certain works, genres, and attitudes reflect the situation at a given historical moment. That is only the first step and not the hardest. The task of criticism is not completed until we have evaluated the significance of the literature of the past for the world of today from the point of view of the historic experience of the present in which were formed our scholarly and critical consciousness. Marxist critics cannot be satisfied to explicate the past; they are seeking to use the past to help solve the problems of the present. Marxist scholarship and criticism thus imply a political aspect which is most repugnant to the habits of thought of many academics. But it cannot be helped because politics is part and parcel of the method. Of these political themes I shall only discuss the issues closest to the teaching of the Marxist theory of literature, i.e., the problem of Utopia and the problem of the historicity of literature.

The students grasp immediately that Coleridge's message can be translated into New Left doctrine—"The revolution is in your head." This is reinforced by the strong smell of opium surrounding the poem since its first publication in

1816, accompanied by Coleridge's story of the man from Porlock. Escape from politics is not only a good idea to many students; the experience of the 1960s has made it an ideological and emotional necessity for many. Even if they agree with my interpretation of "Kubla Kahn," they are annoyed by my claim that the rejection of politics corresponds to conservative politics. What they call Utopia is a personal secession from a corrupt and brutal society, the formation of new communities of like-minded friends and a fraternal quest for higher types of human relationship, *pantisocracy,* with or without drugs.

There are some good literary examples to show that Utopias are also responses to particular social conditions and that they are structured as the negation of those conditions, but always shaped out of the materials at hand in contemporary society. Rabelais' "Abbaye de Thélème" is the exact reverse of a monastery but its happy inhabitants are all aristocrats since, clearly, that was the only social class whose freedom and leisure could symbolize the human possibility of such a regenerated world. It is not long before someone in the class points out that the little communistic groups scattered throughout North America are in the main made up of middle-class students receiving material assistance from home. This discussion yields some real benefits, intellectual and practical. Students start reading about Utopias from ancient to modern. Some get interested in food cooperatives and similar projects. The overall lesson for me, however, is the profound emotional and moral hold of utopian thinking on the American youth who participated in the movements of the 1960s and even on their more conservative successors.

The answer to utopian thinking is the dialectical-materialist interpretation of history which simultaneously explains Utopia as an ideological phenomenon and the reasons for its theoretical and political inadequacy. It is good to read and discuss Engels' *Socialism, Utopian and Scientific,* because to many students Marxism is a form of utopian thought. Of course, Engels' critique of the grandiose social plans of Owen, Saint-Simon, and Fourier does not cover the radically subjective, individualistic, and mystical visions of Coleridge. In the conditions of American life, however, sensitive, restless, and discontented young people of the middle classes almost always start by seeking individual solutions to social problems. They see parallels between Coleridge and thinkers and artists such as Kierkegaard, Nietzsche, Gide, Camus, and Sartre, the mythographers of modern individualism in its various heroic guises. Students can contrast these theories with those of Beckett, Ionesco, Adamov, and Genet, spokesmen for absurdity and dereliction, the comic tragedy (tragicomedy) of the human condition. Peter Weiss' *Marat-Sade* and Brecht's *Good Woman of Setzuan* allow for a good discussion of these issues.

The insistence on the historicity of literature and of all cultural production is a healthy antidote to the universalist ideologies which perceive the different schools and periods of art as a variety of reflections on the eternal constants of human nature. Marxism alone consistently seeks out the emergence of the new as a product of historic experience based on changes in the material and social conditions of life brought about by labor, science, art, and political struggle. A Marxist history of Utopias would, in the first place, show their differences. The idea that human nature changes, that indeed changeability is the *differentia specifica* of human beings, is probably the single most interesting notion to the students. The idea that their capacity to understand the past involves an understanding of their own historical position, of the historicity of their own thought, is certainly the most difficult for them. I began this paper with a polemic against philistine antiphilosophy and anti-intellectualism. Perhaps worse than that is our cultivated absence of a sense of history which makes the past useless as a guide to present problems, the miscomprehended present into a hindrance for understanding the past, and the future into a maze of unforeseeable dangers and potentials, unleashing simultaneously apocalyptic visions of imminent catastrophe and mind-soothing utopian pipedreams.

The student evaluations of this course, written and spoken, show that the principal benefit most of them derive is a way of thinking, an alternative to what they are usually taught; in brief, a new method. Few indeed become socialists because they study the Marxist theory of literature, but almost all appreciate the intellectual perspectives, analytical precision, and immediate relevance of the Marxist approach. They are almost all anticommunist and anti-Soviet. Those, however, who do believe in the socialist transformation of society look to China, Cuba, and Yugoslavia for possible new models of social organization, frequently forgetting the differing conditions which gave rise to revolutions in those countries. At the same time they are aware that the United States will have to find its own way.

Notes

1. Lee Baxandall, *Radical Perspectives in the Arts* (Harmondsworth: Penguin, 1972); B. Lang and F. Williams, *Marxism and Art: Writings in Aesthetics and Criticism* (New York: McKay, 1972); M. Solomon, *Marxism and Art* (New York: Knopf, 1973); G. C. Le Roy and U. Beitz, trans. and ed., *Preserve and Create: Essays in Marxist Literary Criticism* (New York: Humanities Press, 1973).
2. N. Rudich, "Kubla Kahn, Coleridge's Anti-Political Vision," in *The Weapons of Criticism: Marxism and the Literary Tradition in America*, ed. N. Rudich (Palo Alto: Ramparts Press, 1976).
3. K. Marx and F. Engels, *Selected Works* (New York: International Publishers, 1970), p. 28.

No More Teacher's Dirty Looks: Conceptual Teaching from the Bottom Up
Ira Shor

What do most students have to show for their years of schooling? So many of us spend thousands of hours in school buildings, waiting for the boredom to end. We cling to memories of good teachers here and there, but have etched in our minds a grand gallery of our teachers' disapproving faces, much like Macbeth's vision of Banquo's progeny.

Why do millions of people spend so much time in school and come away with so little? What do schools accomplish? "Nothing" is not the answer. Schools keep kids off the streets, supervised while parents are at work, and delay the entry of young workers into the crowded job market. But how much learning is there? Generations of students are drilled in basic reading, writing, and math, yet leave school functionally illiterate. Besides delivering us to adulthood weakly literate, school also keeps us unaware of where we've come from historically, who our friends are, where we should be heading, and what kind of sense we can make of the things going on around us.

Term by term, schools try to habituate young workers to the patterns of society and to the needs of the business world. This is no easy task, and no mean accomplishment, because the students keep resisting most of the way. School is an early preparation of the working class for the dull routines of the adult workworld. Worker-students are no more happy about their adjustment process than are the working adults who exchange teachers for bosses. Schools have a wide variety of mechanisms for weakening student resistance. The institutional goal is a mass psychology of obedience. Lively worker-kids arrive in school wary but curious. They graduate from high school anti-intellectual, resentful, suffering from injured pride, hungry for respect and power, and cynical about themselves and the chance for meaningful social change.

This dehumanizing process retards a wide range of feeling and thought. Virtually lost to workers in America is their class memory of struggle; weakened is their class solidarity; trivialized is their sense of how to analyze things. Their critical thinking about daily life and larger social issues is discouraged by pedagogy which mystifies both philosophy and history. The past is a laundry list of names, dates, and places; or a classless excursion through a theme like "industrialization." Twelve years of lower education and some college seem to have left my worker-students with the conviction that things were mostly bad in the past, but they're surely a lot worse now, and what's the difference anyway because you can't change human nature. Learning that power corrupts and that people are only out for themselves, they are held back from seeing the past, taking hold of the present, and conceiving of an independent future. School does not easily or completely develop this kind of static consciousness. Workers keep wanting to find out more for themselves, to feel more free, more educated, more collective and powerful than they do. Few chances for this come their way, but they don't abandon looking, and are avid fans of movies that show nobodies winning respect. School plays a big role in channeling their aspirations, but school alone is not enough. Joining the massive national education system are complementary social forces in the mass media, the sports culture, and the consumer twilight zone where "buying" is the shape of freedom, power, and pleasure.

Twilight in school can begin dissolving when radical teaching begins. Teachers in a dehumanized milieu can let some light in by devoting class time to consciousness-raising. What has to be raised is the students' sense of history and purpose. What has to be developed is their ability to conceive of a future built on different principles than the present. What makes these tasks especially challenging to radical teachers is that they have to be carried out simultaneously with developing in worker-students deep literacy and conceptual skills. Consciousness-raising is valuable in itself; it is most valuable when taught through one of the concrete skills school has kept away from workers. The arts, sciences, and humanities, as well as reading, writing, and analysis, are fundaments poorly developed in worker-students. Taught singly, literacy, conceptual, or awareness-teaching will be of help to students who have never been exposed to these resources seriously; taught together, they can become mutually propelling.

Teachers who experiment with skill development through consciousness-raising will find themselves confronting much uncharted terrain. One dimension of the problem will be dealing with contradictions among students and contradictions between students and teacher. Sex and race loom large as divisive forces among students. Another contradiction is the division of labor. Students will come from a variety of job backgrounds and levels. Those "higher up" will cling defensively to their toehold of prestige, while those "lower down" will speak in resentful challenge. This whole issue gets writ large in terms of teacher-student divisions. The teacher is a college graduate with an elite salary, teaching students who hold menial jobs and who live in a world of mass culture. The special responsibility of the teacher, as a facilitator of consciousness-raising, is to keep working at seeing things from the bottom up. Worker-students will want to join in the teacher-initiated process only if the studies flow into and through the idiom of mass experience. Both mass culture and high culture were not designed by students or teachers for themselves, but are the cultural forms developed by corporate society for them. Teachers need to become familiar with the language, feeling, and structure of everyday life, drawing upon these resources for class study. The abstract ideas of division of labor, regional and ethnic differences, and conditioned sexism and racism take various forms in the lived experience of students and are most usefully confronted in those concrete forms. Formulations and examples drawn from experience ("money talks," "the little woman," "the welfare Cadillac," "you can't fight city hall," "the nine-to-fiver," etc.) should be a major resource for radical teaching. In Paulo Freire's terms, process-oriented radical teachers initiate an analytic dialogue that problematizes as it uses the student's reality to teach cognitive skills.

Besides integrating pedagogy with immediate experience, radical teachers can speak to their students' needs by developing conceptual skills through exercises in methodology and ideology. Class studies grounded in methodical inquiry can begin to reverse the anti-intellectual effects of mass media and the pace of daily life, which tend to evoke furious and scattered mental habits. The "news" comes at workers in two-minute flashes from melodramatic announcers who make international wars and the birth of mutant ducklings sound equally important. Workers commuting from home to work and to school rush past highway billboards with pseudo-romantic messages promising elusive sexual and social happiness. On the job, at home, in the streets, or in school, workers receive a constant flow of information, as well as orders and commands, from bosses, parents, cops, and teachers. In work or play, repose is rare. From fast foods to quickie sex to instant video replay, daily life is superstimulating. The brain is not made empty, but is left saturated and impressionistic. Minds dominated by mass culture are too crowded and too fast to tolerate the bigness and slowness of radical ideas. Radical teaching can do something about this. The radical classroom has to slow down and conceptualize the habits of mind. This is not the same thing as running a boring or simple-minded course. The work in class should be challenging, intricate, even demanding, but unhurried. If mass culture is shallow thought done quickly, the class should be deep thought done slowly. A class that teaches analytic methods can achieve this by exercising the brain in detailed thinking. Needless to say, workers will agree to take part in the unfamiliar act of prolonged scrutiny only if the work is presented respectfully and is relevant to their experience.

While careful study of analytic methods and of the ideology of everyday life can be an antidote to a racing mind, another resource is comedy. It can help emotionalize interest in demanding mental work. Comedy draws upon the culture of pleasure, here integrated into the experience of education. This can help radical teachers deal positively with the huge resentments working-class students have built up against school. Even radical teachers will have a lot of anger directed at them. Humor in the classroom can ease some of this alienation, but too much ease will signal to students that the teacher is a pushover. Worker-students develop a lot of survival radar in their progress through social institutions, so if they suspect that a teacher or a course is not serious, they will take the class from structure into chaos. Only by trial and error can a teacher find out the right blend of rigor and relaxation. Setting this goal in advance will lessen some frustrations later on. Comedy also achieves a pedagogical effect similar to the use of everyday life for thematic content. Both these methods take the teacher off her or his pedestal. Laughter and daily experience can be egalitarian forces validating the teacher by the voluntary surrender of two teacherly defenses: academic abstractness and professional austerity.

These are some starting points for radical teachers who decide to teach *for* their students instead of just lecturing *at* them. We'll learn in practice how to become a popular intelligentsia. Reversing the effects of school and mass culture, and achieving the widest distribution of intellectual skills, we will travel a long and interesting road.

A Course Called Utopia

I developed a Utopia course for some of the most conservative worker-students I've ever met. Most are white like me, and part of the same class I grew up in; a few are black; about half are women; many have come out of the parochial schools. While the New Left of the 1960s brought many middle-class students to radical politics, the same decade passed my students by. Vietnam and Watergate have made them more cynical about the government, but the burning issues of the last decade have not left much of an ideological trace in their lives. They've taken to marijuana and unisex hairstyles and clothes; they love rock music and sports; they often feel that minorities and women complain too much.

Still, the Utopia course is always well-enrolled. More and more of my students want to find out about "the good life." They're interested in becoming "complete human beings." Despite the forces holding them back (traditional family life, church, school, the mass media, drugs, unemployment), they want some genuine answers. The women seem most serious about schoolwork. The women's movement has helped them get in touch with their grievances. On the other side, the men are more likely to argue, to become defensive, as they uphold their received ideology. We argue plenty, but we manage to laugh a lot also, and sometimes play basketball together. I find myself admiring their toughness, their closeness to life's nitty-gritty problems, their up-front disregard for decorum, their desire for independence, and their enduring desire for knowledge. They're not polite, and they are reluctant to ask for help even when they should. Also, they're very smart, which surprises them more than me.

In the Utopia course we do consciousness-raising around methodology and ideology. Studying methods of analysis and structures for ideas trains us to criticize conditioned habits. It helps us to decode the seeming confusion of daily life, and to discuss new ideas.

The eyes are an excellent place to begin. I slow down the students' furious pace of perception by asking them to concentrate on a stationary object. This is the first step of the Utopia course. We begin immediately with a style of work and a pace of intellectualism different from the experience of mass culture. We are concentrating together, quietly.

After a time, I ask the students to describe on paper, as carefully as they can, what they are seeing. We read our descriptions out loud. I call this step "life description," the breaking down of a thing into its visual components. The students usually find no problem with this. They connect their eyes to the language store in their brains, which pours words through their hands.

Some care should be exercised in choosing the object to be analyzed. I usually start with one of the chairs in the classroom. It's familiar, close at hand, and full of ideology. After taking a chair down the method/ideology road, we consider the automobile, and then the hamburger (eventually getting into why the burger has taken over the American food industry).

Our work with the chair trains us in a method that we can apply to many things besides America's automania and burgeritis. Along the way, philosophical training adds rigor to our impressions. One example of our mental gymnastics is the time I spend carefully examining the difference between "chair" and "seat." If the students agree that our classroom "chair" is a "seat," I then ask, "If a chair and a seat are the same, and a chair and my desk are not the same, then how come my desk can seat six people?" We puzzle out that answer, conceptualizing how "seat" describes many surfaces which can accommodate the act of sitting while "chair" denotes an object predesigned *only* for sitting.

The simple chair proves to be fairly versatile as an object by which methodology can be taught. The stimulation of the mind to make a lot of verbal sense out of a single object sparks a good deal of energy. That energy carries us into Step 2—the "diagnosis."

I explain Step 2 as the investigatory phase of our beginning method. In "life description," we mostly used our eyes. In "diagnosis," we begin using a lot of critical, conceptual, and intellectual skills. Our diagnosis elaborates the object we're considering into its total social, political, and historical context. I ask the class to consider the chair as a problem, a human problem. What does it mean for us to have it? Where do its construction materials come from? Where is it made? Who made it? How did it get to us? Why was it made like it is? Is it a good thing for us to have? What's good or bad with it? Who decided we should have it? When did it enter human history? How did people live before they had it? Could we do without it?

We begin to lay out something like the following:

The chair was built by a private corporation. It was mass-produced by unionized labor in a factory. The workers are semi-skilled and paid by the hour. The chair is constructed from metal, fiberglass, and plastic, and form-styled as a narrow bucket seat. The metals are extracted from the earth by miners and smelted into ingots. The synthetic materials are produced in other factories.

Attached to each chair is a movable writing surface, which is a kind of small desk. These chairs were shipped to our college by truck or train, where groundskeepers unloaded them into the classrooms.

The chair is hard and uncomfortable and only designed for right-handed people. It is hard so as to be durable, and uncomfortable so that students won't fall asleep in it. It is generally too small for male students. The design of the chair makes it hard to look anywhere except straight ahead, usually at the teacher, rather than at the other students. The chairs are cheap and stack on one another. They also interlock into neat rows. Evening cleanup crews set them up that way, to make their sweeping easier.

This chair was purchased for students to sit on but students had no part in making it, transporting it, selecting it, or purchasing it.

This monologue emerges as a model synthesis of each student's diagnosis. No single analysis is so thorough, but compositely, the class pieces it together. For all of us, it is an achievement to recreate a total economic process. This kind of work demystifies what we know as commodity relations. The origins and the meaning of a familiar commodity become accessible, not mysterious. One political role of commodity culture is to mystify the reproduction of daily life, so that workers never feel their creative power in the making of the things they use. If the origins of daily life are mysterious, working people can never see themselves as *actors,* as the very people who make everything we have. (Lukács, in *History and Class Consciousness,* analyzes this in depth.) When the Utopia course uses method and ideology to comprehend commodities and immediate experience, we make clear what the human sources and human implications are in everything we live through. This is one way that schoolwork can impart a sense of power.

Students in the Utopia class begin to see that we use the chair but didn't design it or choose it. It is uncomfortable. Would they build or pick uncomfortable chairs for themselves? Does the college president sit on a chair like this? Would people buy a chair like this for their homes? What's the difference between public life in an institution and private life in your house? This last question has led to useful discussions on the alienation of work from pleasure. Using home-chairs as some kind of counter-model from the student's personal life, I ask them what kinds of seats they would want in their classrooms. They come up with their own alternatives: bigger chairs, upholstered chairs, old wooden chairs, padded benches, floor pillows, used couches, etc. They think up improvements, practicing what mass culture forbids—the self-design of a noncommercial commodity.

When we discuss how uncomfortable the chair is, we get into the behavioral principles of its design. You can't fall asleep in this kind of chair. You can't doodle graffiti on its rock-hard formica desk. You can't slouch. You can't turn and whisper to another student. The chair is an academic straightjacket, designed to rivet a student's attention toward the teacher at the front. The next question I ask should be obvious: Why does so much effort have to be put into keeping the student's attention? They have a quick answer: School is a boring waste of time. Why don't we change school to make it more important instead of making school-chairs more uncomfortable? This line of inquiry provokes a prolonged exchange between students, in which they share experiences of school. The discussion is reality-confronting, skill-developing, and consciousness-raising, started by methodical analysis of an immediate, familiar object.

We also have gone on to consider how elite colleges are furnished. The high-tuition sanctuaries of higher education are often decorated with rugs on the floor, soft chairs, reposeful lounges, spacious halls, art on the walls, wood doors and paneling, indirect lighting, and even draperies. When we acknowledge that our "budget" junior college is a tile, cinderblock, and formica-fluorescent wonderland, the question of class analysis is very immediate. Our public college is as shabby as public housing and as functional as a factory. Thus, our simple classroom chair proves a central function of dialectical method—you can get anywhere you want to from any place you start. We are sitting on social theory.

So far the first method in the Utopia course can be laid out like this:

> *Step 1: Life Description.* Seeing the thing. A component breakdown of the object, process, or situation.
>
> *Step 2: Diagnosis.* The investigation. Locating the thing in its total time and space, its total human implications; the thing as a problem.
>
> *Step 3: Reconstruction.* The solution. Rebuilding, so that it serves people's needs.

I present this structure as a problem-solving method and as a model for the consciousness of Utopia. Step 3 is the leap into the future. When people just abandon society and set up an ideal way of life, we call that Utopia. Steps 1 and 2 represent one thought process which leads Utopians to Step 3. Practicing this method, my students exercise their ability to conceive alternatives.

There is another visual way to represent this method, which adds to a student's sense of how our present society developed. It looks like this:

1. This square is the thing being analyzed. "Life description" breaks it down into its components.

2. This figure represents the thing in its immediate societal space. The rectangle around the square begins the "diagnosis." For instance, how does X relate to other things like it in society? Where does X fit into our way of life?

3. This figure represents the thing in its *global space*. The larger

rectangle demonstrates that the thing in our way of life has a relation to the rest of the world. How is X experienced in China or France? How does our having X affect China and France?

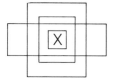

4. This figure shows the thing in its immediate *time*, as well as its national and international space. The horizontal rectangle represents the immediate timespan of the thing. To the left of X we ask: Who made it? Where and when? How did it get to us? What process produced it, marketed it, distributed it to us? Why did we buy it? When? Where? To the right of X is the immediate future. How will X look tomorrow, next month, next year? Does it change, get used up or thrown away, recycled, stored, made more valuable, etc.?

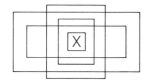

5. This is the thing in its long-range *time*. The larger horizontal rectangle is the long-range time block. To the left is the past. In the middle is the present. To the right is the future. The long-range past out of which X came tells us who invented or set up X, when, and why. What did people do before X existed? What made X necessary and possible at the time it appeared? The future time span answers two questions: Utopia and Dystopia. If the future is to be Utopia, who will make it and how? If the future of X is to be the same or get worse, who brought it to us and what more will they do to X so that it satisfies our needs even less? How would X look if it were to serve people's needs better?

This structural paradigm for conceptual thinking (which one student named the "Utopia graph") automatically locates anything in its fullest time and space, and begs the question about the future. What we have now (the present) came to us out of an immediate social/economic process and a long-range historical development. Who is dominating the direction of society? Where are *they* likely to take X? Where would we take it if X were to satisfy our needs better in the future than it does now? We've used this graph for the car and the hamburger. Before the fast-food industry monopolized the restaurant business, there used to be many small family-run eateries, many of them ethnic, and most of the food was fresh-cooked and tasty. Now? Restauranting is dominated by the fast-food industry, with its processed and nutritionless food, tasty only by virtue of pickles and ketchup.

Using this method to analyze the car and the burger not only places us in daily life, but develops a theory of monopoly capital in very existential terms. Everyone uses cars and eats burgers. But many of us also live in neighborhoods where McDonald's is replacing the family restaurants, and where bad mass transit makes a car a necessity. Moreover, everyone is being bombarded by the media to buy sexy new car models and to love superburgers. Join these recognitions to the class's acknowledgment that fast foods fit into the suburbanization and automobilization of America, and the going gets tough and exciting. It's exciting because so much gets brought together. But it's tough because so many working-class needs are tied to the social process that cars, drive-ins, and suburbia represent.

Most workers need their own cars and want their own private houses to live in. If we discuss in class an American future with more mass transit, and with jobs closer to home, and with fewer cars, the method asks them to convert their conditioned dreams. They hate mass transit. It's dirty, uncomfortable, slow, expensive, and dangerous. The private car is quick, but polluting and not so cheap. Further, it represents freedom as well as a personal lovenest for underemployed young adults who can't have sex where they live, in their parents' houses. When our method asks students to leap to a reconstructed future where mass transit is better than the private car, it makes a tremendous emotional and intellectual demand. The public sector, which has brought us decrepit mass transit (along with boring schools), has so dominated us that it's hard for students to believe in a positive public power that can serve the people's needs, whether it be the need for food, work, transportation, or sex.

Imagining reality created by people as their own government is what the utopian phase of our method calls for. That effort demands great intellectual clarity if we are to develop models of the future we ourselves can believe in. What grows in some students' minds is a recognition, shared by Utopians and political radicals, that we will be happy and healthy only if we ourselves design our future. Utopia becomes understood as a dream and a process, of people who figure out who they are, what they need, and how to go about getting it. Sometimes the force holding back the utopian future is seen as the private profit system. The utopian accounts we read keep pointing to the ideologies of self-management and cooperative economy. The importance of these values keeps getting reinforced as we dissect how Utopians try to set up a new society. A critique of monopoly capitalism, or a validation of workers' control, are not easily or best done in lecture form. They are abstractions until our methods and our study of ideology and Utopia makes them concrete. They are also values that provoke the students' conditioned fear of socialism. Some students gain a critique of the system from the process of our study, but they don't take action from their new knowledge, and they're not especially optimistic about getting their ideas realized in history. Our classwork is only a starting point for challenging ruling ideas.

To make ideology tangible, I work on comparing two things, and on a method for extracting ideology from experience. Comparison and ideological extraction become accessible through our study of several utopian communes. We analyze their components and compare what they have in common. To clarify what it means to extract from existential details a value structure, I offer a model:

> *Name of idea:* Pastoralism.
>
> *General definition:* The urge to live a simpler life; less dependence on machines; no waste or conspicuous consumption; closeness to nature; emphasis on simplicity.
>
> *Life examples:* Make own clothes; wear hair natural; wear loose-fitting outfits; eat organic food; bake own bread; build own shelter; live in extended families.

As an intellectual model, this begins to train students in conceptualizing experience. The "life examples" are drawn from the accounts of communal life we read. The "general definition" is a generalization about what the life examples mean. The "name" elevates the generalization to linguistic brevity, refining a whole category of experience into an easily digestible notation. A sense of what ideology is grows from the students' successive conceptualization of experience. To get into this method, we first, as a class, generally characterize two communes. Then we compare their lives with our own. Lastly, we break into workgroups to characterize specific areas, like work, money, sex, free time, etc. From these themes, each group develops its generalizations and names. This method serves us as a model for the conceptual habit of mind.

What I've found is that the "name" level is the hardest for students. Further, they often have trouble distinguishing generalizations from specific life details. In subsequent projects, when I have the students plan their own utopian commune based on our developed ideology, they write militant general manifestoes about the utopian life, but have to rewrite their papers before they can nail down *specific* mechanisms for implementing utopian ideas. For this level, I am often called on to provide terminology. They find it very difficult to come up with conceptions or abstractions which name their own experience or their self-designed utopian alternatives. Here is one ideology for a secular Utopia that I developed with the class after weeks of discussion:

Utopian Ideology

1. *Self-organization*—set up own work rules, schedules, government; change rules easily.
2. *Egalitarian democracy*—open discussions of all rules and issues; government open to everyone; one vote for everyone; less bureaucracy and hierarchy; easy to remove leaders and change the government; manual work shared by all.
3. *Collectivism*—sharing everything; jobs, tools, knowledge, expertise, money, goods, necessities, living space; no emphasis on careers; little emphasis on possessions.
4. *Experimentalism*—openness to new things, new ways of doing things; continuous testing of relationships, in work, in division of labor, salary, and sexuality, etc.
5. *Holism*—attempt to merge work and play, home and the job, public and private lives; a rejection of living the alienated life, a piece of you here, a piece there.
6. *Aestheticism*—merging art and work, art and life; desire to liberate the creativity in each person, on the job and in spare time; greater emphasis on handicrafts, manual arts.
7. *Cooperatism*—desire to spread communal feeling; a criticism of individualism; emphasis on self-expression without encouraging selfishness; a moral concern with other people's needs and well-being.
8. *Pastoralism*—urge to live a simpler life; less technology and machines; no waste or conspicuous consumption; organic food, loose clothes, natural hair; closeness to nature; emphasis on sincerity and simplicity.
9. *Activism*—participation in life; no spectators; urge to do and not just watch; people encouraged to do as much as they can; people learning to do things for themselves; people do a variety of jobs, not tied to one job all the time.
10. *Tribalism*—home close to work; home as place of work; all people thought of as family; each generation close to the others, no hostility of age groups; each generation teaches the

next; responsible feelings for all people lived with; no family breakups, as kids mature they stay close to home; mutual dependence.

Following our work on methods and ideologies, we take this ideology and use it to plan our own rural Utopias, a utopian salary policy for urban workers, and to write such things as a Free Labor Manifesto (a declaration or model of the conditions under which labor would make us feel free and whole). Sometimes we restructure the hierarchical division of labor we uncover in such places as schools and hospitals. We also go on to apply the methods and the extracted utopian ideology to various novels (like Skinner's *Walden II* and Vonnegut's *Player Piano*). At one point I asked my students to treat the communes we were studying as the immediate future in the Utopia graph, and then to go back in time and recreate the former lives of the communal people in such a way as to explain why they chose to leave their previous lives and become Utopians. This exercise in imagination turns out to be immensely real. In recreating the previous lives of the communalists, the students articulate their own grievances and needs as the basis for justifying the abandonment of society. The fiction of the commune's past reveals the reality of the students' present.

The method of extracting ideology and the three-step life description/diagnosis/reconstruction method fit into each other in the following manner. The three-step method is placed on its side and becomes a model for action as well as thought:

Life description (1)	T
Diagnosis (2)	I M
Reconstruction (3)	E

There is a time span because each step precedes the other in thinking and acting. The Utopians choose Utopia after analyzing and diagnosing the evils of their society.

Next, I ask if any of these steps are part of any other method we have discussed. Someone in class realizes that Steps 1 and 3 are really "life examples," a step in the method to extract ideology. Both materially describe something in life—a thing, a situation, or a way of living. So this recognition enables us to move in space as well as time:

Space

Name	Conceptual definition	Life description (1)	One time period
Negations ↑↓		Diagnosis (investigation) (2)	Time transition
Name	Conceptual definition	Life description Reconstruction (solution) (3)	New time period

Space

Students have called this configuration the "horseshoe" or "the open doughnut." As my students watch how all the methods fit together, I ask what's missing. They see that the "names" of the ideologies are not connected. This physically demonstrates that the utopian future is philosophically and existentially in another dimension. The paradigm also shows how important the diagnosis is. Diagnosis, the most dialectical moment of thought, is the cementing and transitional block between the present and the future. It's the mental pivot of time.

The "horseshoe" or "open doughnut" is a structure that can be used as a mental puzzle. I ask my students to take each of the ten utopian ideology points and place them in the bottom level of the horseshoe. Then I ask them to work backward and develop the rest of the boxes. What they come up with is the negation of Utopia and also an existential and ideological description of some of the features of our own society. This kind of exercise leads to the thoughtful recognition that much of what we have now is the opposite of the best we need. Working-class students are so alienated from social institutions that they hardly need to learn that the system's hurdles and daily life are not good for them. They know this. What this prolonged study accomplishes is to offer a depth to their intuitions and recognitions. More than just depth, these methods offer and name what some of the alternatives could be. These methods also provide students with the opportunity to hone mental skills in designing options, and giving these options more tangible reality. The structures as a whole train students to conceptualize experience and to existentialize conceptions. They can unfreeze a student's sense of time. Thought and life become more unified and fluid in motion from one time zone to another. Radical teaching like this can begin to transform what Lukács described as "reified consciousness," the great mass product of commodity culture.

By the term's end the conceptual sharpness in many of my students becomes startling. Not only have I been immensely enlightened by doing this course with my students, but it has been encouraging to find out just how much serious brainpower remains in worker-students, despite all the years of school fatigue and mass media deluge. The Utopia course equips them with some mental habits for resisting dehumanization. Utopia, studied as a thing in itself, as an ongoing process of daily life, and as a critique of American society, offers a stimulating medium for teaching systematic and creative thought. It is one starting point for the development of new consciousness.

Teaching Feminist Politics
....
Joan B. Landes

The women's liberation movement in the decade of the 1970s often appears to have been successfully packaged by the mass culture industry so that it exists only as a phenomenon of the commodity sphere. On the one hand, we find palatable versions of feminism served up in commercial time slots in order to increase product sales; on the other hand, the movement is disparaged by hostile pundits on television talk-shows and entertainment serials or ridiculed in advertisements. The effect of either tactic is to rob the women's movement of its real social content. As a result, feminists can be challenged by skeptics to locate their movement in *real*— that is, nonbroadcast—time and space. One possible, though certainly not the only, answer to those who ask where the women's movement is to be found is that it exists in and around the college campuses of this country. Indeed, one might convincingly argue that it was the contradictory experience of women in the sector of higher education that spawned many of the most significant groups in today's movement. Moreover, no appreciation of contemporary feminism is possible without a prior understanding of the intellectual traditions to which it is indebted. And, the women's liberation movement continues to be reflected in the recurrent struggles waged by feminist students to establish or retain women's studies curricula and to foster the hiring and retention of feminist teachers.

It was in just such a context that I was hired to my first university post and asked, in addition to my other responsibilities, to develop a course in feminist politics. (The only other feminist offering at this institution had encountered strong opposition to its permanent inclusion in the curriculum; by the time I left, however, two related courses had won this status.) The course I devised, called "Women, Power, and Politics" and later renamed "Theories of Women's Liberation," was by no means easy to organize. At first it appeared that there were few "classics" in the field around which to draw up a syllabus (as it turned out there were quite a few), and that the conventional literature in political theory and social science offered little further encouragement. Yet despite these initial difficulties, the course was directly related to my own subsequent theoretical and political education as well as the subject matter of my doctoral dissertation. Indeed, to a significant extent I view the dissertation as the product of a several year dialogue between my students and myself, as a reflection of a joint project to achieve mutual theoretical consciousness of the issues raised within the women's movement.

Varying the Setting

I taught the course for two years in its original setting, a traditional small private university. Each time the course attracted an equal number of male and female students, and a strong minority of black students—again equally divided between men and women. With the exception of the black students, whose origins were in the urban working class, most students were products of professional middle-class or other nonworking-class suburban and small-town rural backgrounds. Their attitudes ranged from commitment and sympathy toward a feminist perspective to outright hostility or a "what's-in-it-for-me?" attitude. Their academic preparation varied. Along with liberal arts students, the course drew engineering, business, and education majors, two "faculty wives," and one female faculty member. Accordingly, I found among these students a very uneven receptivity toward theoretical questions and readings.

More recently I offered the course in a small experimental liberal arts college whose students are drawn preponderantly from nonworking-class backgrounds, with a few important exceptions. Most of these students had been exposed to feminist issues through prior attendance in other feminist studies courses. Moreover, the existence of an active women's center, a multiplicity of feminist organizations on- and off-campus, and a large number of faculty from a variety of disciplines working in women's studies provided a congenial context for the course. The students in this setting were until recently all women and did not include any black or Third World students. Several were sympathetic to separatist political strategies, as a result of wrestling with this issue in their personal and sexual lives.

The course was conceived as a seminar, although the mix between lectures, student presentations, and class discussion varied from time to time. The class size never exceeded twenty-five. As a result, it was possible to remain flexible by experimenting with several forms in order to achieve spontaneity on the part of class members without sacrificing a rigorous approach to the course material. In other words, it was deemed important for the students to subject their own views of feminism, women, the family, and the sexual struggle to a systematic critique. This required an ability to situate prior conceptions within a structured social reality, and this in turn obliged the students to become familiar with historical changes in women's and family life, and to locate different theoretical versions of feminism within modern social movements. Over the years in which this course was taught the feminist literature became more theoretically self-conscious and the course evolved in the direction of feminist theory rather than women's politics. It became necessary to present appreciably more material in a lecture format in order to provide students with the background from which to read critically the rapidly multiplying feminist texts. At the same time, I tried to remain sensitive to the need for dialogue within the classroom, avoiding the oppressive habit of "talking at" students without listening to their questions.

To an important extent, the evolving content of feminist writings dictated a new sensitivity to form. Pedagogical clichés about the feminist classroom no longer seemed appropriate to this new situation. Not surprisingly, the transition to a more traditional format met with mixed reactions. Many were appreciative and relieved to treat their feminist class with the same seriousness as they profferred toward other respected academic subjects. They welcomed the fact that the course would not decompose into a series of loosely structured rap sessions. At the same time, others insisted that the feminist classroom is and should be a haven from more oppressive academic situations. They emphasized the need to transform the classroom into an arena for open discussions of feelings and personal experiences as a way of arriving at the truth about ourselves as women. They viewed theory itself with some suspicion. It had been in the past the special province of men; it required of us an alien language and an abstract mode of thought which they regarded as opposite to the personal, intersubjective, and emotional mode in which women best articulated. For these students, what did not emerge directly from feminist practice was understood to be elitist, patriarchal, and dominating.

To the extent that such objections were raised within the course, they reaffirmed my increased awareness of the interpenetration of form and content. The view of the feminist classroom advocated by these students had to be related to a broader tendency within the movement to separate thought and feeling, mind and body, affirming the latter of these two polarities as the authentically feminist mode of being. Likewise, on a theoretical level many radically minded feminists sought to isolate woman from man, the family from economic life, and the sexual revolution from the class struggle. Within the course, these related perspectives were juxtaposed to the classical antinomies of liberal thought with respect to the individual subject and society. The feminist antipathy to theory and the desire to ghettoize women's studies were situated as part of a broader empiricist tendency within American culture by which only subjective experience is treated as an authentic fact. The process of grappling with these dimensions of the subject led to a reorganization of the course materials and to a revision of the original conception of the course.

Changing Perspectives

The course was initially conceived as a radical version of a politics course. It sought to make visible the ways in which women are excluded from positions of power in all institutional arenas of modern American society; to demonstrate the ideological dimensions of women's powerlessness and alienation in popular culture as well as social science theory; and, finally, to move toward the elaboration of a theory of women's oppression which might account for historical changes in the organization of family life as well as the social-psychological aspects of women's oppression today. Over time, as the course was transformed into one in feminist theory, the latter objective came to predominate.

Whereas many of the reading selections used in the earliest version of the course were provocative for students newly charged by feminist concerns, it became clear that they were often based on an eclectic use of materials, combined with positivist notions of social science and underlying liberal goals. As a result, these writings were usually insensitive to the theoretical dimension of feminist arguments and uninformed as to the relationship of earlier feminist movements to liberal, Marxist, and Freudian thought. For example, we read an article by Naomi Weisstein entitled "Kinder, Küche, Kirche as Scientific Law: Psychology Constructs the Female,"[1] which was influential in the early years of the movement. From the standpoint of experimental psychology, Weisstein assaults clinical psychology and psychiatry for amassing theory without evidence. The source of their errors in technique is located in Freud's practice. Freud's antifeminism is presented here as a direct consequence of his antiempiricist, and therefore false, conception of scientific research. Although Weisstein is concerned with the important task of situating the individual woman within her social surroundings, she, like many other feminist writers in diverse disciplines, reasserts the positivist prejudices of her own discipline and proposes the extension of laboratory techniques to the study of woman. She accepts uncritically the empiricist attack on Freud and reproduces it as an original feminist insight. Similarly, other contributions from the standpoint of sociology or economics documented inequalities suffered by American women, but gave only a partial view of these problems by focusing primarily on middle-class subjects.[2]

All of these writers lacked an overall social and historical framework from which the specific inequalities which they documented could be situated. They treated psychological problems as functions of recorded attitudes and behavior and never dealt with the dimension of unconscious mental processes. All such writings allowed students to declare themselves as feminists without challenging the accepted notions of mainstream social science. Feminism in this context amounted to a bold insistence that women are a legitimate subject of investigation, but offered no unified body of theory about what feminism is. To the extent, then, that feminist writings were deficient in theory, students were apt to substitute their own versions of women's theory. Thus, among my students in this period I often encountered a tentative agreement on the view that all women by virtue of their sex share a common fate which transcends group, class, and national boundaries. The family was seen as an important locus of oppression, affecting women's fate in all arenas of social life. It was only with the digestion of Shulamith Firestone's *The Dialectic of Sex* [3] that these tacitly held arguments were organized into an explicit theory of sex class. Prior to assimilating Firestone's arguments, students confronted the accumulating mass of detail on their own oppression, as well as the cross-cultural experiences of women, with a cruder, but related, version of sex-class theory. In fact, the notion that all women are oppressed at all times in all places seemed to have the advantage of allowing students to be completely eclectic in adopting evidence for their position from a variety of feminist writers without considering the possible conflicting implications of these different positions. However, as the contributions to feminist theory proliferated, it became more and more difficult to avoid recognizing that important differences among feminists existed, differences expressed on a political as well as a theoretical level. It was around these differences that I came to organize the theoretical writings in the subsequent versions of the course, situating sex-class arguments as one of many perspectives on the "woman question," the view that individual women are oppressed by virtue of the universal social situation which seems to derive from their special nature, defying historical change.

Significantly, my earliest attempts to grapple with the assumptions grounding different feminist positions were advanced by the presence of black women and men who were less willing to accept with complacency the opinion that women's oppression is a unique phenomenon, separate from the historical experiences of black and working-class people, affecting all women of different classes in the same manner. Also, the literature by black feminist writers suggested a different interpretation: these writers began to link the particular exploitation of black women to the historical dynamics of capitalist social life,[4] and many of the most provocative articles suggested a Marxist analysis. Rather than setting women against blacks or workers as special groups with a special oppression, like commodities which one is asked to choose between, these writers urged that the particularity of any one group's exploitation has to be situated in terms of an integrated theory which transcends all attempts to "naturalize" the inferiority of the oppressed group and thereby legitimate social subordination.

That black feminists were beginning to confront nationalist and separatist ideologies within the black movement was received initially with considerable shock and surprise by black women students who wanted to reject the women's movement as a white bourgeois phenomenon. Yet their own need to grapple with the alienation they experienced as black *women* was what had propelled them, hesitantly to be sure, into a course in feminist politics. All of these contradictions came together when they discovered black feminist writers who were attempting to link the social relations of black women and men within the family and the labor force to the logic of capitalist development. Some of the antagonisms that the black women and men felt toward other students were thus given an added dimension: they were rooted not only in race but also in class differences.

It was in this context that our reading of the nineteenth-century contribution of Frederick Engels, *The Origin of the Family, Private Property and the State,* assumed added importance. There is no other book in the library of feminist studies which is so often the object of attack. On careful inspection, however, one discovers that Engels is either faulted for not doing something which he never intended, or that his argument is misrepresented and then rejected. The political significance of these attacks is, of course, that having dispensed summarily with Engels many feminist writers then return unwittingly to a liberal approach without ever confronting the full scope of Marxism. Engels is often accused of offering a monocausal or economic determinist account of women's oppression. In fact, he suggests a multidimensional but coincidental series of social relationships whose emergence together contributes to the developing oppression of women. He rejects the argument that women's inferiority is rooted in her physical weakness or her sexuality and reproductive role. In other words, he situates these facts within a broader set of historical events. He cautions that human reproduction, like production, expresses an historically precise set of social relationships: "The social organization under which the people of a particular country live is determined by both kinds of production: by the stage of the development of labor on the one hand and of the family on the other."[5] For those who would insist that reproduction is a natural phenomenon, that biological sex differences have universal political and social implications, or that sex is a variable to be discretely added into any account of social experience, Engels provides an important corrective.

The reassessment of Engels' analysis helped to locate the precise demarcation of theoretical differences within the women's literature. My own discovery of a rapidly growing body of new Marxist feminist writings only confirmed my judgment that a decisive split within the literature—as within the women's movement—was between liberal feminist and Marxist feminist perspective. I concluded that what had been interpreted as a variety of radical alternatives to bourgeois or liberal feminism more often than not had devolved back into a liberal perspective.[6] I also began to discover ways in which certain very distinctive positions *within* liberal feminism were deeply indebted to a variety of traditions within modern social theory, such as functionalism, methodological individualism, existentialism, Weberianism, and structuralism—an important confirmation of my suspicion that any attempt to grasp the theoretical directions in the feminist movement without considering their relationship to contemporary thought was bound to go astray. A unity within the movement inspired solely by such slogans as "sisterhood is powerful" could no longer, I believed, ignore the fact that liberalism and Marxism emerge out of radically distinct ways of viewing social life.

The course took a new turn at this juncture, reflected in the reorganization of the syllabus. I sought to bring forward the differing sets of social and philosophical assumptions about women and men within the literature. I identified the major works within each tradition and suggested some of the ways in which they differed according to the criteria they employed for selecting and organizing the "facts" in light of problems differently perceived. In this way I came to emphasize, for example, the differences between analyses which stressed the "woman question" and those which emphasized the social relations of women in different groups and classes in capitalist society; or the differences between those works which focused on the status of the family unit and those which attempted to investigate capitalism from the standpoint of the family. Through this process I hoped to enable students to become conscious of the distinctions embedded in their prior commitments to one or another version of feminism.

The balance of reading between Marxist and non-Marxist material changed dramatically from the first years of the course as I incorporated the recent contributions to Marxist feminism. The new weight given to the latter selections emerged from the ongoing critique of liberal feminism within the course. The new Marxist-feminist literature advanced

considerably many of the incomplete or inadequate formulations of Engels by theoretically investigating the character of
women's labor in the home under capitalism, as well as its
relationship to wage labor; by critiquing the liberal division
of social life into private and public spheres; and by replacing
the abstract "woman" of liberal theory with a series of
concrete individuals whose relations to one another are, to an
important extent, determined by their class position. Further, we found the most rewarding selections to be those
which did not merely reproduce outworn statements but
which sought to apply Marx's method to a previously un-
explored set of social problems.

Once more, however, the specific composition of the class
helped to bring forward certain important questions about
the literature. For example, the continuing appeal to my
most recent students of such non-Marxist formulations as
radical feminism or radical lesbianism revealed the suggestive-
ness of their analyses of women's sexuality and the striking
inattention to these questions by many Marxist feminist
writers. In response, I moved to expand our consideration of
Freud's writings on women's sexuality, prompted as well by
the attention given to Freud in Juliet Mitchell's important
study *Psychoanalysis and Feminism.*[7] I situated Freud's
writings as a major influence on contemporary feminism, of
equal stature to those of J. S. Mill or Marx and Engels.

In addition, the writings of Sheila Rowbotham and Eli
Zaretsky were especially well-received by the class members,
for they suggest that many of the considerations of liberal
and radical feminists might be relevant to a Marxist-feminist
approach. They are concerned with issues of personal life and
sexuality. In my own work and within this class, I sought to
find the basis for recapturing and regrounding the insights of
liberal feminism on women's sexual objectification within an
expanded Marxist-feminist approach.[8]

Over the four years I have given this course, I have witnessed an increasing theoretical sensitivity and sophistication in the written work of students. I have also watched a number of students graduate and take positions with unions whose major constituency is white collar women workers or with groups advocating particular attention to women prisoners. Others have gone on in their studies to address the theoretical and historical issues surrounding the changing organization of family life, the nature of sexuality in capitalism, or the relationship of women houseworkers and wage earners to the current fiscal crisis in capitalism.

Some students have expressed considerable discomfort with the directions taken by feminist theory as presented in this course. As stated above, such discomfort is often expressed as an attack on theory as such. While it has never been my intention to win over my students to a set point of view—indeed, I have wished to show how my own ideas have continued to evolve in the framework of the course—such criticisms have provoked me continually to rethink the importance of the theoretical endeavor for advancing socialist praxis in the women's movement. If in women's studies courses devoted to theory one frequently encounters a typically pragmatic insistence on "relevance" and immediate politics, the issues must be squarely faced rather than avoided. I have tried to indicate here my own attempts to establish the relevance of the theoretical enterprise and to make explicit the underlying theoretical assumptions which ground even the most antitheoretical positions. My provisional conclusion is that an effort must be made to show how the theory-practice relation, as differently conceived, is itself a point of contention within the feminist literature. As Russell Jacoby has suggested, the attacks launched in some of the literature on monogamy, theory, leadership, and relations between men and women as forms of exclusion and privilege help to confirm the subjective predilections of many readers. Jacoby says:

> What is perpetually lost under the sway of immediacy is a dialectical analysis: monogamy as both human and inhuman—as the bad refuge from a worse world and a bad solution for a better world; theory as insight into objectivity as well as elitism. To see only one moment is to trade the worse for the bad; no theory instead of elitist theory, inhuman fragmented relations for damaged human ones. The dialectical path is elsewhere.[9]

Overcoming repression requires a comprehension of the historical forms of that repression as well as of the theoretical attempts to objectively grasp its contours. The first approach contests the characterization embodied within the "woman question," which is, by implication, a timeless puzzle that can never be solved. The second is required to bring to all issues a depth and perspective which is frequently obscured by the requirements of day to day action for liberation. In line with this second requirement, this course has attempted to recover and express the contours of a dialectical theory of women's liberation. At the same time, almost by definition, it has had to face the contradictions that have emerged throughout its history and that will have to be confronted repeatedly in the future. After all, these dilemmas only reflect the reality of the underlying movement which called this course into existence and to which it has hoped to make a contribution.

Notes

1. New England Free Press, 1968.
2. See, for example, Betty Friedan, *The Feminine Mystique* (New York: W. W. Norton, 1963), and Alice Rossi, "Equality Between the Sexes: An Immodest Proposal," in *Roles Women Play*, ed. Michele Hoffnung Garskof (Belmont, Ca.: Brooks/Cole, 1971).
3. New York: Bantam Books, 1970.
4. See *The Black Woman*, ed. Toni Cade (New York: Signet Books, 1970). Despite the promising insights offered in this anthology, there is to date no major theoretical or historical work on black

women, class relations, and family life, a subject which demands serious attention.

5. New York: International Publishers, 1972, pp. 71-72.
6. Consider in this regard Simone de Beauvoir, *The Second Sex* (New York: Modern Library, 1968), and Firestone, *The Dialectic of Sex.*
7. New York: Pantheon, 1974.
8. See my "Women, Labor, and Family Life: A Theoretical Perspective," *Science and Society*, XLI (Winter 1978).
9. Russell Jacoby, *Social Amnesia: A Critique of Conformist Psychology from Adler to Laing* (Boston: Beacon Press, 1975), pp. 115-16.

Action and Reaction:
Teaching Physics in Context
....
David Jhirad and Al Weinrub

Course Description

The audience for this course was composed of about 250 sophomores, the vast majority of whom were nonmajors in the physical and biological sciences. The main objective of the first semester was to convey, in a historical sequence, an understanding of the evolutionary and revolutionary aspects of the two main themes in the development of the physical sciences. These are the conceptual structure of the theories, and the institutional framework within which these theories have developed.

Since these themes are coupled to an extent that is dependent on the theory and the historical epoch involved, we felt that a critical method for examining that interaction was an important priority. Through a consideration of some crucial eras in the history of science and technology, we hoped to provide a tool for evaluating the role played by science and technology in contemporary capitalist societies. This seems to be especially important when dealing with students whose attitudes to affairs scientific and technological are largely shaped by the counterculture ethic, i.e., they regard technology as the demon, rather than focusing on the entire institutional fabric of capitalism which decides the development and use of technology.

The course began with an analysis of the institutional and conceptual foundation of physics today. In fact, since Al's first lecture came the day after the Attica massacre, it was devoted to how science and technology in this society provide methods for repression, control, and murder. It was magnificently received.

The lecture on the institutional aspects of contemporary physics dealt with the nature of the research establishment in the United States, including the various kinds of laboratories and employers, the number of physicists, and the size and scope of government agencies and funding. Some attention was devoted to the social relations *within* science (competition, hierarchies, criteria for advancement, professional societies and publications), as well as to the social function of basic and applied work.

The first unit of the course included an attempt to describe the assumptions, methods, and flavor of modern physical science, with some discussion of the role played by theory, experiment, mathematics, technological tools and apparatus, and research teams. Journal papers were used to illustrate these different ideas.

We then attempted to trace our two parallel and interacting themes from Greek cosmology and astronomy to the Newtonian synthesis. We dealt with the development of astronomical perspectives and cosmological models from their earliest beginnings in Egypt, Babylon, and Greece to the Copernican revolution and Kepler's laws. An attempt was made to situate the Copernican revolution in the context of the social upheaval that accompanied the transition from feudalism to capitalism, as well as the secularization of intellectual investigation and the shifting roles of church and state.

The third topic was concerned with the theme of motion and movement in the pre-Galilean and Galilean era. This was followed by a section we called "Galileo in Context," which treated the social and economic transformation of Europe from the fifteenth to the seventeenth century, the breakdown of feudalism, and the rise of a merchant class. There was an analysis of such questions as the union of intellect and craftsman from Leonardo to Galileo, Galileo and the military-industrial complex, conflict with the church, and a comparison with the role of science and technology in China in the same period.

The section on the Newtonian revolution was an attempt to embrace a number of different dimensions, i.e., Newtonian dynamics, universal gravitation, the Newtonian synthesis, "Newton in Context," and the philosophical aspects of determinism, causality, and the Newtonian world machine. The discussion of "Newton in Context" centered on the relationship between science and society in seventeenth-century England, and included topics such as Francis Bacon, the role of the Royal Society, and the utilitarians.

The concluding section of the first semester was concerned with conservation laws, energy, and the Industrial Revolution. This was an examination of such concepts as work, heat, and temperature, as well as steam engines, power, and the storage and transitions of energy. We concluded with an account of the manner in which energy is transmitted, and this led into a discussion of waves and wave phenomena.

Analysis

While ambitious in design, the course met with only limited success. Billed as a required course in physics for nonscience majors, it had a lot of student antipathy to contend with. Students came in feeling hostility toward anything scientific, convinced of the irrelevance of physics to their major interests, or frightened of their inability to handle the mathematical and abstract character of physics. Some exhibited a combination of these attitudes.

But the real struggle was not the effort to counter feelings of hostility or indifference, but to counter a certain mental or intellectual idea of what science is all about. To put it succinctly: anything technical was considered rightly physics, anything social, philosophical, historical, political, or economic was deemed extraneous. Thus *their* definition of what physics was, and therefore of what was important to our studies, was so narrow as to make it difficult to convey the central theme—that technical details cannot be considered independently of their social context. Students found it difficult to grasp the totality of physical concepts—when and how they emerge, why they flourish for a time, what brings about their downfall. In most students' minds, history, sociology, philosophy, science, etc., were distinct, fragmented disciplines and not merely different aspects of the changing social and productive relations of society.

This fragmented intellectual approach was very difficult to overcome, even with the great variety of material in the readings and their emphasis on an integrated view of science. The dichotomy in the students' minds between "science" and "everything else" apparently has been reinforced by many years in an educational environment built upon disciplines and specialization rather than on broad integrated understanding.

The other major difficulty with a course of this type is more difficult to deal with. The character of the course was such that its principal orientation was intellectual rather than practical—it dealt with an understanding of the development of physical ideas rather than with the direct application of these to present-day technology. This raised the question of relevance, and whether such an introductory course in conceptual physics should be given in the first place.

For many of us, our knowledge of Newton's laws, for example, is not used much in our day-to-day lives. Why, then, is such a course important as part of liberal education and why is it worthwhile for radicals? Its value to liberal education is that it points out the scientific foundation of Western civilization, glorifies the achievements of individual scientists, and attempts to outline the rational scientific methodology that has laid the foundations for technological progress. Thus Newton's laws are of fundamental interest in the liberal academic tradition.

For the radical, the value in teaching Newton's laws does not lie in worshipping Newton's intellectual genius, but rather in understanding the general ideological climate accompanying the birth of capitalism, in seeing that science in the seventeenth century was a starting point for the new productive relations because it provided a philosophical break with the past, and in viewing seventeenth-century science as an outgrowth of the technology needed for the expansion of the industrial and mercantile sectors of the economy. Thus teaching Newton's laws can help provide an understanding of the function of science in capitalist society. We should not look at science as an end in itself, but should view it in the context of history and the present time.

Such a course finds its relevance, then, in contributing to a different way of viewing science, by emphasizing its social functions, its productive functions, and its ideological functions.

On Teaching Marxism
....
Bertell Ollman

At many American universities, Marxism G2010 or Communist Theory V1106 or Socialist Thought A2242 are no longer "know your enemy" kind of exercises, and the number of serious courses on these subjects is constantly increasing. Unfortunately, the opportunity they offer for promoting a true understanding of Marxism is frequently lost, either wholly or partially, under the weight of problems inherent in the university context. Having taught both undergraduate and graduate courses on Marxism for almost a decade—mainly at New York University, but also at Columbia University, Union College, and the old Free University of New York—I would like to share with other Marxist teachers my experiences in dealing with these problems.

There are three main problems facing any university teacher of Marxism: the bourgeois ideology of most students, the social and ideological restraints that are part of the university setting, and the absence of a vital socialist movement. To be sure, the same difficulties confront any radical teacher no matter what the subject matter, but the forms in which they are expressed and their disorienting effect vary considerably, and so too must the strategies for dealing with them.

The absence of a vital socialist movement makes most students approach Marxism too much in the spirit of another academic exercise, just as it confirms them in the belief—

before study begins—that Marx's analysis cannot be correct. The classroom situation, whatever one does to humanize social relations, remains locked inside a university structure that is itself forced to play a certain preparatory role within society at large. Students take Marxism for four credits; for some it counts toward their "major"; for all it is a step toward their degree. Given a society with restricted privileges, some kind of grading is necessary at each stage of the education process, as in life generally. All of this affects how students prepare for a course, any course, so that all but the most committed treat the acquisition of knowledge (and often understand it) as the means to a good grade.

There are also ideological elements in the classroom situation which continually gnaw away at the foundations of a Marxist analysis. The very presence of a Marxist teacher who is allowed to teach Marxism is conclusive evidence to some that bourgeois freedom works—just as students from modest backgrounds often take their own presence in class and in the university as proof that extensive social mobility and equality of opportunity really exist under capitalism. Even the fact that the course is offered by a particular department reinforces the alienated notion of the division of knowledge into disciplines and predisposes students to view Marx as essentially an economic or a political or a philosophical thinker.

But undoubtedly the major hurdle in presenting Marxism to American students is the bourgeois ideology, the systematic biases and blind spots, which even the most radical bring with them. This ideology reflects their own class background, whatever that may be, but also their position in capitalism as young people and students. There is nothing in bourgeois ideas and ways of thinking that doesn't interfere with the reception of Marx's message, but the scrambling effect of some ideas is clearly greater than that of others. In my experience, the most troublesome notions have been students' egotistical and ahistorical conception of human nature; their conception of society as the sum of separate individuals, and with this the tendency to reduce social problems to problems of individual psychology (the whole "blaming the victim" syndrome); their identification of Marxism with Soviet and Chinese practice; and of course the ultimate rationale that radical change is impossible in any case. Much less destructive and also easier to dislodge are the intrinsically feeble notions that we are all middle class, that there is a harmony of interests under capitalism, that the government belongs to and represents everybody equally, and that history is the product of the interaction of great people and ideas. Underpinning and providing a framework for all these views—whether in the form of conclusions or assumptions, and whether held consciously or unconsciously—is an undialectical, factoral mode of thinking that separates events from their conditions, people from their real alternatives and human potential, social problems from one another, and the present from the past and the future. The organizing and predisposing power of this mode of thought is such that any attempt to teach Marxism, or indeed to present a Marxist analysis of any event, is doomed to distortion and failure unless accompanied by an equally strenuous effort to impart the dialectical mode of reasoning.

I originally thought that students who *chose* to take my course on Marxism—the department doesn't exist where this is a required course—would be relatively free of the worst effects of bourgeois ideology, and it just may be that a survey of the whole university would show a tilt in critical consciousness in their favor. I certainly attract most of the self-consciously radical students, but it has become clear that the great majority of my students—whatever the sense of adventure or morbid curiosity that bring them to class—suffer from most of the distortions mentioned above. And even the radical students, as I have indicated, have not escaped the ideological effects of their bourgeois conditioning and education.

The problems one faces in teaching Marxism that come from the absence of a socialist movement, the university context, and the students' own bourgeois ideology permit neither easy nor complete solutions. Still, how one approaches and organizes the subject matter, where one begins and concludes, the kind of examples used, and especially what one emphasizes have considerable influence on the *degree* of success (or failure). My own courses on Marxism on both the undergraduate and graduate levels lay heaviest stress on the dialectic, the theory of class struggle, and Marx's critique of bourgeois ideology. These three theories are explained, illustrated, questioned, and elaborated in a variety of contexts throughout the term.

The dialectic is the only adequate means of thinking (and therefore, too, of examining and presenting) the changes and interactions that make up so large a part of the real world. Incorporating the dialectic, Marxism is essentially the attempt to exhibit the complexities of capitalist processes, their origins, and the possibilities for their transcendence (all of which is conceived of in terms of relations, where the conditions of existence of any process—like its potential for development—are taken to be a part of what it is). Unlike bourgeois social scientists, who try to relate and put into motion what they conceive of as logically independent and essentially static factors, Marx *assumes* movement and interconnectedness and sets out to examine why some social forms appear to be fixed and independent. The problem of bourgeois social science is similar to that of Humpty Dumpty after the fall, when all the king's horses and all the king's men could not put Humpty Dumpty together again. Once reality is broken up epistemologically into externally related objects, all ties between them—just as their own changes of form and function—become artificial and of secondary importance in determining their essential character. In fixing them in time and space, the ever changing boundaries between things in the real world are systematically wrenched out of shape. My emphasis on the dialectic, therefore, can be seen as a recognition of the fact that one must understand the sense of "interconnection," "reciprocal effect," "movement," and "transformation" in order to grasp correctly whatever it is to which Marx applies these expressions. Aside from its obvious importance in Marxism, the need I feel to give special emphasis to Marx's theory of class struggle derives from the absolute inability of most students to think in these terms. Like most Americans, they slide in their thinking from the individual to "everybody" without passing through the mediation of particular groups. Thus, for example, when responsibility for an act goes beyond its actual perpetrator, everyone is said to be guilty. This is the logic (if not the politics) behind Billy Graham's request that we all pray to be forgiven for the sins of Mylai and Watergate, a request that most people can deny only by upholding the equally absurd position that Calley and Nixon are solely responsible. The middle terms are missing. Marxism is an analysis of capitalism that is organized around such middle terms (groups), the most important of which is class. Without a notion of class, which enables us to consider human interaction on the basis of interests that come out of people's differing relations to the prevailing mode of production, none of Marx's theories can be understood.

The theory of class struggle also contains the apparently contradictory ideas that individuals have been made what they are (that along with their class they are the product of social conditioning), but they don't have to stay made (that along with their class they can transform existing social relations). Paradoxically, it is when one understands the degree to which an individual is a social product, and how and why this has occurred, that he or she can transcend the conditions and become the potential creator of a new and better future. To set this dialectic of necessity and freedom into motion is another reason I emphasize the theory of class struggle.

Capitalism differs from all other oppressive systems in the

amount and insidious character of its mystification, in the thoroughness with which this mystification is integrated into all its life processes, and in the degree to which it requires mystification in order to survive (all other oppressive systems relying far more on direct force). The importance of bourgeois ideology is reflected in the space given it in Marx's writings, which are throughout critiques of capitalist practices and of the ways these practices are ordinarily understood. Our own accounts of Marxism, therefore, must at every point combine a description of how capitalism works with a description of how these workings are dissembled in both common sense and "learned discourse." In universities, where bourgeois ideology is dispensed in every classroom, the need for such a two-level critique is greater than it would be in other settings—in factories or neighborhood centers, for example. Furthermore, the longer exposure of graduate students to the more refined forms of bourgeois ideology calls for a correspondingly greater stress on the criticisms of such ideas in graduate courses.

In preparing my own critique, I start from an awareness that bourgeois ideology is both an expression of the real situation and a product of conscious efforts to manipulate people's understanding, for the same conditions that are reflected in bourgeois ideology give rise—however confusingly and haltingly—to a correct understanding of capitalist processes. The fact is that while bourgeois ideology is systematic, it is also unfinished, inconsistent, contradictory, and constantly fighting for its life against a science of society whose most complete expression is Marxism. In class, my main contribution to this ongoing struggle is to insist at every turn that bourgeois ideology is made up of partial truths— ideas that are not so much false as severely limited by conditions of which the speaker or writer is unaware—and that these partial truths serve the interests of the capitalist class. In this manner, bourgeois ideology is transcended rather than denied outright. Focusing on immediate appearances, most bourgeois accounts of capitalism succeed in reversing the actual dynamics of what is taking place. Marx summarizes the net effect of such practices when, referring to Luther's description of the Roman mythological figure Cacus, who steals oxen by dragging them backward into his den to make it appear they have gone out, he comments, "An excellent picture, it fits the capitalist in general, who pretends that what he has taken from others and brought into his den emanates from him, and by causing it to go backwards he gives it a semblance of having come from his den."[1] My critique of bourgeois ideology, like Marx's, has the double goal of unmasking it as a defense of capitalist interests and reappropriating the evidence of immediate appearances into an account that captures the true dynamics of capitalist society.

The actual division of Marxism into lecture topics, and the ordering of these topics, is determined by the requirements of effective exposition, given the peculiar problems mentioned above. I begin with a discussion of the current crisis in our society, illustrated with stories and statistics from the capitalist press, in an effort to reach general agreement on what needs to be explained. Then, I devote at least one session to each of the following: an overview of Marx's analysis to clarify its systemic character and to provide a rough map of the areas into which the course will take us; the dialectic; Marx's treatment of the fact/value distinction; the theory of alienation; the labor theory of value; the materialist conception of history; the theory of the state; the critique of bourgeois ideology; Marx's vision of communism; his theories of class consciousness and revolution; and finally—if time allows—his method, with special emphasis on its utility for our own research. I cannot hope to repeat my lectures in this space, or even to mention all the subjects that come up, but it may be useful to go through these topics one at a time to provide concrete illustrations of my pedagogical strategy. Readers of the following should keep in mind that my intention is not the ordinary one of using a scaffolding to construct a building but of using the building to display its scaffolding.

Lecture 1. I begin the first class by asking students to take out a piece of paper and write for fifteen minutes on why they are or are not Marxists. Rather than collecting these papers, I ask students to keep them until the end of term when I want them to answer the same question (either as part of a take-home final or as an addendum to their term papers), in light of their work in the course and what they have said at the start. My aim is to involve students personally in the subject, to jolt them into a recognition that Marxism belongs to their lives as well as to the curriculum, and consequently that they are as much a part of the subject as they are people studying it. I also want to make them conscious as soon as possible of their main objections to Marxism, so they can reflect on them and test them in their readings and in our discussions. Finally, I want to provide them and myself with a benchmark by which to judge some of the effects of the course.

The substantive part of this first session is devoted to parading, with the aid of appropriate newspaper stories, the worst problems of our society—poverty, unemployment, malnutrition, social and economic inequality, racism, sexism, etc. The message is that there is a lot that is wrong, but that we have to understand it better before we can hope to change it. Paradoxes are used to highlight the apparent absurdity of poverty in the midst of so much wealth and to indicate the presence of underlying contradictions. If contradictions are incompatible trends rooted in the structure and organization of society, paradoxes are the flotsam and jetsam that float on the surface of these trends, and as such they offer good clues to the existence of contradictions. My favorite paradox is found in the exchange between Secretary of Agriculture Butz and a reporter who asked him if he thought it would help resolve the world's food shortage if we all ate one hamburger a week less. Butz responded that he intended to eat one hamburger a week more to help deal with the more serious problem of low cattle prices.

Students, particularly beginning students, need to hear in clear, simple language exactly how Marxism differs from what they already know and believe. Toward this end I distinguish between liberals, radicals, and Marxists in the following manner: liberals—which I say includes most students present—view capitalism's problems one at a time. Each problem has an independent existence and can be understood and even solved in a way that does not bring in other problems, or does so only incidentally. Thus the slogans, "one thing at a time," "first things first," etc. Radicals, on the other hand, recognize a pattern in these problems. For them, these problems are linked together as part of the necessary life processes of the capitalist system. They are correct in holding capitalism responsible, but if they are only radicals, and not yet Marxists, they don't really understand how this system gives rise to these problems: the mediations between the parts and the whole are missing. Marxists analyze the workings of capitalism to make sense of the patterns that radicals only see and liberals still have to learn about (Marxism is obviously much more than this, but for present purposes this will do). At the end of the session I try to make explicit—with the help of students—some of the patterns that emerge from the problems listed earlier. These patterns generally have to do with the power of money in capitalist society, the fact that people are willing to do almost anything for money, the great gap between the rich and the poor, the tie between being rich and powerful and being poor and powerless, and the class-biased character of our laws and their administration.

An attempt is made here, as in all later sessions, to involve students in discussion, and questions and comments are taken at any time, but I am very careful not to let the discussion overflow in all directions. The organic ties between all the elements of Marxism and the different levels of difficulty involved require a more ordered presentation. There are many ways to present Marxism, but following wherever the free association of students leads is not one of them. When necessary—and it happens quite often—I explain why I can't go into a particular topic at the moment it is raised and tell students in what session it will be dealt with.

It is also during this first class that I make it clear that I am a Marxist and that this will affect my choice of materials, the emphasis I give them, and, of course, my interpretation, but that it will not affect my honest examination of the facts or my willingness to hear other opinions. Every social science professor has a point of view. The fact that I announce mine and other teachers do not is, possibly, a more important difference between us than the fact that I am a Marxist and they are not. I have been open and have warned students what to expect, while they have hidden behind a specious neutrality (misnamed objectivity) from which they sally forth to surprise students at every opportunity. After this admission, I am often asked why the university allows a Marxist to teach. If a radical student asks the question, he or she is usually saying "What kind of a Marxist can you be?" I defend myself from this implied criticism by explaining how unusual, personally and politically difficult, and historically overdue this event is. The nonradical student uses this same question to proclaim his or her belief that academic freedom and complete freedom of speech really exist in America. I answer that the opportunity for such courses emerges from the contradictions in the university's functions (preparatory, humanist, and scholarly), and its need for legitimation in a world where Marxism is taken ever more seriously.

Lecture 2. The second session is devoted to trying to give students some sense of the systemic character of Marx's analysis, i.e., what it means to have capitalism as the object of study, as a reflection of the complex interdependence and developments found there. It may be that in Marx's day, or even in Europe today, one would not have to insist on this point; but most Americans don't know what it is to have a total view of any epoch, in part because they don't have a total or systematic view of anything, and in part because they don't know what constitutes an epoch. Grasping the relevant time framework is especially difficult for people who oscillate in their thinking between this minute and forever as easily and automatically as they move between the individual and everybody. Before offering the specifics of Marx's analysis, I think it is important to make students aware that its holistic quality derives in large part from the choice of a spatial and temporal object that is different from any they have ever contemplated.

To claim that Marxism is systemic, that it is a complex, organic whole whose parts cannot be grasped separately, is not to say that it is a closed and finished system with definite answers to the problems of the past, present, or future. It was such a misinterpretation of his views by some French followers that led a frustrated Marx to proclaim, "All I know is that I am not a Marxist."[2] Marxism is unfinished and, like reality itself, is open to all the revisions and corrections made necessary by new empirical research. But if Marxism is not a closed system, it remains a system of such interlocking parts that a full study of any single part implies a study of them all.

In providing an overview of Marxism I make use of the techniques described in *The Ragged Trousered Philanthropists* by Robert Tressell.[3] I ask five or six students to take the part of workers, I play the capitalist, and we reenact the primal exploitation scene that goes on daily in every capitalist factory (my only revision is that where Tressell uses bread, I use scraps of paper). In depicting the relations between workers and capitalists, I find it useful—here as later—to compare them both objectively and in the consciousness of the participants with the relations of oppression in other systems, particularly in feudal and slave societies. The charade goes on to show how surplus value gets distributed and does so in a way which makes very clear the ties of function and interest that link the different sectors of capitalist life. I avoid using Marxian concepts until the broad outlines of the situations to which they apply have been established. When the terms "exploitation," "class struggle," "value," and "surplus value" are finally used, I take special care to point out that they refer to complex sets of relations and not to things. Students are prepared in this way for what will be a major topic in the next class—the dialectic.

I consider this game from *The Ragged Trousered Philanthropists,* which I've used in dozens of classes, the most successful teaching device I have ever used. It really gives students a sense of the broad scope and systemic character of Marx's analysis, its central concern, and the way important theories are connected—all in a painless and even amusing manner. It is crude, oversimplified, and leaves out some essential elements of social life—all this I readily admit—but it does help to bring Marxist theory and the objects it studies into focus.

In this session I also discuss why so much of the debate over Marx's ideas goes on at cross purposes. Marxists believe that most bourgeois social scientists assume precisely that which needs to be explained, chiefly the unequal distribution of wealth and power and the character of social relations which result from this, and then set out with great fanfare to explain what may justifiably be assumed, the lowest common denominator features that characterize any social grouping. Social scientists, on the other hand, often criticize Marx and Marxists for drawing conclusions about the relationship between economic and noneconomic factors in history on the basis of too little evidence, and for not taking account of the exceptions. Marx's hypotheses, they claim, have yet to be proven. But Marx was not concerned with collecting evidence to prove a set of hypotheses that apply to all societies. He is faulted for what he did not do, did not think could be done, or could be done with only trivial results. His project was to reconstruct the workings of an historically specific social system—capitalism—whose workings are taken for granted and treated as natural and unchanging by most social scientists engaged in the building and testing of ahistorical hypotheses.

Finally, it is in this session that I deal with such preliminary matters as problems in translating Marx, the recent availability of certain key works, and the role of Engels in Marxism. With minor qualifications, I regard Engels as coequal spokesperson with Marx on the doctrines of Marxism and treat him as such for the remainder of the course.

Lecture 3. The dialectic (though it has been operating all along) is introduced under its proper name only when students begin to feel the need for it. How does one come to understand a social system composed of a multitude of constantly changing and interacting parts that has a real history and a limited number of possible futures? How does one study it to capture both its essential character, the way of working which makes it different from other social systems, and that dynamic which has brought it to its present state and will carry it to whatever future awaits it? How does one think of the results of such a study and through what steps and forms does one proceed in presenting these results to others? The dialectic is the only adequate means for thinking and dealing with such a subject matter.

My account of the dialectic stresses its roots in the philosophy of internal relations which holds that the irreducible unit of reality is the relation and not the thing. The relations that people ordinarily assume to exist *between* things are viewed here as existing *within* (as a necessary part of) each thing in turn, now conceived of as a relation (likewise, the changes which any "thing" undergoes). This peculiar notion of relation is the key to understanding the entire dialectic, and is used to unlock the otherwise mysterious notions of totality, abstraction, identity, law, and contradiction. In the interests of clarity, these notions are examined in Hegel as well as Marx and contrasted with their equivalents in Aristotelian logic and its watered-down version—common sense.

The philosophy of internal relations also accounts for Marx's understanding of language as a social relation, his use of what appear to be elastic meanings, and the total lack of definitions in his works. On the basis of this conception, words are taken to mean what they describe, with the result that Marx's major concepts mean—at their limit—the analysis made with them. Marx seldom uses a concept in this full sense, but neither does he stick to the core notion meanings that are carried by tradition and clearly understood by non-Marxists. What he does ranges between the two, with actual usage depending on the context. This practice makes it very difficult to know what Marx is saying on any occasion without an understanding of the dialectic (which supplies the framework and the possibilities), his analysis (which supplies the actual content), and the context (which determines how much of this content is relevant). Students are warned that they can have only a superficial understanding of Marx's theories until they learn the fuller meanings of his concepts, which in turn hinges on their progress in understanding his theories. In the sessions to follow, I explain, I will be concerned with developing both Marx's analysis of capitalism and, beginning with core notion meanings, the fuller definitions of the major concepts with which he makes this analysis.

In the philosophy of internal relations, truth is linked to the notion of system: statements are more or less true depending on how much they reflect in extent and detail the actual complexity of the real world. The criteria for judging whether Marxism is true, therefore, go beyond its correspondence to capitalist reality to its completeness and coherence as a total interpretation. Hence the irrelevance and/or insignificance of those rebuttals of Marx which focus on the odd exception. Marxists, as is well known, generally stress practice as the test of the truth of Marxism, and there is a sense (which I cannot develop here) in which this is so. Unfortunately, for non-Marxists—which means for most of my students—the "test of practice" can only be understood as the fact that revolutions occurred in Russia and China, the policies currently followed by these regimes, or the feeble efforts by workers and working-class parties to make a revolution in the West. As practices go, none of these do very much to convince people that Marx's analysis of capitalism is correct. On the other hand, people do begin to gravitate to Marxism insofar as it provides a more complete and coherent understanding of their lives and their society than they had before. I urge students to use these criteria in judging Marx's theories.

If I begin to discuss the dialectic by opposing it to common sense in order to establish its distinctive character, in my conclusion I try to point out that common sense also contains elements of the dialectic. Children, and less educated people in general, often operate with a rough, unconscious dialectic, while those who have benefited from an education that is constantly breaking down processes and wholes without putting them together again do so much less or not at all. It is important that students see that formal education in America is in large part training in how to think undialectically.[4]

What of Marx's materialism? In most treatments of Marx's philosophy, his dialectic and his materialism are coupled. I believe this practice has led to a serious confusion over the various senses in which Marx can be said to be a materialist, because—unlike the dialectic—his materialism cannot be abstracted very easily from its real content. Marx's materialism *is* the particular relations he sees between people, nature, and society, including ideas. (I treat Marx's conception of human nature in the fifth lecture, and his materialist conception of history again in the seventh lecture.) When this content is abstracted, all that remains of Marx's materialism is his opposition to various idealist positions which view the world as the effect and/or expression of disembodied ideas, and the methodological imperative (one, however, which admits exceptions) that we should begin our analysis of problems with their material aspects. What is to be avoided at all costs is the presentation of Marx's materialism as the belief that only matter is real, or that matter comes before ideas (since the concept "matter" is already an idea), or that ideas never affect matter, or that one should *never* begin an analysis from the vantage point of ideas. In every instance, such claims are undialectical, and the last two prejudge—incorrectly, as it turns out—the results of empirical research. Since the prevailing ethos is no longer idealist in the sense mentioned above, and given the dangers of misinterpretation at this early stage, my own presentation of Marx integrates his materialist philosophy with its real content, except in the treatment of method at the very end of the course, where materialism re-emerges as a methodological principle regarding priorities.

Lecture 4. A major constituent of bourgeois ideology is the belief that the facts we know are logically independent of the values we hold. It is what permits people who disagree on facts, if these are viewed broadly, to treat their disagreement as one of values, while holding that the latter are beyond rational examination, i.e., one that takes account of the conditions and interests in which values emerge and flourish. To maintain that Marx himself subscribed to this logical distinction makes it possible to agree with him on his description of capitalism while disagreeing with his socialist solution simply because one believes in other values. It also makes whatever is labeled Marx's values appear as arbitrary and as ultimately unconvincing as the values of anyone else.

Marx does not accept a logical separation between facts and values, and, on the basis of his philosophy of internal relations, could not. On this conception, judgments cannot be severed from the people who make them and the conditions (including real alternatives) in which they are pronounced. In this session I work out the meaning of the dialectic for the entire sphere of ethics, other people's ethics and what are said to be Marx's. It should be clear that what is at stake here is the status of Marx's whole critique and with it the grounds on which one can reasonably accept or reject it. Marx does not condemn capitalism on moral grounds but analyzes it (and the views of those who praise or condemn it) in a way that confronts present conditions with their real alternatives. Rather than an external ideal, communism—or what is usually taken to be the basis of Marx's value judgments—is the extension of patterns and trends found in the present that Marx has projected into the future, given the new priorities that would be established by a socialist government. The content of this projection is treated in the session on Marx's vision of communism, but its logical status as part of the world of fact is clarified at this time. The great majority of students operate with the fact/value distinction, however, and it is a very difficult task to get them to see how Marx could have done otherwise.

Finally, to help bring out the ideological dimensions of the fact/value distinction, I make a special effort to recount its history from the time of Hume, along with its uses and ramifications in modern social science.

Lecture 5. From Marx's philosophy I proceed to his theory of alienation rather than to any of his other theories. I do this in order to force an early confrontation of Marx's conception of human nature with the individualistic conception held by most students, and also because of the connections this enables me to make between Marx's analysis and the students' own life situation. As Marx's conception of human beings in capitalist society, the theory of alienation is a cross between Marx's conception of human nature in general and the special conditions of capitalism. In expounding such concepts as "powers," "needs," "appropriation," "activity," "natural," "social," "species," and "freedom," with which Marx integrates both society and nature into humanity, as part of his conception of human nature, I am careful to stress the reliance of this conception on his dialectic. Later I show how the theory of alienation, which focuses on the separation and dissembling of these elements, cannot be conceived of outside of the foregoing conception of human nature and its underlying dialectic. The language of separation only makes sense in a context where a unified whole of some sort is already assumed to exist.

In displaying the four basic relations of alienation—between the individual and his or her activity, product, other people, and the species—I make the point that most students will soon be workers and that whatever their status and material rewards, the relations Marx describes will apply to them. Studying, I remind them, is but a temporary respite in the life of a worker. We then examine what forms these four basic relations of alienation take in politics, religion, and finally—with special emphasis—in education. Applying this framework to general feelings of student malaise invariably strikes a responsive chord. It is here, too, that the limitations on learning anything, especially a radical critique of society, within the alienated context of a capitalist university receives the attention due it.

In discussing Marx's conception of human nature and his theory of alienation, it becomes clear that he is concerned with the typical, rather than with the unique, individual, or with the unique individual insofar as he is typical. The social types of greatest interest to him are classes that are products of alienated social relations, as well as co-instigators of the dynamic that gives rise to these relations. Classes in struggle over their interests are the human subjects of Marx's analysis. Given his conception of human nature, no other subdivision of mankind carries the same influence. Given his broader subject matter—the real history of the capitalist mode of production—no other subdivision of the human species is as relevant. It is important that American students, for whom this mode of thinking is so foreign, see the necessity as well as the advantages and limitations in Marx's choice of class as his human subject. As for limitations, I point out that interests do not translate easily into motives, a quality possessed by unique individuals, and that the attempt to do so has led to some of the more serious, vulgar distortions of Marx's analysis.

Lecture 6. There is still another advantage in treating Marx's theory of alienation before the labor theory of value. This is that it enables me to bring out better the social relations inherent in the latter theory, because the labor Marx has in mind in discussing value is alienated labor, with all that entails in the way of relations between the producer and his or her activity, product, fellow human beings, and the species. Likewise, value can now be seen as that which happens to and can be done with the products of alienated labor just because of its alienation, or, alternatively, as the form this alienation takes when viewed from the vantage point of its products. Both use- and exchange-value exhibit these effects. After clarifying the social content of labor and value, most of this session is devoted to the metamorphosis of value, the fetishism of commodities, and the theory of crisis, understood not only as a crisis in accumulation and consumption but also as a social crisis. Facts from our present crisis are used as illustration. At a time when the standard of living of the working class throughout the capitalist world is going down, Marxists bear a heavy responsibility to present clearly—and frequently—the only explanation of this social disaster that makes any sense.

Lenin said that it is necessary to read Hegel's *Logic* before one can truly understand *Capital,* and I am very much in sympathy with this view. But this is not a recipe for how to teach the labor theory of value to beginners. Hegel is even more difficult to understand than Marx, and it seems perverse to prepare students for Marxism with something that is even more difficult, even easier to distort. In this course, Hegel is dealt with directly only in the session on the dialectic, but his presence is felt throughout. The central position accorded the philosophy of internal relations in the dialectic, and the use of internal relations as the framework in which to set Marx's other theories, gives my interpretation of Marx a very Hegelian cast. This is never clearer than in my presentation of the labor theory of value.

At the very start, I try to get students to see that Marx's labor theory of value is not an economic theory, narrowly understood, but a theory about the workings of capitalism viewed from the vantage point of the production and exchange of commodities. The question to which Marx addresses himself in the first volume of *Capital* is, "Why is labor represented by the value of its product and labor-time by the magnitude of that value?"[5] This is not a question about how much things cost or even why they cost what they do. Following Smith and Ricardo, Marx can assume that labor is responsible for the bulk of these costs. What he sets out to study are the historical conditions in which prices come about in the first place, in which all the things that people produce are available for exchange—indeed, are produced with such exchange in mind. In unravelling the social conditions which make this process both possible and necessary, Marx also shows how, in the very act of reproducing these conditions, contradictions emerge that point to the demise of the system. The main tendencies that lie at the core of these contradictions—the concentration of capital in fewer economic units, the expansion of capital throughout the globe, the falling rate of profit, the disappearance of the middle class, and the pauperization of the working class—are sometimes called Marx's predictive economic theories. It is the failure of these predictions unambiguously and permanently to come true that is all that many know (or care to know) about Marxism. It is important to make clear to students that these predictions are really projections of tendencies Marx found in his research, but that since they are often countered by other tendencies (the tendency of the rate of profit to fall, for example, by the tendency of capital to expand), what actually transpires and when requires continual study.

The widespread acceptance of the economistic interpretation of Marx's labor theory of value shows how essential it is to recover Marx's actual questions, which make all his theories, his answers to these questions, accounts of the workings of an entire social system. These theories differ in the sector and problems from which they take off, and each is organized around a distinctive set of concepts, but the systemic pretension of each theory is the same. The labor theory of value, the theory of alienation, the materialist conception of history, the theory of class struggle, the theory of the state, and the theory of ideology do not, in the final analysis, deal with different subjects, but with the same subject differently. Rather than a series of externally related sectoral analyses, Marx offers overlapping analyses—some more, some less worked out—of the same capitalist reality. In presenting each of these theories I try to bring out the special contribution to our understanding that comes from approaching capitalism from this vantage point (chiefly the privileged access it gives us to certain kinds of information and the insights that come from ordering reality in this manner), and the ways it sustains and qualifies the analyses undertaken from other vantage points.

By this point in the course most students are able to grasp

the uniqueness of Marx's project and something of the manner in which he sets out to achieve it, but as yet only a few really understand or accept his analysis. Taking the theory of exploitation found in the labor theory of value, it is useful to address this hiatus directly and, in the process, to examine our own class positions in the light of Lukács' observation that of all classes the proletariat is best placed to grasp the Marxian totality.

Lecture 7. Unlike most Marxists, I take the materialist conception of history to be mainly a theory about capitalism, where the history referred to is the origins of capitalism, and not a theory about history in general, where capitalism is but the major illustration. Consequently, most of this session is devoted to an account of the real history of the capitalist mode of production and especially to the transition from feudalism to capitalism in western Europe. The story revolves around contradictions that arose in the reproduction of then existing conditions of production which, at a certain point, burst asunder the social and political forms in which production was taking place, and how the reproduction of the conditions of capitalist existence, now under new forms, have given rise to its own peculiar contradictions. Coming after discussions of alienation, class struggle, and value, an effort is made to discuss the unfolding of these contradictions on these different levels. From the facts of this evolution it is possible to draw (and Marx does draw) certain conclusions regarding the role and influence of forces and relations of production, economic processes generally, and class struggle that have a wider applicability. In every case, however, these conclusions admit the kind of exceptions that Marx himself often introduces when examining specific social formations.

Most students come into the course holding a caricature of the materialist conception of history in which "economics" is supposed to be the cause of everything people do and think and of all that happens in history. To counter this crude economic determinism, it is important to distinguish the determinism expressed in special conditioning and limited alternatives from the metaphysical determinism that denies choice altogether, and to illustrate this difference in Marx's treatment of real historical personalities. The influence Marx often attributes—because this is what his studies reveal—to political, scientific, cultural, religious, geographical, and still other factors must also be brought out.

In combating economic determinism, however, there is a serious danger—and one that I myself have often succumbed to—of overreaction, in which case students are left with a picture of Marx as an eclectic thinker not that different from other eclectic thinkers they know. We are operating in an academic environment where, along with everything else, "economics" is important (hence, the absurd claim that "we are all Marxists now"). For most, however, such eclecticism is merely an excuse for not studying any area in depth, so it is not surprising that the organic connections between areas are likewise neglected. Marx made these connections his subject matter, but his explanation accords a special role to the mode and relations of production, and it is this special role that our account must try to capture. If most students caricature Marxism as economic determinism, they also have little understanding of economic processes or their importance, and I have come to believe that in explaining the materialist conception of history the latter is our immediate problem. Consequently, I now begin my presentation with a heavy stress on economic processes and gradually qualify it in the manner and direction suggested above. The opposite distortions of economic determinism and eclecticism are avoided by leaning first in one direction and then in the other. This holds both for the account of the real history of capitalism and the conclusions Marx draws from this account for the rest of history (history organized in other ways).

Lecture 8. The state has already come into earlier discussions of alienation, class struggle, the labor theory of value, and especially the materialist conception of history, although the picture we got of the state's function and history differed somewhat with each theory. Approaching the state directly permits a fuller grasp of its character and a more adequate estimate of its influence, just as it casts a new, political light on alienation, classes, value, and the mode and relations of production. But just as the state, conceived of as a relation, serves as another dimension for the examination of capitalist society, the various aspects of the state, also conceived of as relations, serve as complementary dimensions for its examination. The institutions of government, the dominant role of the ruling economic class, the objective structures which maintain the cohesion and equilibrium of the social system, political parties, political socialization, the state's function in the reproduction of value, the illusory community (the alienated social power) and the hegemonic political ideology are all aspects of the state, and interpretations which focus only on one or a couple of these aspects—as so many Marxist accounts do—are necessarily lopsided and distorting. For example, in the recent *New Left Review* debate between Ralph Miliband and Nicos Poulantzas, the real issue is not, or rather should not be, whether the state is the executive committee of the ruling class or a set of structures which maintain the cohesion and equilibrium of the social system, but how it can be both and what it means for it to be both. Without a firm grasp of the dialectic, and in particular its foundations in the philosophy of internal relations, Marxist scholars are no more immune to one-sided, ideological interpretations of Marxism than their bourgeois counterparts. Marx himself dealt relatively little with the state. He planned to do a systematic study of it but like so many of his other projects this was sacrificed to the demands of his political economy. For this reason—and also because of the important ways the capitalist state has changed in our century (particularly, in its economic role and with regard to socializing people to the status quo)—there is a great need for serious Marxist studies in this area.

In my interpretation of the Marxist theory of the state, each aspect of the state relation is itself treated as a relation within which to unfold the workings of the state as a dimension of capitalism. I have found this to be one of the most successful illustrations of Marx's dialectical approach which discovers change and interaction within the very units—relations—that undergo it, and seeks to understand and explain these processes through frequent changes of perspective. It is in discussing the state, too, that the class biases in capitalist institutions and practices become clear to everyone, and that the many radical but hitherto disconnected facts and intuitions that most students have begin to connect up and make Marxist sense. All along I have told students that there is a big difference between patches of critical knowledge or occasional insights, which anyone can have and which lead to nothing in particular, and a critical analysis which integrates such facts and insights into a systemic whole. Lincoln, after all, recognized that labor produces all value; Woodrow Wilson saw that our nation's laws serve the interests of the capitalist class; and even Eisenhower could warn us of the growing influence of a military-industrial complex. But by themselves, outside of a comprehensive analysis, such insights remained barren of further understanding and politically led nowhere at all.

Lecture 9. In this session I sum up the Marxist critique of bourgeois ideology, a critique which has already appeared as aspects of other theories throughout the course. The main emphasis is now on how bourgeois ideology in its various forms functions to serve capitalist interests. Starting with pro-capitalist solutions to common problems, we examine in turn how capitalism is treated as the natural form of society, the mystification involved in mistaking appearances for essences, the substitution of concepts that don't allow an adequate comprehension of their subject matter for those that do (or could), the division of knowledge into separate and competing disciplines, the use of the abstract individual or the sum of such abstract individuals as the human subject of study, and finally the definition of fact/value, cause/ effect, freedom/necessity, nature/society, and reason/feeling as absolute opposites (so that any "thing" must be one or the other). Bourgeois ideology is present in the forms that promote divisive, static, and unsystematic (i.e., undialectical) thought, as well as in its not too surprising conservative content. Throughout, I stress that bourgeois ideology not only serves capitalist interests openly, but also when it confuses people, or makes them pessimistic and resigned, or makes it difficult for them to formulate criticisms or to imagine alternative systems.

Marx's critique of bourgeois ideology is as concerned with how these ideas and concepts arise (as a result of what activities, at what juncture in the class struggle, within which groups, in what connection to other ideas and events, etc.) as it is with their role in reproducing existing conditions. Since the origins of bourgeois ideology have received most of the attention up to this point—particularly in the sessions on the theory of alienation, the labor theory of value, and the materialist conception of history—it is primarily the role of ideology in society that concerns me here. My main effort is to get students to see bourgeois ideology as a piece, and the great variety of positions in practical politics, social science, and common sense as just so many versions of the same thing. Again, I stress that what these positions have in common is not that they are completely false, but that they are partial (though not recognized as such), that they are generally limited to appearances (hence, for Marx, unscientific), that they disregard the real history and actual potential of

their subject, that they confuse the real relations between
their elements, and that as a function of possessing just such
qualities they are biased in favor of the capitalist class.
Lecture 10. From the first day of the course, students ask,
"How would a 'Marxist society' be different?" Many, if not
most, believe that such societies already exist in the Soviet
Union, China, and Cuba, and that it should be easy for me to
respond. My answer, which I generally have to repeat again
and again, is that this is a very difficult question and that I
cannot approach it without some preparation. First, it is
absolutely essential to grasp that for Marx, communism was
to succeed capitalism and that the seeds of communism are
already present within capitalist society. It is necessary,
therefore, to examine Marx's analysis of capitalism to see
what he found that led him to believe in the possibility of
communism. In short, the various theories with which Marx
explained the workings of capitalism must be of prior concern. Second, the elements in Marx's vision of communism
are interdependent (no one or several of them can exist or
even be conceived of correctly without the others), so that
only a systematic account that ties these elements together
can avoid serious distortions.

Putting off students' requests for information on communism does not mean I consider the subject unimportant.
On the contrary, it is of such importance, particularly today,
that great care must be taken to circumvent the many ideological traps that await its telling. As is well known, Marx
never devoted an entire work to communism, but the raw
materials for it are scattered throughout his writings. Among
his reasons for not doing so, undoubtedly, was a fear that it
would appear too much like science fiction and that many
people would confuse him with the Utopian socialists for
whom such accounts were the main stock in trade. Another
objection Marx must have had to addressing communism
directly and systematically is that it is not a very effective

way—as compared to analyzing exploitation, for example—of raising workers' class consciousness. Today, however, no one is likely to confuse Marxism, even with the addition of an explicit conception of communism, with other socialist schools whose very names are difficult to recall. Furthermore, given the success of bourgeois ideology in getting people to accept the Soviet and Chinese models as "ideal" Marxist societies (presenting us with Marx's picture of our own future), a return to Marx's vision of communism may be a necessary complement to the analysis of exploitation in raising the consciousness of any oppressed group in modern capitalist society.

My account of Marx's vision of communism begins by making clear that we are really talking about two different societies, a first stage, socialism, also called the "dictatorship of the proletariat," which is essentially a transition period of indefinite duration, and a second stage of full communism. Most of the session is devoted to the first stage and, in particular, to showing how practical, rational, and democratic are the reforms Marx foresees. Wherever possible I try to locate these changes within the technological and organizational possibilities of modern capitalism, given the priorities that would be adopted by a new socialist government. It is here, and not before, that meaningful comparisons can be made between Marx's vision of world socialism and those isolated societies that have tried to build socialism under such trying conditions. In reconstructing the sketchy picture Marx paints of full communism, I again emphasize its logical status as part of the present grasped as a process, and clarify its role as the point of ultimate reference within the theory of alienation and as the probable future of mankind within the materialist conception of history.

In my opinion, one should not try to show that communism is inevitable, only that it is possible—that it is indeed based on conditions inherent in the further development of our present ones. After all, communism is almost never opposed because one holds other values, but because it is said to be an unrealizable ideal. In these circumstances, making a case for communism as a possible successor to capitalism is often enough to convince people that they must help to bring it about.

Lecture 11. I present Marx's ideas on class consciousness and revolution *after* presenting his vision of communism, because I want once again to make the point that the latter—as a projection of existing patterns and trends—belongs to his analysis of capitalism. As such, Marx's vision of communism is—at least in broad outline—part of what class conscious workers understand and part of the reason that socialist revolution is desirable. To study revolution without paying attention to its real causes and attainable goals (such as occurs in most bourgeois courses on revolution) is to get lost in a maze of practical politics, where there is no more reason to favor one side than the other.

Marx had no specific theory of revolution, of the steps and mechanisms by which capitalist society is to be overturned, unless we choose to view the whole of Marxism in this light. He was not committed, in other words, to any one strategy or form of organization as the means to make the revolution. Both his comments and his practical political activities show an enormous flexibility in response to the specific conditions of time and place. Despite what bourgeois scholars would have us believe, Marx—like every other socialist revolutionary—was opposed to violence, but he objected far more to the violence done daily to the working-class majority by a minuscule capitalist minority than to the violence that might be required to right this situation. According to Marx, the actual degree of violence in a revolution is, in any case, determined by the way the supporters of the status quo choose to defend it. Where revolutions have led to bloodbaths, this was generally the work of the counterrevolution—France in 1848 and 1871 (in our century, China in 1927, Germany after 1933, Spain after 1939, Indonesia in 1965, and Chile in 1972). Given the position that so many students take—of being against violence in the abstract—it is important that they realize the greater violence done by capitalists and, indirectly, by those, like themselves, who permit the capitalists to continue their oppression.

The one constant in Marx's approach to revolution is the belief he had that in one crisis or another the working class would come to see its class interests and would act upon them in a massive, organized, and effective way—which brings us to the theory of class consciousness. Marx always focused on the conditions in which this consciousness would emerge—indeed was already emerging—and hardly at all on the character of the people who were being called upon to respond. His masterly analysis of alienation was never integrated into his theory of class consciousness, so that the continued refusal of the mass of workers to become class conscious in conditions which should have made this possible remained a mystery that only drove him back (as it has most of his followers) to reexamine underlying conditions. It is in this area that I feel Marxism is in most need of revision. My own contribution here is an attempt to expand Marx's theory of alienation to include some of the findings of modern psychology (particularly the early work of Wilhelm Reich) and to integrate this expanded conception of alienation with the theory of class consciousness. As part of this revision, I also argue that Marxists must pay greater attention to the "politics of everyday life," both in our analyses of how capitalism works and in our strategies for changing it.

In this session I also introduce for the first time some of the Marxist political parties, their strategies and political activities, and briefly analyze why they have been so unsuccessful (the relative material well-being of American workers, the greater social mobility in the United States as compared to other capitalist countries, political repression, racism, the Cold War, etc.). I am neither very favorable toward, nor particularly critical of, these parties. Not having a comprehensive strategy for achieving socialism, I urge interested students to explore the various alternatives for themselves. Delaying the discussion of revolution to the end of the course means that students do not have to come to a decision on whether a revolution is possible until—with the aid of Marx's analysis—they understand the forces which make it both likely and desirable. Approaching the subject of what workers are or want or are capable of directly, as happens in so many discussions of revolution, usually leads to pessimism and its concomitant, political apathy ("Why bother?"), and undermines whatever interest exists in learning Marx's analysis. Studying Marx's analysis first, approaching workers' class consciousness as a problem within this analysis, permits a view of the possibilities and limitations inherent in our situation that is at once realistic and challenging. Understanding how capitalism works permits people to contribute more effectively to the struggle for socialism, knowing all the while that to do any less is to aid the other side.

Lecture 12. In graduate courses I try to leave a session at the end to summarize my remarks on Marx's method—to do for the dialectic, in other words, what Lecture 9 does for Marx's critique of bourgeois ideology. If the theory of alienation, the labor theory of value (particularly the discussion of exploitation), and the materialist conception of history are of most interest and have the greatest impact on undergraduates, it is Marx's philosophy, the critique of bourgeois ideology, the theory of the state, and his method that graduate students seem to find most relevant to their special concerns. Already committed to teaching and/or to some kind of serious research, they want to know how Marxism can help them in these tasks. It is very difficult for them—as it was for most of us—to make the necessary transition between the subjects treated early in the course and their practice as teachers and scholars. I consider this transition of such importance that it is the subject of a term-long seminar; in my lecture course on Marxism it occupies only the final session.

I divide Marx's method into four interlocking phases or moments: (1) philosophy, which can also be divided into ontology and epistemology (stressing the process of abstraction by which Marx establishes the units of reality); (2) inquiry, or how Marx proceeds from doubting everything (the skeptical stance he takes before the world of appearances) to studying it in just these units, whose changes and interactions as parts (expressions) of the capitalist system are his real subject; (3) intellectual reconstruction, or how Marx pieces together and clarifies for himself the results of this inquiry; and (4) exposition, or how he presents this understanding to others. Viewing the forces that produce change and the possible changes produced as a part of what anything is, the dialectic encourages us to expect change and to look for it, just as it helps us eventually to find it. It is this which makes the dialectic "in its essence critical and revolutionary," and underlies my course-long concern to have students think dialectically.[6] Most discussions of Marx's method focus on his philosophy or on his exposition, with the strategy Marx followed in *Capital* as the center of attention. I try to rectify this imbalance and particularly the neglect of the moment of inquiry, which is the aspect of method that is most discussed in non-Marxist works in this field. In treating this moment, I consider it very important that students see both the possibilities in and the limitations of standard social science techniques in gathering information for a Marxist analysis.

Exposition is a social relation between a writer (or speaker) and a chosen audience, whose mode of thought, interests, knowledge, and biases must be carefully considered before determining the order and form of presentation. I illustrate this point with Marx's occasional essays as well as with

Capital and—if time permits—with my own presentation of
Marxism in this course. Ideally, the session and the course
then concludes with student criticism of the strategy I used
in teaching them Marxism.

On rereading what I have written I am forced to admit that
this outline includes not only what I have done, but what I
have tried to do and what, on reflection, I believe I should
have done and will try to do in future courses. Readers will
also have noticed that some major aspects of our subject—
such as the origins of Marxism, nineteenth-century social and
political history, Marx's own life, the various schools of
Marxist interpretation, and the standard criticisms of Marxism—are not treated in separate sessions. To some extent,
they are integrated into discussions throughout the course—
with undergraduates getting more history and biography and
graduates a greater variety of interpretations and criticisms—
but it is also true that I have chosen to underplay these
topics. My main goal is to have students understand Marxism
not as intellectual history, political biography, or partisan
rhetoric, but as the only adequate analysis of capitalism
today; and given this end—and the limitations on time—it is
simply that other topics have been given a higher priority.

What are the practical results of my course on Marxism?
How can one judge them? Most students who answer the
question, "Why are you or aren't you a Marxist?", indicate
at the end of the course that they now accept Marx's analysis, though the majority are still wary of the label "Marxist."
Where this happens, these students know better than most
comrades with whom I have talked when and how they
adopted a Marxist outlook. I have always been amazed at
how little socialists, who are forever trying to effect a change
of consciousness in others, have reflected on the circumstances surrounding their own change of consciousness. For
most, the break with bourgeois ideology seems to have taken

place behind their backs, so that at one moment they considered themselves liberals (or worse) and then a little later—without quite noticing the transition—they considered themselves socialists.

If non-Marxists see my concern with such questions as an admission that the purpose of my course is to convert students to socialism, I can only answer that in my view—a view that denies the fact/value distinction—a correct understanding of Marxism (or any body of scientific truths) leads automatically to its acceptance. I hasten to add that this is not reflected in my grading practices where non-Marxist students (i.e., students who don't yet understand Marxism) do at least as well as the rest of the class (would that so much could be said of Marxist students in classes given by bourgeois professors). Furthermore, I do not consider that I introduce more "politics" into my course than do other social science professors, or that I am more interested in convincing students of the correctness of my interpretations than they are of theirs. If my concern with a teaching strategy suggests manipulation (whereas, supposedly, their concern with pedagogy is morally neutral), I can only reply that the truth being what it is, I have no interest in lying, or in hiding any facts or in misleading students in any way. Along with a growing number of socialist teachers, however, I have become very concerned with pedagogy because we have learned (usually the hard way) that truth doesn't always win out in the struggle with half-truths and lies, that it doesn't always forge its own means of expression, and that the very complexity of a Marxist analysis invites confusion and easy caricaturing. In addition, often our own personalities and shortcomings come between what we have to say and our audiences, while these audiences have undergone an ideological preparation that all but immunizes them against our message. The need so many socialist teachers feel to work out ways of presenting Marxism effectively implies, of course, an equal interest in the process by which students learn and understand Marxism, which is but the other side of the coin. And given the identity that I and most Marxists see between understanding Marxism and accepting it, this means, too, a concern with the process by which one becomes a socialist.

Becoming a socialist is obviously a process that varies with each person, but judging from my own frequent but highly informal inquiries there are certain experiences and insights that have a disproportionate influence in triggering or speeding up this transformation. Among these experiences are the following: undergoing a particularly brutal example of capitalist exploitation (or seeing it happen to one's parents or other loved ones); becoming involved in radical political activity, even of a minor sort, and being treated as a socialist by others (it is surprising how many comrades told me that they only knew they were socialists or were becoming socialists when people who disagreed with them said as much); living socialist relationships and finding them humanly more satisfying; having socialist friends and coming to take their assumptions for granted; knowing a socialist whose wisdom or kindness or courage one admires. Among the intellectual events that constitute major breakthroughs in the process of becoming a socialist there are the realizations that one has been consistently lied to; that the personal oppression from which one suffers is shared by others and is socially determined; that the path on which our society is traveling leads to economic and social disaster; that the problems of capitalism are interrelated and cannot be solved individually; that classes exist and the class struggle is real; and that the socialist ideal represents a morally superior way of life. This last shows that even though ethics has no place in Marxism (see Lecture 4), people may come to Marxism by an ethical route.

A course on Marxism, such as the one I have outlined, provides the occasion for many of these insights but for only a few, if any, of these experiences. Nowhere else do Marxists have so much freedom and time to present their case to non-Marxists. Still, I have come to believe that unless a course on Marxism is coupled with experiences at work or in some kind of political struggle, benefiting from the emotional jolt that such experiences bring, its effect on most students is likely to be minimal and probably short-term. But the fact is that the daily life of most people, including my students, contains many examples of oppression and struggle, and occasionally of cooperation. For them, it is an opportunity to study Marx's analysis of capitalism that has until now been missing. Where the most painful of these experiences are still to be lived, however, as is the case with students who have never looked for or held a job or raised a family, Marx's analysis may take years to bear political fruit. With such people, it is through experiences to come that the Marxism they study now will have its full impact, an impact that these experiences alone would probably not produce. This delayed-action effect makes it impossible to estimate with any accuracy the influence of socialist teachers, and has led many, among both friends and foes, to seriously underestimate it.

Still another impediment to acquiring a socialist consciousness in the classroom is the irrational tie that exists between the ideology of most people and whatever emotional equilibrium they have attained, so that an attack on one is felt as a threat to the other. The struggle to make sense of the world within bourgeois categories is experienced by them as a need as well as a choice. One of the reasons they cling to their ideology, therefore, is because it is "comfortable," and when studying Marxism makes what they believe increasingly untenable, many students experience real anxiety. For even as its rationalizations begin to falter, bourgeois ideology offers its adherents the acceptance and respect of their own families and of society's leaders, and, perhaps more important, the emotional security of having been right all along. No one finds it easy to admit that what he or she has been thinking and doing for many years is mistaken (this becomes harder with age, as there is more to justify and less time to make amends). Against this, what do we have to offer? In the absence of a socialist movement and without a circle of socialist friends, the transition to adopting a Marxist outlook—for all its intellectual excitement—can be a cold and lonely affair. To be sure, students differ in how much they need comradely support in making this transition and in how much support they are already getting. And if time permitted, the need itself could be analyzed within the framework of Marx's theory of alienation, expanded to include Reich's theory of character structure. The point remains, however, that the classroom in which their bourgeois ideology is being dismantled does not provide the continuity of contact and emotional security that many students need to extend their critical thinking to its logical conclusions and embrace Marxism. In the years to come, a change in their personal situations or in the political climate might produce different results.

Consequently, though many students write at the end of my course that they are now Marxists, I consider—for the reasons given—that the real effect of the course both on them and on their more resistant peers will not be known for some time.

Appendix

Readings. There are two major problems here: students, particularly in graduate classes, vary a great deal in how much Marxism they have read; and there are few writings by Marx and Engels that deal with only one or a few theories at a time. I am not wholly satisfied with my solutions to either of these problems, but this is what I have done. First, I ask beginners to read either the Mehring, Berlin, or McLellan biographies of Marx, "The Communist Manifesto," and Engels' *Socialism: Utopian and Scientific* before doing any other reading for the course. They simply need to get some feeling for the range and tone of Marxism before setting out to understand it in a systematic fashion. The two sessions at the beginning of the term in which we prepare to study Marxism give them the time to do most of this reading. Second, the reading for each lecture is broken down into works for beginners and works for advanced students. Many works, of course, are so important that I ask beginners— especially as the course progresses—to try to read them, though I warn them of the difficulty. I tell the advanced students to read the works on the beginners' list first, if they haven't already done so (except in the case of selections), and then go on to other works. I also suggest that they use the course as an opportunity to read/finish *Capital* I and III, and urge them to investigate at least one other interpretation of Marx besides my own for each of the topics covered. Everybody is asked to read my book, *Alienation,* so that I can devote most of the lecture time to elaborating on its content and to other matters.

Term Paper. Usually, the only requirement for a grade in the course is that students produce one or two term papers. Once students choose a term paper topic, there is a tendency for them to read less for class sessions. I ask them, therefore, not to settle on a topic until we are about two-thirds of the way into the course. This also enables them to get a foundation in the subject and to see the range of topics it offers before committing themselves to research in a certain direction.

Taking Notes. I have found it very helpful in my own reading of Marx to devote separate pages in my notebooks to his key concepts. Marx never supplies us with definitions, but we can more or less reconstruct them by collecting examples of what he says about these concepts and of how he uses them in his various works. As relations, as aspects of the whole which offer different vantage points for its examination and comprehension, each successful reconstruction will also be a version of Marx's analysis. Consequently, I urge students at the very start of the course to put aside separate pages in their notebooks for such concepts as "labor," "capital," "value," "commodity," "class," "mode of production," "relations of production," "alienation," "ideology," "private property," and "freedom." It is not a matter of writing down everything that is said about these concepts, but the effort to record what seems most important or unusual will prove very rewarding as the patterns both within and between each group of comments begin to emerge.

Notes

1. Karl Marx, *Theories of Surplus-Value* (Moscow: Progress Publishers, 1971), p. 536.
2. Karl Marx and Friedrich Engels, *Selected Correspondence*, ed. and trans. Dona Torr (London, 1941), p. 472.
3. Robert Tressell, *The Ragged Trousered Philanthropists* (London, 1965), pp. 209-14; to be published in paperback by Monthly Review Press, 1978.
4. Marx's philosophy has proven the most difficult subject to summarize in this outline. For a more detailed account see my book, *Alienation: Marx's Conception of Man in Capitalist Society* (New York: Cambridge University Press, 1971), particularly Chapters 2 and 3 and Appendix I; in the second edition (New York: Cambridge University Press, 1976), see "In Defense of Internal Relations," Appendix II. This subject is treated from another vantage point in my article, "Marxism and Political Science: Prolegomenon to a Debate on Marx's Method," *Politics and Society* (Summer 1973).
5. Karl Marx, *Capital*, vol. I (Moscow: Progress Publishers, 1958), p. 80.
6. Ibid., p. 20.

"The Great Money Trick"
from
The Ragged Trousered Philanthropists
••••
Robert Tressell

"Money *is* the real cause of poverty," said Owen.

"Prove it," repeated Crass.

"Money is the cause of poverty because it is the device by which those who are too lazy to work are enabled to rob the workers of the fruits of their labor."

"Prove it," said Crass.

Owen slowly folded up the piece of newspaper he had been reading and put it into his pocket.

"All right," he replied. "I'll show you how the Great Money Trick is worked."

Owen opened his dinner basket and took from it two slices of bread but as these were not sufficient, he requested that anyone who had some bread left would give it to him. They gave him several pieces, which he placed in a heap on a clean piece of paper, and, having borrowed the pocket knives they used to cut and eat their dinners with from Easton, Harlow, and Philpot, he addressed them as follows:

"These pieces of bread represent the raw materials which exist naturally in and on the earth for the use of mankind; they were not made by any human being, but were created by the Great Spirit for the benefit and sustenance of all, the same as were the air and the light of the sun."

"You're about as fair-speakin' a man as I've met for some time," said Harlow, winking at the others.

"Yes, mate," said Philpot. "Anyone would agree to that much! It's as clear as mud."

"Now," continued Owen, "I am a Capitalist; or, rather, I represent the Landlord and Capitalist Class. That is to say, all these raw materials belong to me. It does not matter for our present argument how I obtained possession of them, or whether I have any real right to them; the only thing that matters now is the admitted fact that all the raw materials which are necessary for the production of the necessaries of life are now the property of the Landlord and Capitalist Class. I am that class: all these raw materials belong to me."

"Good enough!" agreed Philpot.

"Now you three represent the Working Class: you have nothing—and for my part, although I have all these raw materials, they are of no use to me—what I need is—the things that can be made out of these raw materials by Work: but as I am too lazy to work myself, I have invented the Money Trick to make you work *for* me. But first I must explain that I possess something else beside the raw materials. These three knives represent—all the machinery of production; the factories, tools, railways, and so forth, without which the necessaries of life cannot be produced in abundance. And these three coins"—taking three halfpennies from his pocket— "represent my Money Capital."

"But before we go any further," said Owen, interrupting himself, "it is most important that you remember that I am not supposed to be merely 'a' capitalist. I represent the whole Capitalist Class. You are not supposed to be just three workers—you represent the whole Working Class."

"All right, all right," said Crass, impatiently, "we all understand that. Git on with it."

Owen proceeded to cut up one of the slices of bread into a number of little square blocks.

"These represent the things which are produced by labor, aided by machinery, from the raw materials. We will suppose that three of these blocks represent—a week's work. We will suppose that a week's work is worth—one pound: and we will suppose that each of these ha'pennies is a sovereign. We'd be able to do the trick better if we had real sovereigns, but I forgot to bring any with me."

"I'd lend you some," said Philpot, regretfully, "but I left me purse on our grand pianner."

As by a strange coincidence nobody happened to have any gold with them, it was decided to make shift with the halfpence.

"Now this is the way the trick works—"

"Before you goes on with it," interrupted Philpot, apprehensively, "don't you think we'd better 'ave someone to keep watch at the gate in case a slop comes along? We don't want to get runned in, you know."

"I don't think there's any need for that," replied Owen, "there's only one slop who'd interfere with us for playing this game, and that's Police Constable Socialism."

"Never mind about Socialism," said Crass, irritably. "Get along with the bloody trick."

Owen now addressed himself to the working classes as represented by Philpot, Harlow, and Easton.

"You say that you are all in need of employment, and as I am the kind-hearted Capitalist Class I am going to invest all my money in various industries, so as to give you Plenty of Work. I shall pay each of you one pound per week, and a week's work is—you must each produce three of these square blocks. For doing this work you will each receive your wages; the money will be your own, to do as you like with, and the things you produce will of course be mine, to do as I like with. You will each take one of these machines and as soon as you have done a week's work, you shall have your money."

The Working Classes accordingly set to work, and the Capitalist Class sat down and watched them. As soon as they had finished, they passed the nine little blocks to Owen, who placed them on a piece of paper by his side and paid the workers their wages.

"These blocks represent the necessaries of life. You can't live without some of these things, but as they belong to me, you will have to buy them from me: my price for these blocks is—one pound each."

As the Working Classes were in need of the necessaries of life and as they could not eat, drink, or wear the useless money, they were compelled to agree to the kind Capitalist's terms. They each bought back and at once consumed one-third of the produce of their labor. The Capitalist Class also devoured two of the square blocks, and so the net result of the week's work was that the kind Capitalist had consumed two pounds' worth of the things produced by the labor of the others, and reckoning the squares at their market value of one pound each, he had more than doubled his capital, for he still possessed the three pounds in money and in addition four pounds' worth of goods. As for the Working Classes, Philpot, Harlow, and Easton, having each consumed the pound's worth of necessaries they had bought with their wages, they were again in precisely the same condition as when they started work—they had nothing.

This process was repeated several times: for each week's work the producers were paid their wages. They kept on working and spending all their earnings. The kind-hearted Capitalist consumed twice as much as any one of them and his pile of wealth continually increased. In a little while— reckoning the little squares at their market value of one pound each—he was worth about one hundred pounds, and the Working Classes were still in the same condition as when they began, and were still tearing into their work as if their lives depended upon it.

After a while the rest of the crowd began to laugh, and their merriment increased when the kind-hearted Capitalist,

just after having sold a pound's worth of necessaries to each
of his workers, suddenly took their tools—the Machinery of
Production—the knives away from them, and informed them
that as owing to Over-Production all his storehouses were
glutted with the necessaries of life, he had decided to close
down the works.

"Well, and wot the bloody 'ell are we to do now?" demanded Philpot.

"That's not my business," replied the kind-hearted Capitalist. "I've paid you your wages, and provided you with Plenty
of Work for a long time past. I have no more work for you to
do at present. Come round again in a few months' time and
I'll see what I can do for you."

"But what about the necessaries of life?" demanded Harlow. "We must have something to eat."

"Of course you must," replied the Capitalist, affably; "and
I shall be very pleased to sell you some."

"But we ain't got no bloody money!"

"Well, you can't expect me to give you my goods for
nothing! You didn't work for me for nothing, you know. I
paid you for your work and you should have saved something: you should have been thrifty like me. Look how I
have got on by being thrifty!"

The unemployed looked blankly at each other, but the rest
of the crowd only laughed; and then the three unemployed
began to abuse the kind-hearted Capitalist, demanding that
he should give them some of the necessaries of life that he
had piled up in his warehouses, or to be allowed to work and
produce some more for their own needs; and even threatened to take some of the things by force if he did not comply
with their demands. But the kind-hearted Capitalist told
them not to be insolent, and spoke to them about honesty,
and said if they were not careful he would have their faces
battered in for them by the police, or if necessary he would
call out the military and have them shot down like dogs, the
same as he had done before at Featherstone and Belfast.

"Of course," continued the kind-hearted Capitalist, "if it were not for foreign competition I should be able to sell these things that you have made, and then I should be able to give you Plenty of Work again: but until I have sold them to somebody or other, or until I have used them myself, you will have to remain idle."

"Well, this takes the bloody biskit, don't it?" said Harlow.

"The only thing as I can see for it," said Philpot mournfully, "is to 'ave a unemployed procession."

"That's the idear," said Harlow, and the three began to march about the room in Indian file, singing:

"We've got no work to do-oo-oo!
We've got no work to do-oo-oo!
Just because we've been workin' a dam sight too hard,
Now we've got no work to do."

As they marched round, the crowd jeered at them and made offensive remarks. Crass said that anyone could see that they were a lot of lazy, drunken loafers who had never done a fair day's work in their lives and never intended to.

"We shan't never get nothing like this, you know," said Philpot. "Let's try the religious dodge."

"All right," agreed Harlow. "What shall we give 'em?"

"I know!" cried Philpot after a moment's deliberation. " 'Let my lower lights be burning.' That always makes 'em part up."

The three unemployed accordingly resumed their march round the room, singing mournfully and imitating the usual whine of streetsingers:

"Trim your fee-bil lamp me brither-in,
Some poor sail-er tempest torst,
Strugglin' 'ard to save the 'arb-er,
Hin the dark-niss may be lorst,
So let my lower lights be burning,
Send 'er gleam acrost the wave,
Some poor shipwrecked, struggling seaman,
You may rescue, you may save."

"Kind frens," said Philpot, removing his cap and addressing the crowd, "we're hall honest British workin' men, but we've been hout of work for the last twenty years on account of foreign competition and over-production. We don't come hout 'ere because we're too lazy to work; it's because we can't get a job. If it wasn't for foreign competition, the kind-'earted Hinglish capitalists would be able to sell their goods and give us Plenty of Work, and if they could, I assure you that we should hall be perfectly willing and contented to go on workin' our bloody guts out for the benefit of our masters for the rest of our lives. We're quite willin' to work: that's hall we arst for—Plenty of Work—but as we can't get it we're forced to come out 'ere and arst you to spare a few coppers toward a crust of bread and a night's lodgin'."

As Philpot held out his cap for subscriptions, some of them attempted to expectorate into it, but the more charitable put in pieces of cinder or dirt from the floor, and the kind-hearted Capitalist was so affected by the sight of their misery that he gave them one of the sovereigns he had in his pocket: but as this was of no use to them they immediately returned it to him in exchange for one of the small squares of the necessaries of life, which they divided and greedily devoured. And when they had finished eating they gathered round the philanthropist and sang, "For he's a jolly good fellow," and afterward Harlow suggested that they should ask him if he would allow them to elect him to Parliament.

Some Remarks on Ollman's
"On Teaching Marxism"
.....
Martin Sklar

I am among those who still believe Marx's theory of value is relevant to modern political economy, not only as an ethical axiom but also as a regulative principle of inquiry; who believe, from my own long studies as a U.S. historian, that U.S. history offers as good a record as that of the history of any society in corroborating the power and efficacy of Marx's social theory; who believe that by and large Marx's forecasts and prognostications about the course of history in modern capitalist societies, made within the framework of his systematic theoretical diagnoses, have proved generally accurate; and who believe that Marx's theory of freedom (and its relation to necessity) remains unsurpassed on scientific, philosophic, and ethical grounds.

I also share, with virtually all avowed Marxists, in other basic concepts or ways of thinking: for example, the dialectical method, or reasoning; the indissolubility of fact and value; the concept of alienation and its implications; the belief in socialism as a stage in history prepared for by capitalism and succeeding it—hence periodization of historical development in terms of modes of production and property-class relations; evolutionary progression (or cumulative human development) by means of revolutions; the class character of post-tribal society and of the state, and class struggles as central to historical reality and historical development of humanity.

Yet I do not believe in "Marxism" in the sense it is commonly conveyed by proponents and opponents alike, and as conveyed in Ollman's paper. This refers not necessarily to specific elements as presented in the paper, nor to certain more general characterizations found there (though I do have some differences in each case), but rather to the *aura* with which "Marxism" is ordained and conveyed, amounting I believe to a reification of a body of knowledge and mode of inquiry into a canon of prescribed truths, or emblems of frozen authority.

I believe the very notion of Marxism to be utterly alien to Marx's system of thought and, I like to believe, to his own way of thinking personally.

One way of getting at what I am trying to suggest is to say that the idea is not to teach and to learn Marxism, but to teach and to learn about history and our current reality—in the course of which our thinking expresses and critically reflects upon the social body of knowledge and modes of inquiry that form the legacy of developing human consciousness, and that include the contributions of outstanding thinkers. The idea is to learn about, to change and adapt, our own consciousness as the outcome and further development of the historical course of human consciousness, and more particularly as the ongoing development of modern consciousness expressing humanity's social relations and their transformations.

It is as preposterous to understand modern consciousness, and modern social reality, including our own, without reference to Marx as it is to do so without reference to Freud, or Darwin, or Weber, or Einstein (etc.).

We study Marx's thought (like others') as a guide to our own consciousness, to the consciousness of our own epoch, and to comprehending historical reality generally, that of the past and present, and its future tendencies. We also study Marx's thought, as we do that of other eminent thinkers, to change, deepen, and extend our consciousness.

Otherwise, if we say we are studying Marxism—rather than human reality—as our basic object, we are really searching texts, and authorized (or heretical) commentaries upon texts for, and awaiting, something like a pentecostal descent of the True Revelation. Instead of using our brains and our experience to understand and change the world, we are "using" the texts to gain self-justification, to acquire Grace, while the world goes on quite merrily without reference to us. Because, after all, it *is* a secular world, as the Billy Grahams, Charles Colsons, and James Carters well know.

By all means, then, study the thought of Marx, and offer the best possible courses in the thought of Marx, and that of the other worthy thinkers (and the course Ollman offers is one I'd like to attend myself), but not Marxism as some eternal canon of Truth, or as sacred texts set apart or "above" the rest of the human world of thought.

There is no intent here to criticize Ollman's strategy in the presentation of Marx's thought in the course he outlines. I think it is quite effective for its purposes—learned and comprehensive. It is rather the broader context he establishes, the devotional elixir he bathes it in, to which I take exception. That broader framework does make a difference in teaching and in the learning that results.

Marx is presented as something of a heaven-sent messenger, set off from the rest of humanity, bearing the Truth in the form of precepts and doctrines equally set off from the rest of human consciousness. That presentation violates Ollman's own principle of "internal relations" which he so effectively formulates in his book, *Alienation*.

Setting Marx (and Marxism) apart, or above, is a way of setting ourselves (as socialists, or Marxists) apart. It is a principal way the bourgeois intellectuals and political leaders happily and with serious intent set us apart, and by which we dutifully oblige them. It is time we let Marx (and Marxism) rejoin the human world, and let ourselves, too. It is time, that is, to understand Marx's thought, and our own, as integral to modern human consciousness, generated by and expressing conditions of the capitalist epoch and its developing outcome: a development that includes an unprecedented acceleration in the growth and transformation of physical and social scientific thought and method (for which Marx eminently, among others, laid the foundations and the subsequent course of which they anticipated). This modern consciousness includes also the maturing of rationalistic ethics grounded in the expanding horizons of human knowledge and activity as the essence of human freedom, or the actualization of more and more of the potentials latent in human being.

More specifically, in much the larger and most penetrating body of his works, Marx clarified widely held and time-honored views, and brought them into a critical focus upon the study of society in general and upon capitalist society in particular. Marx did this more powerfully than any other single thinker of his time and—in so comprehensive a way—perhaps since. In so doing, he affirmed, expressed, and developed much of the best and most profound in human thought to his time; so that to evade Marx is to evade the intellectual legacy that many of the evading intellectuals themselves acclaim, and also to evade a critical understanding of contemporary historical reality. A serious study of, and attention to, Marx's work (as with those of others) is indispensable for a critical understanding of contemporary historical reality and its development. Their evasion or suppression represents a psychic mutilation, and the sickness that comes with repression and the inexorable return of the repressed in neurotic modes.

The scandal of American higher education has resided not so much in the absence of courses on *Marxism* as in the absence of the serious study of Marx's thought *in the appropriate courses.* The provincial neglect and falsification of Marx's thought that has passed, in the United States, for intellectual sophistication would be laughed out of court as scholarly incompetence, if not grounds for denial of tenure, almost anywhere else. But this situation is changing; the scandal is lifting, along with changing historical circumstances.

One who has studied the classical social theorists of the nineteenth and early twentieth centuries must, it seems to me, be struck by and acknowledge the large degree of common agreement among them, as much as the differences. In the evasion and neglect of Marx's thought American intellectuals have by and large evaded and obscured those aspects of the thought of other great social theorists that are similar to and corroborative of Marx's (and, vice versa, Marxians are similarly guilty). In so doing American intellectuals have come dangerously close to desiccating, fragmenting, and denying the power of our common legacy of consciousness. It is such suppression of consciousness that preordains the widely noted and feared "decline of Western civilization," as if we were caught in the clutches of the proverbial death wish. For it severely weakens a common awareness of the community of thought and values, of available alternatives forged in human experience, and hence the vital capacity for variability and adaptation.

As a result, we lose sight of the real differences among great bodies of thought, and understand only vaguely the real alternatives before us. We often fabricate nonexistent differences, by not first establishing the common ground underlying the universe of human discourse, embracing the broadest range of thinkers, who at first glance seem to be only at loggerheads. We magnify superficial differences, ignore profound areas of agreement, and often as not never get to those real and substantial differences that *are* there. It is symptomatic of this condition that in the United States today not only the political leaders of major and minor parties alike, but also the intellectuals, are unable to articulate the great issues of our time, in the face of their own intensely felt need for it. We have crises and proclamations of crises on every hand, but nowhere is there a convincing formulation even of the nature of the crises, let alone their resolution. There is an intellectual power failure, no less enervating than the recurrent energy shortages, in the United States and in the world at large.

Turning to Ollman's paper in some of its detail may clarify what I am trying to convey.

At the paper's outset, bourgeois ideology is portrayed onesidedly (and in violation of Ollman's own principle of internal relations) as an obstruction to his students' learning about Marx's thought. Yet the bourgeois modes of consciousness are also, historically, intimately linked with Marx's thought. They are a key condition of its emergence and maturation, and, more broadly, of the socialist outlook (just as the rise of the bourgeoisie creates the proletariat, and capitalism prepares the way, establishes the conditions, for socialism). Concrete elements of bourgeois ideology that, for example, flow *into* the socialist (and Marx's) outlook include:

—the idea of self-determination and individuality *in* society, and *in* the world;

—the idea of human being as social and political and economic being;

—discovery of material foundations of society;

—bourgeois economic determinism (which becomes something else in Marx);

—the scientific-utilitarian outlook;

—the idea of "progress" through "reason" and material development, i.e., evolution;

—ever growing awareness (through division of labor and market relations) of interdependency among individuals, classes, nations;

—the idea of government by consent of the governed: republican institutions (democracy more broadly);

—the idea of equality under the law;

—the idea of the right to life, liberty, happiness in society;

—the concept of property in one's self;

—the theory of labor as the source of value, and the idea of the dignity of labor.

In the later, corporate stage of capitalism:

—internationalism;

—corporative (cooperative and social) quality of production, distribution, social existence generally;

—conscious regulation and planning of economic affairs and social arrangements;

—systems-thinking.

(These latter represent more points of convergence between Marxian and later bourgeois thought, the latter to a significant extent borrowing and adapting from Marxian and socialist thought.)

Bourgeois ideology, then, is not only a "major hurdle"; it is also a major condition and opportunity. Every ideology, as Ollman's principle of internal relations suggests, is a genetic system of contradictions harboring its own negations.

"There is nothing in bourgeois ideas and ways of thinking," Ollman writes, "which doesn't interfere with the reception of Marx's message." I would submit, however, that at the same time there is much that leads directly *to* it, and little that does not, at least indirectly (except I would not use the term "message"). In further discussing his students' ideology as an obstacle to understanding Marx, Ollman observes that it reflects their class background and their position in capitalist society as young people and students. In strict Marxian terms, this ideology should be (and is) pregnant with contradictions embracing socialist implications *and* thinking, as well as convergences with Marx's thought as such. Actually, in the course of his discussion Ollman indeed recognizes that there *is* much of substance with which to work in the students' ideology. How could it be otherwise, if one holds that capitalism establishes the conditions for socialism, including the conditions of consciousness? Conversely, if the ideological situation were as barren as Ollman asserts, that would be rather strong evidence, within the principles of Marx's theory, that socialism cannot be regarded, on inductive grounds, as the concrete historical "negation" of modern capitalist society—or at least of modern *U.S.* capitalist society, which would vindicate the American-exceptionalists.

Similarly, at the outset of his paper Ollman designates the university setting as an obstacle to teaching Marx's thought. This, too, is one-sided. As a key institution of bourgeois society, the university also offers large opportunities. Take, for example, two of the major, contradictory ideas of the university and its corresponding role:

1. The idea (and reality) that the university serves the society (business, the state, etc.); that it is utilitarian and practical in orientation; that higher education should be useful, organically related to society and its needs, not simply for parasitic or indolent elites.

This conception of the university acknowledges the nondisinterestedness of the university, its subordination to the imperatives and prescriptions of capitalist society and capitalist interests. It also, however, implies a critique of that state of affairs; it raises the question as to which interests in society, which values, the university should serve, what kind of society it should serve, what purposes, and how and by whom those purposes should be defined. The conception also implicitly affirms the interrelatedness of theory and practice, social purpose and technology, fact and value. It also, by the way, suggests parallels for students to consider between the role of education in the United States which they take as quite natural, and that of education in socialist countries, whether China, the Soviet Union, Cuba, etc.

2. The idea of the pursuit of knowledge, art, science, for its own sake, wherever it may lead, apart from utilitarian, immediately practicable, or exploitable, interests and purposes; the idea of "value-free" objectivity: knowledge should not

simply serve power or vested interests; the value of disinterested pursuit of knowledge and the truth.

This conception of the university effectively acknowledges the dangers of subordinating education to class interests and class power, to business and the state. It implies the disparity between critical knowledge and the going ideologies, myths, interests, suppressive forces of the capitalist society at large, and the obligation to reveal and dispel them.

The conflicting ideas of the university in Western society express its contradictory roles. The university has always harbored both contemplative and practical activity, both critics and servants of society. It has always been integrally related to the reproduction of essential social functions as well as to the generation of innovative (including revolutionary) tendencies. This is as true of the medieval and pre-industrial bourgeois universities (seminaries, colleges) as it is of those in modern times. The universities have been, at one and the same time, the citadel of conservatism and the breeding ground of dissident, radical, and critical thinking.

It is no anomaly, therefore, that Marxists or socialists are to be found teaching in the U.S. universities, or that courses on or including the study of Marx and Marxism are to be found there. The anomaly to be explained, rather, is their relatively lesser frequency and sophistication, their relatively later appearance, in U.S. universities than in those of other countries. The explanation would involve reference to the special circumstances of U.S. history as well as to the general Marxian theory of class domination. It would not, however, involve the implication Ollman conveys to his students, that there is something strange, embarrassing, or contrary to Marxian theory, in his teaching a course on Marx's thought, or in a Marxist or socialist working, in a university in U.S. society.

Ollman designates the absence of a vital socialist movement in the United States as an obstruction to the teaching of

Marx's thought. Just as much an obstacle, no less than an
opportunity, in teaching Marx's thought, conceivably, could
be a universal socialist ideology, as seems to be the case in
many socialist countries today. It is true that in the United
States there are no political parties that go by the name of
socialism, or the name of Marx, and that also have a large
popular constituency. Most students accordingly do not
come to the university from family and broader cultural
backgrounds with roots in a political and intellectual identity
of that sort. Yet the conclusion drawn from this by most
U.S. Marxists, that a socialist tradition is virtually absent
from the U.S. political universe as a vital force, is superficial and ahistorical. Socialism in the United States does
not appear in the forms and language of other countries
and past times; but that does not mean that socialist values,
ideas, goals, and political objectives are not real components
of the U.S. political universe, only that they have to be
identified and brought to explicit consciousness in the forms
in which they do appear in this country's concrete history.
Most U.S. Marxists in this respect permit appearances to
dominate their thinking about realities, contrary to their
own strictures about the need to penetrate appearances and
bring realities to consciousness, no less to make the latent
actual. It might also be observed that the absence of a powerful, overtly socialist party in U.S. politics may serve as an
advantage in the teaching of Marx's thought: there is no
eminent party or tradition with overbearing prestige and
entrenched doctrines to interfere with the study of theory
and conditions, or for that matter obstruct the building of a
political movement freshly geared to present-day conditions.

   Now I'd like to turn, in thinking about teaching Marxism,
to a question that relates more particularly to American
circumstances. In other countries, Marxism offers a convenient term of reference to identifiable and substantial
bodies of scholarship, social and political theory and ideas,

philosophy, aesthetics, etc.—i.e., to a definite living intellectual tradition. It refers as well to major political movements and parties. In those countries, therefore, studying Marxism involves studying real aspects of one's own society's history of consciousness and sociopolitical development. In the United States, however, the body of substantial, professedly Marxist thought, until very recently (and the situation *is* changing), has been so thin as to be nearly invisible. Similarly, with respect to professedly Marxist political movements. Among U.S. Marxists there is incessant squabbling over who among them are or are not *bona fide* Marxists. But what is peculiar to the American disputants is not their disputes, but that in settling them to their own satisfaction they make appeal largely to foreign texts and authorities, and very little if at all to those of U.S. vintage.

In the United States, that is, to study Marxism is in effect to study Europe, Asia, Latin America, Africa, the Middle East, everywhere except the United States. It is another version of the all-too-American flight to "new frontiers" and exotic climes, to expatriated adventures or genteel tourism: a twentieth-century jet-set version of the pioneers' flight from society's reality into "new beginnings"—and away from history. It becomes the ultimate ahistorical act in the name of the quest for historical consciousness.

Having said these things, let me also say in conclusion that its specific topics and readings make of Ollman's course a valuable introduction to Marx's thought, and more, a valuable guide to the advanced study of Marx's thought, to many of the profound questions raised by it, and to their implications. It also seems to be well suited to indicating the relevance of Marx's thought to the comprehension of contemporary reality. But, following from the foregoing, I would do certain things differently:

1. I'd explore and emphasize the common ground shared by Marx and other significant thinkers before him, during his own time, and afterward.

2. I'd explore the ways in which Marx's thought has fed into the current streams of social theory, historiography, anthropology, philosophy, etc., as well as into large portions of everyday consciousness—and bring that to a more emphatic awareness.

3. I'd explore, *on that basis,* the differences between Marx's thought and others', and between his thought and that of avowed Marxists after him.

4. I'd explore the relationship (including the differences) between Marx's social theory and socialist and communist political ideology and practice.

5. I'd explore why it was that though Marx and other nonsocialist, nonrevolutionary thinkers shared wide areas of agreement, Marx nevertheless developed concepts and explored in directions other thinkers closed to themselves.

6. I'd explore the relevance of class stratification, class conflict, and a class culture to that parting of the ways.

Finally, I'd take Marx out of the ghetto of Marxism, and the rest of us socialists (including Marxists) with him. That is, I'd bring Marx back down to earth, to the secular world, so that his thought, and thought subsequently inspired or informed by his, may depart from the realm of sects, of the anointed elect, of sectarianism, and rejoin the broad human stream where it may play its part in replenishing the soil of human consciousness and practice.

Part IV
......
Toward Socialist Relations in the Classroom

Toward a Marxist Theory
and Practice of Teaching
....
Bruce M. Rappaport

Introduction

I am really excited about being a Marxist teacher. I enjoy teaching: the communication and sharing and creating of information. After quite a few years of struggle, I have found something to teach that really explains the world and how to change it—Marxism.

I am currently working on an analysis of the theory and practice of this kind of teaching. What I want to do here is share, in an abbreviated form, some of my thoughts and ideas on the subject. These ideas have developed through discussions and work with other teachers, particularly at the May 1964 Socialist Sociology Conference in Boulder Creek, California, through work and study that I have done with people in Reevaluation Counseling,[1] through a careful reading of an article on teaching by Shierry Weber and Bernard Somers,[2] and through my own practice.

Most of the available writing on radical/Marxist pedagogy concerns itself primarily with content issues, such as course outlines, books, themes, etc. In this article I want to focus on the less discussed problem of teaching methodology, make a preliminary attempt to develop a Marxist theory of teaching, and suggest and discuss a few practices that follow from this theory.

Two Types of Teaching Styles and Their Problems

We can clearly reject the traditional bourgeois style of
teaching, with its authoritarianism, class and intellectual
snobbery, and deliberate design that reproduces the hierarchical division of labor so crucial to capitalistic society.
However, we need to scrutinize other styles of teaching
whose problems are not as clear.

The first of these involves teaching Marxist content while
relying on a traditional style of teaching. Lectures, harsh
criticism, competitive grading, etc., are used in this instance
not so much for asserting bourgeois superiority over the
students but out of a sincere conviction that people must
learn Marxism "no matter what we have to do to get them
to do it." This behavior is a form of putting "economics"
rather than "politics" in command. The emphasis, in other
words, is on an accumulation of knowledge, regardless of the
method, just as the USSR has been accused of aiming at
"socialist accumulation" even if it entails using capitalist-
type incentives. Mao has criticized such an approach in economic situations; in the academic world it ignores the general
political context of what we are about. It is not the accumulation of Marxist knowledge that is our aim for our
students (or ourselves), but the development of revolutionaries, free of bourgeois values such as competitiveness and the
approach to learning as an individualistic cram process.

A second tendency goes to the other extreme. The teacher,
genuinely concerned to avoid the authoritarianism of the
traditional classroom, uses the "do your own thing" style of
teaching. The basic content and structure of the course are
left up to the students and the class "flows" according to
their expressed wishes. In the political world, Lenin called
such a style "spontaneity." A revolutionary/teacher abdicates
responsibility by not leading people who have less knowledge
about the issues under study. Such behavior confuses leader-

ship with domination. Having a leadership role in one area does not make one "superior" to other people in all areas. A teacher is one who in a particular situation has more information. Outside of that particular context, the teacher remains a peer or a student. In bourgeois-dominated universities, the teacher role frequently gets generalized into a position of superiority and domination over the students. Beyond the confusion about leadership, the "do your own thing" style of teaching often allows the most aggressive students, usually upwardly mobile males, to dominate the class, and negates chances for real participation for all students. Such "structurelessness" really produces a highly structured situation, built on the attitudes and roles of the students' prior capitalist socialization.

It is important to note that, in both cases, the mistakes that are being made are not motivated by ill intent or malicious revisionism. Both styles represent genuine, if mistaken, attempts to deal with the problems that teachers face in trying to be revolutionaries and teachers at the same time. The first mistake, authoritative teaching patterns, tends to arise from a desperate effort to get Marxist ideas across. This same desperation, particularly in the 1960s, sometimes moved us to act too hastily and without the revolutionary patience that is so crucial. The second teaching pattern, the "do your own thing" style, seems to derive from either the fear that we, as teachers, may be acting like all those authoritarian types who were our teachers, or from genuine concern to treat everyone as peers and equals.

The Contradictions in Radical Teaching

If excessively authoritarian and anarchistic methods are inappropriate, what is the more correct approach to the problem of being a radical or Marxist teacher? Conventional college teachers see teaching primarily in terms of course content. They assume that being an effective teacher means becoming more and more of an expert in one's own subject matter. As Marxists we should see the task of effective teaching in a different light. Obviously, we are concerned with communicating radical and Marxist analysis, not bourgeois ideology; but the issue is a deeper one. The notion that ideas do not exist in a vacuum but in a particular social context is critical to Marxism. It follows that the teaching of ideas must involve paying close attention to the social context of the teaching and learning situation. The task for a Marxist teacher, then, is not only to develop the best possible Marxist analysis but to find ways to communicate this material in a manner that takes into account a Marxist analysis of the classroom situation, namely, the role of teacher and student, the socialization process, and the false consciousness of many students that will decrease their receptiveness to revolutionary ideas.

The most basic contradiction that we face as Marxist teachers in a capitalist society is our involvement in learning and teaching in a society which needs to systematically deprive its members of their inherent intelligence. To briefly sum up the main points of this argument:

1. Human beings are inherently characterized by the possession of enormous intelligence. While rigid, blind, or slow thinking abound in this and other societies, all the evidence indicates that this deficient behavior does not stem from any lack of inherent intelligence. It is rather the result of the suppression of intelligence that occurs in a class-stratified society.

2. Why does a capitalist society require this suppression of intelligence? To put it briefly, the smooth operation of a capitalist system requires that people be trained in very specific ways designed to make them an easily disciplined labor force.[3] This kind of training is hardly conducive to the development of clear thinking and analysis but, in fact,

requires that this kind of thinking be narrowly channeled. Furthermore, the maintenance of ideological control by those in power requires that working people be trained not in critical thinking but only in rigid, indoctrinated forms of thought.

3. Clear thinking is most difficult when we find ourselves in a painful or distressing situation. In this context, critical thinking can be controlled if learning can be associated with fear and anxiety. American schools, for instance, through their authoritarianism, competitiveness, class, racial, and sex-role biases, have created generation after generation of people who associate learning and thinking with isolation, helplessness, and anxiety. It is no wonder that study after study indicates that people think more clearly when they start public school than when they finish it, and that learning in this society, instead of maintaining its inherent excitement, has become associated with drudgery.

4. If pain distorts thinking, then people can be effectively indoctrinated if unrelieved pain or distress can be associated with a particular experience. Information we take in when we are in a stressful situation gets "locked into our brain." It is taken in unanalyzed or sorted out, and later experiences which contradict this information seem to be ignored or distorted. The intensity of the hysteria that accompanied the teaching that "communism and socialism are evil" has made it difficult for us to argue persuasively for socialism or communism, even with the clear and concrete examples of the value and beauty of these kinds of social systems.

5. Self-respect seems closely tied to the ability to hold onto, develop, and use our inherent intelligence. Feeling worthless, inferior, and invalidated creates a general kind of pain in a person's life that becomes a pervasive deterrent to both effective action and clear thinking. We have all felt the experience of how hard it is to study when we feel depressed. The pain of the depression interferes with clear thinking in a

way different in degree but not in essence from the inter-
ference created by being hit over the head with a stick.
Stratification is at the heart of a capitalist system; this stratification results in the systematic destruction of self-respect of
the masses of people in a capitalistic society. It is this kind of
pervasive depression among our people that creates a passive
citizenry and places a severe damper on intelligence and clear
thinking.

All teachers in a capitalist society confront these contradictions and barriers to thinking and learning. For Marxist teachers, these barriers are particularly intense since Americans
have been indoctrinated to view this kind of analysis as sub-
versive and dangerous. It is hardly surprising, then, that many
people have found teaching in general, and Marxist and radical teaching in particular, a very difficult job. A certain
amount of defeatism and cynicism has been common regarding our ability to do radical teaching in this society,
especially in public schools. While such feelings are understandable, contradictions are really *not* defeats but indica-
tions of both the possibility and inevitability of change.
While capitalism makes teaching difficult, the crisis produced
by the system creates an ever increasing need for our students
to understand what is going on. On the one hand, previous
schooling has been so rigid and limiting in this society that it
creates barriers to our teaching effectiveness. On the other
hand, this means that students are all the more in need of
finding an analysis that both makes sense of the world and
points to the means of change. As Marxist teachers we can
offer an effective way of understanding the world and, quite
crucially in these often depressing times, a powerful sense of
optimism about change.

Teaching Marxism means dealing with all these contradictions and, consequently, we have to be prepared to put a
good deal of energy into dealing with problems that are normally not the concerns of teachers. This includes: (a) the
negative and debilitating associations people have with being

in school situations; (b) the feelings of invalidation and helplessness carried by our students which interfere with their ability to learn and act; and (c) the painful associations that our students have with specific topics, such as racism, sexism, and communism.

Marxist Teaching Practice

Below are brief summaries and suggestions for dealing with the difficulties that we face in this kind of teaching.

The Classroom Situation: The Class Environment. The most immediate problem that teachers face in the classroom is that many students come to class expecting the worst; they are depressed both by these expectations and by their day-to-day lives and work activities. We probably have all looked across a classroom, excited about what we are about to teach, only to realize that half the students are looking back at us with blank stares, rather mechanically taking notes, their heads and hearts somewhere else. What we need to do is to learn how to shift the attention of these students in a positive direction—not to be pollyannas, but to get these people out of their depression so they can hear what we are trying to communicate. Moreover, this is an important part of the fight against the defeatism and pessimism that is such a major barrier to the development of a revolutionary movement.

1. To break out of the doldrums of the beginning of class, have everyone (including the teacher) pair off with someone he or she does not know. Have them tell each other their names and something *new and good* that has happened to them lately. The result is a focus on something positive, a break in the isolation of students through the exchange of names and some personal, but not intimate, information.

2. Give students a chance to ventilate some of their trapped feelings about classes, readings, etc., by dividing the class into small groups in which each member gets an equal

amount of time to "speak bitterness," i.e., to talk about the difficulties they have had in the past with classes, speaking bitterly, angrily, dramatically.

3. In a small group activity similar to that above, give students an equal amount of time to say something about an author whose writing particularly irritates them, as if the author were in the class, e.g., "What would you like to say to Durkheim?" In both this exercise and the one above, it is important to emphasize that these groups are to explore feelings about school and related readings. These activities are not substitutes for critiques of the readings or for suggestions for changes in the class (something that will be discussed later).

4. Encourage students to do things that break the tension of the classroom and free their attention for the discussion: encourage laughter, and plan certain days when students bring things to entertain each other. When the atmosphere of a discussion gets too tense, have students pair off and talk about their feelings before you continue.

The Classroom Situation: Isolation in the Class. Capitalism is so concerned with teaching individualism and competition that working together is typically labeled "cheating," even though it has been clear for years that a friendly and supportive situation increases the amount of learning and thinking that can go on in a classroom. As socialists, however, we recognize the enormous political and practical importance of collective effort and feel that collective work means not only serious teamwork but, very importantly, a sense of caring among the people working together.

1. As a "requirement" for the course, ask students to learn the names of the others in the class; have each student and the teacher introduce themselves to the other people in the class.

2. As often as possible, divide the class into small discussion and work groups, providing each with a specific problem.

Encourage people to study together, write group term papers, and structure the course to encourage this kind of shared work.

3. Encourage students to ask each other for help. Illustrate how "thinking out loud" can clarify ideas.

4. Have groups of students divide the readings for reports. Each student should do all the regular reading, and also be responsible for teaching a portion to the other students.

The Classroom Situation: Competition and Inequality. Challenging the socialized competitiveness of our students and the traditional inequality of classrooms requires establishing alternative structures to traditional methods of teaching.

1. "Think-and-listen" groups: have small group discussions in which each student has an equal amount of time and is required to use it without interruption. Even comradely comments should be discouraged. This sounds overly structured, but the normal, supposedly free-flowing discussion is often dominated by a few aggressive and articulate students, usually whites rather than Third World people, and males rather than females. The think-and-listen form of discussion gives everyone a chance to think out loud. The lack of interruption allows the speaker to focus on his or her *own* thoughts and ideas. Sometimes there are complaints about this system, from both those who are afraid to talk and those who are afraid not to, but generally it works out quite well. This type of discussion can be followed up by more traditional ones, but initial structure seems to be crucial at the beginning.

2. For the same reasons, even in one-to-one exercises time should be divided equally and students should be encouraged to refrain from interrupting.

3. As teachers, we should participate as much as possible in all of the exercises. There is no point in pretending that we do not have power in the classroom. We can give our "news

and goods," however, like everyone else, participate in "speaking bitterness," and take our turn in the "think-and-listen" exercise.

4. Weber and Somers suggest a "grievance and flattery committee," made up of students through whom other students can bring their comments and criticisms anonymously to the teacher. Teachers, of course, should encourage students to come directly to them with such comments, but this system provides a way for students who are still too heavily socialized to make their complaints in person.

The Classroom Situation: Presentations. As Marxists, we do have important information to convey to the people in our classes. The problem is to find ways to do this so that people can listen critically and give us feedback to guide our work. Long lectures followed by question and answer periods are inadequate.

1. In this regard, one very useful procedure is the following schedule for a class session: some kind of "news and goods" exchange between students to start the class; a short lecture on the day's topic; one-to-one or small group think-and-listen discussions to focus questions about the lecture material; questions and answers, discussion, and then more lecture with the whole class; small-group work organized around questions assigned by the instructor; and a report to the whole class from each discussion group. While the teacher is actually presenting quantitatively less information, much more material is actually learned. The class discussions are usually much livelier, and the teacher conveys more information.

2. Have two or three students present a report summarizing the previous class. This can be oral, but preferably with written copies for everyone. This reviews the previous class discussion, gives students a chance to be "teachers," and also to see their comments in print.

Validation and Invalidation in the Classroom. As noted

earlier, destruction of self-respect and invalidation necessarily pervade a capitalist society, creating a concomitant
passive citizenry and apathetic students and teachers. Traditionally, problems of self-respect are relegated to counselors,
therapists, or encounter groups. If we are to effectively communicate revolutionary ideas and actions, however, I think
we have the responsibility to confront these problems in our
own classrooms.

1. Maximize the number of opportunities to point out the
strengths of students. This does not mean ignoring mistakes,
but rather putting a great deal of emphasis on identifying and
commenting on their strengths and successes. It means making supportive criticism, indicating our full confidence in a
student's potential for growth. This is difficult because as
academics we have been trained to do just the opposite, i.e.,
to look for failure and to criticize. We must, however, recognize that this is not China, where criticism can be very strong
without being destructive because people live in a society
which consistently validates them. In capitalist society, harsh
criticism only reinforces feelings of helplessness and pessimism. (Incidentally, this may be something to keep in mind
in movement criticism and self-criticism sessions.)

2. Encourage students to validate themselves and each
other by discussing the problem of invalidation, followed by
one-to-one sessions among the students where they describe
something they like about themselves, something they did
well, or something they did well despite their socialization,
e.g., women being strong, workers fighting against bosses;
people validating *one another* for a problem they dealt with
clearly and forcefully.

3. Halt put-downs in the class by noting how this plays into
the hands of those who want to control and manipulate.
While self-criticism is important and should be practiced, put-
downs serve to do the enemy's work, encouraging invalidation and passivity.

4. Teachers can set an example by projecting an image of self-worth. This is important but difficult since teachers, too, have grown up in this invalidating society and often resort to self-denigration in an effort to bring themselves down to the student's level.

5. Analyze and discuss the class, race, and sex-role stratification that is the basic force behind invalidation. Such discussion is crucial if students are to understand the degree to which they are manipulated by capitalism's inherent stratification processes.

6. Counter the pessimism that is part of the invalidation process by using materials that show people fighting back and emphasizing the contradictions in the capitalist system rather than its horrors; and by organizing one-to-one and small-group sessions where people discuss ways in which they have resisted the system and acted to change it.

Painful Associations with Important Topics. As noted earlier, some of our understanding of the world has come to us in such an emotionally distorted way that it is difficult to change it. Quite frequently a Marxist teacher wants to deal with just this understanding, which usually contains elements of false consciousness. To do so, students must be given opportunities to work through the associated feelings of distress and fear. The precise technique varies with the particular subject matter under discussion. When discussing sexism, for instance, I have found the following exercises useful:

1. Give students a chance to talk on a one-to-one basis or in a think-and-listen small group about the experience of oppression by sexism and the anger and hurt produced by it. This is most effective when done in mixed pairs of men and women, sharing information on an equal time, no interruption basis.

2. Create role-playing situations in which people act out their feelings of oppression and alternative ways of combatting the problem.

3. Counter the pessimism that may arise from a discussion of sexism to prevent the analysis from degenerating into guilt and defeatism by using readings and discussions of changes that have been made by radicals here and abroad and the impact of such changes; and by using one-to-one or group exercises where people share experiences of acting in nonsexist ways despite sexist barriers.

Relevance. Making the class content relevant to students obviously involves more than just including contemporary examples. It seems to me that relevancy means (a) validating people's experiences by having them relate what *we* say to their *own* experiences and provide feedback in the light of these experiences (in one-to-one and think-and-listen sessions, and in class discussion); and (b) emphasizing that correct ideas come from actual social practice. To illustrate this point, we might ask students to analyze one major change in their ideas and the sociopolitical events that underlay this change. Relevancy also means paying close attention to the class background of our students—but I do not mean adjusting the material to meet bourgeois conceptions of what different classes of people are capable of studying. We need to be concerned with more than just choosing examples that are related to the actual lives of our students; we also need to emphasize the successful struggles of people from the same class backgrounds as our students.

Using These Techniques. In trying to use these techniques, we are likely to run into resistance and cynicism. This should not be surprising considering the longstanding classroom experience as a place without humane, validating, or emotional contact. Two things are important in alleviating the discomfort of teachers and students experimenting with these new forms of teaching. First, it is crucial to explain why we are using them. I usually begin my classes with a discussion of the problem of schools and the difficulty of learning in a capitalist society, helping people make the connections between their own painful school experiences and the capitalist system, and the creation of a passive and indoctrinated workforce. I then use some of the above techniques, pointing out exactly how each one is designated to deal with these problems.

It is important to ask people to do these exercises with confidence and humor. My own embarrassment rather than a realistic assessment of what students will and will not do is the main obstacle to *my* trying new methods. I have consistently found that if I ask students to "just try" the exercises, they sometimes snicker a little but go ahead and often enjoy them.

The Classroom and the Movement: A Brief Note

The contradiction between teaching revolutionary ideas and analysis in a capitalist system that opposes genuine learning and thinking is very real, but, like all contradictions, it offers an opportunity for revolutionary change. Interestingly enough, some of these ideas for teachers may be useful for the Left in general. What I have described as problems in the classroom are also problems in our own meetings, discussions, or get-togethers. They take the form of pessimism, criticism that is mostly invalidating, self put-downs, and "open discussions" where many people are actually stifled or excluded. We shouldn't feel defeated by this problem; rather we need to find concrete ways of dealing with the contradictions within our own movement.

* * * *

In the last few years, many of us have been involved in some serious reassessment of our politics and our attempts to build a revolutionary movement. My participation in that collective struggle has raised some serious questions in my mind about the content of this article, which I wrote a number of years ago. While I think it had basic strengths, it is heavily pervaded by a petty bourgeois, opportunist analysis of the world. The article correctly calls for "paying close attention to the social context of the teaching and learning situation." In reality, the central fact of all aspects of a capitalist society, including the schools, is the way in which social production is expropriated for the benefit of the ruling class. In American society, this context is imperialism, the division of the world into oppressor and oppressed nations with a white oppressor nation in the United States dominating both internal oppressed (black or Chicano/Mexicano) and Third World nations. The schools play a key role in the maintenance of this system. In my article, however, it is not this that is discussed, evaluated and struggled with. The focus is on psychological problems, such as alienation, social roles, loss of self-respect, etc., instead of the deeper problems of which these are only symptoms. There is no discussion of such things as the tracking of poor whites, the special and critical oppression of Third World and women students, or the reenforcing of white and male privilege.

Putting "process in command" is another major problem. While the question "What good does it do to have a good idea and not know how to get it across?" is discussed, what is *not* asked is "What is the point of having good teaching techniques if you do not have the right thing to communicate in the first place?" Teaching/propaganda skills are important—and the article makes some contributions in this respect—but given the continuing history of revisionism and opportunism in the American and world communist movement, *content* and *correct line,* not the form and method of communication, are *primary.*

Finally, as Mao says that correct ideas do not fall from the sky, so neither do bad ideas and so neither does an overemphasis on process. The constant focus on teaching techniques, in my article and in my teaching, helped me avoid some sticky questions related to my class, national, and sexual privilege. Privilege, especially male and white privilege, is the very basis of imperialism. For those of us who are white and male, what does it mean to further add the privilege of the teaching role itself? How do the various forms of power we enjoy affect what we teach, what political movements (especially Third World and women's) we support on and off campus? How does all of this affect our students? Given that concrete practice in the world (mentioned only fleetingly in the article) is so central to real learning, how can we begin to put serious energy, in and out of the classroom, into the desperately needed building of a party that would create and guide communist practice? These are only a few of the questions which I think get ignored in the search for good teaching techniques.

I hope you will join me in struggling with these issues.

Notes

1. Reevaluation Counseling is a form of peer-group counseling whose basic theory has a great deal in common with a Marxist analysis. It has provided for myself and others a large number of powerful techniques for systematically dealing with the myriad of psychological barriers that we face in trying to be effective in a capitalist world.
2. Shierry M. Weber and Bernard J. Somers, "Humanistic Education at the College Level: A New Strategy and Some Techniques," unpublished ms., 1973.
3. On this see Samuel Bowles, "Unequal Education and the Reproduction of the Hierarchical Division of Labor," in *The Capitalist System*, ed. Richard Edwards et al. (Englewood Cliffs, N.J.: Prentice-Hall, 1972); and Herbert Gintis, "The New Working Class and Revolutionary Youth," *Socialist Revolution* 1, no. 3 (May–June 1970).

The Social Relations of the Classroom: A Moral and Political Perspective
···
Jean Bethke Elshtain

Much of the continuing debate over radical teaching focuses on issues of pedagogical method or "technique." Nontraditional teachers ask themselves: Is it possible to break down "artificial" and destructive relationships of dominance and submission within my classroom? Can I assist students in an effort to cast off passive modes they have internalized as a result of years of socialization into deference toward authority? Shall I attempt to reorder dynamics in my classroom in order to undo the damage done to students within hierarchically structured classes? Can I engender and sustain a sense of "community" within my classroom? These imperatives are felt by all radical teachers but most particularly by those who identify themselves as feminists; indeed, "hierarchical," so-called "traditional, male-dominant" classrooms are frequently castigated as constituent features of a repudiated male approach to teaching and learning, a mode linked to blustering and authoritarian displays of power.

In the discussion which follows I position myself against the popular trend as I mount an attack on pop-psych pedagogy and what I term the "therapeutic classroom." I shall argue that a concentration upon teaching strategy, method, and technique, however well meant, is based, first, on implicitly demeaning assumptions about students; second, on certain empiricist and mechanistic models of mind which lie within the heart of classical liberal thought; and, finally, on an instrumentalistic and therefore reductionistic understanding of the meaning of human thought and action.

The psychoeducational strategy which emerges from these interrelated assumptions is, in the long run, self-defeating for the radical teacher who sees his or her task as the articulation and defense of a critical theoretical perspective. Instead, pop-psych pedagogy encourages a solipsistic and substanceless "deep subjectivity"[1] and a strained and phony warmth which some, in moments of bland delusion, call "community." The vision of human liberation which emerges from the therapeutic classroom is not so much social or political as it is individualistic and antisocial, although it appears in the guise of the former.

I begin with the assertions of those radical teachers who have defended the deployment of a variety of strategems and techniques which are designed to reinstill in students some sense of "self" which the "system" has "invalidated" and to create, within their classrooms, a "positive atmosphere." First, the proponents of this approach see their strategy as therapy for students who are, by definition within their model, distressed, and for teachers who are likely to be.[2] The guiding presumption appears to be a vision of contemporary reality which falls just this side of the apocalyptic: if the dreadful hasn't already happened it probably will this semester. The university is depicted as a hideous place which is "not usually a fit place for anyone to be," an "ecological disaster area."[3] The hours spent within this destructive, disaster-riddled environment are pleasureful neither for them nor for anybody else. One prototypical articulation of the classroom-as-group-therapy position draws on techniques from elementary school experimental teaching methods as well as therapy. This makes sense, of course, as a particular mode of psychological theory and practice serves as one wellspring of the model. For the strategy which evolves from this theory to be effective, the teacher is urged to face certain tough "facts." The first tough fact is that "students are experiencing distress (boredom, painful feelings, numbness, general misery) much of the time"; moreover, this distress, somewhat like arsenic poisoning, is "accumulated ... and brought into each new class setting. Students are preoccupied with what is going on in their personal lives, or simply numb and deadened, worn down by a lot of bad experiences from their pasts, both in and out of schools."[4]

The portrayal of students as distressed, lost, numb, depressed, isolated, helpless, dominated by feelings of worthlessness, inferiority, anxiety, and invalidation, propelled by incompletely expressed and painful "unfinished emotional business" which makes them appear "stupid, tense, rigid, and repetitive"[5] is the depiction of a state of near-catatonia which would seem to make of these hapless and distorted half-persons fit candidates for roles in Marat-Sade rather than participants in a classroom. My analogy is not overdrawn. The classroom "strategy" which flows from this bleak portraiture of subjects who are not so much *alienated* as *anomic*[6] is a therapeutic technique designed to "change the psychological climate of the classroom to allow for personal growth, pleasure, and the learning of what is usually called content."[7] The task which has top priority is finishing all emotional business so that something called "natural" learning can occur. The teacher makes room for all the emotional business to be completed by eschewing both the "authoritarian scholar-lecturer" model in which the teacher "knows the subject matter thoroughly and sets up rules for the classroom and for evaluation based on his or her own standards" (a mode said to make students "feel stupid" and to increase their "level of pain"), together with the "let chaos reign" approach. The preferred mode is one which calls for the teacher who "radiates self-confidence and pleasure in the exercises to be done" to implement a set of stratagems.

According to two of its celebrants, this alternative classroom model involves the repudiation of an "authoritarian" insistence upon rules through the replacement of such rules with techniques. One central feature of the technique is an announcement by the teacher of the specific terms of "what will be expected."[8]

The distinction between "setting up rules" and deploying techniques coupled with "expectations" may seem precious or trivial; in fact, it is quite important as it serves to lay bare the presumptions imbedded implicitly within the two approaches. In the first model ("authoritarian scholar-lecturer") one finds an image of what is presumed to be a *coercive* classroom—although there is nothing in the description per se which precludes *persuasion* rather than coercion as the predominant pedagogical "method" within the traditional classroom. If it is possible to avoid coercion within the traditional approach, *manipulation* is unavoidable within the pop-psych model. Through a series of strategems or games the teacher helps students to get to the place he or she wants them to be—hence the emphasis on "skillful management" and "good vibes." The unstated assumption, of course, is that student preferences, were they known, would be found to mesh with those of the teacher-therapist who knows best.

Manipulation as "good vibes" and nonthreatening warmth slides all too easily into an overtly coercive model: everyone *has* to participate. Unfortunately, radical teachers who have written on the subject have failed to tackle this issue head-on. One radical instructor, for example, declares that the techniques he espouses as part of a "Marxist teaching method" are likely to run into "resistance and cynicism from the students." No matter. Such resistance can and should be ignored as its source is simply the residue of all the "bad experiences students have had in other classrooms." Despite student resistance, even "snickers and embarrassment," the pop-psych teacher-therapist forges forth undauntedly until he or she too not only *enjoys* the exercises but *insists* upon them. Why the insistence? There is no point, after all, "in pretending that we do not have *power* in the classroom."[9] To accept this weak defense of the teacher's power is to countenance the use of power as manipulation—surely a more insidious, because disguised and dishonest, exercise of power than old-fashioned, open coercion. Power which comes masked in the mandate to "feel good" cannot be confronted directly by the student. Coercion, however, can: the students are being bullied and they know who is doing it. Within a manipulatory framework students, not unlike patients in an asylum, do the "exercises" for their own good not because they necessarily see a point to them but because the teacher has the power to "insist" upon them.

What are some of the techniques utilized to create a "positive atmosphere" and to "counteract distress"? One suggestion, designed to help students establish ties with one another so that they will "feel good" is the "cocktail mix," a period during which students are asked to write conversational topics on tags which they then pin on their shirts and blouses. Tagged students wander the classroom, seek out someone with an interesting tag, and talk for ten minutes. Then it's time to make new tags in order to "facilitate" fresh conversations. A second tactic is "news and goods" which should occur at the beginning of each class period.[10] "News and goods" consists of sharing something "nice" with the class. The teacher should participate by sharing some piece of his or her personal life (a work of art, perhaps, or a song). This creates "good feelings" which further buttress classroom "community."

Advocates of the therapeutic classroom favor an intense and insistent breaking-up of the class into small groups which, in turn, break and re-form at regular intervals. A "typical" two-hour class on Hegel's *Phenomenology* (students are encouraged to refer to Hegel as "Georg"), as it is depicted in one formulation, calls for some *eight* separate class segments—most of them running five to ten minutes (including a ten minute intercession). "News and goods" leads off followed by talking to the "person next to you." A fifteen minute lecture on "basic Hegelian concepts" ensues. Following this dose of instant "Georg" students are given five to ten minutes for questions, whereupon they break into small groups for a twenty-minute "Hegel rap." These small groups, in turn, intermingle and merge with others for an additional fifteen minutes. During the final class segment each student is asked to "share" insights garnered during the two-hour flow chart. (By this time the Owl of Minerva, with battered wings, has undoubtedly gone to roost.)

The purpose of such small-group activity is, according to its aficionadoes, to counteract the prevailing presumption that intellectual work "is often accompanied by the feeling of doing lonely, isolated, hard labor."[11] Finally, the teacher-therapist counsels students on what to do with all those "bad feelings that come up while studying."[12] Yelling and screaming appear to be the preferred methods—with the proviso that one shouldn't disturb or "freak-out" others and thus increase their pain. It seems doubtful that "bad feelings . . . while studying" will arise too often, however, as neither papers nor examinations are graded and students are asked to set their own goals and to do their own evaluations. Because the teacher must turn in a grade, a *contract* system is institutionalized which enables "anyone to get an A who chooses to do the necessary *quantity* of work."[13] The stress is clearly on form or externality with little or no reference to content. The "trappings," not the "substance," of intellectual work is stressed.

The only point at which content seeps into the pop-psych strategy is contained in the imperative that the content of what is being taught must "seem" relevant *right away*; if it doesn't relate to immediate social or personal issues, we say, then it is *really useless* and we are exploiting the students by teaching it."[14] This is a position not unlike one attacked by Gramsci as implicitly reactionary when he lamented the burgeoning of vocational schools ("those designed to satisfy immediately produced interests") and the demise of the traditional, formative, or classical school. The thrust toward practicality, with its concomitant penchant for the immediately usable, was only "apparently" democratic; in fact, Gramsci concluded, "it is destined not merely to preserve social differences but to crystallize them in Chinese complexities."[15]

Those pedagogical techniques I have sketched are defended by many radical teachers as comprising *in themselves* a critique of capitalist domination and ideology. Yet these are the very methods regularly deployed in "progressive" elementary and secondary schools (hardly bastions of critical thought) in the clear recognition that the techniques alone criticize nothing! Indeed, as a "softer" approach to instruction, such techniques serve as a more deceptive and opaque and thus effective support of the prevailing order. To assess whether or not the articulation and defense of a critical consciousness is being mounted in a classroom, an evaluation of substance is necessary. Students may sit in circles, wander the classroom, rap, wear tags, share "news and goods," even hold hands and sing songs and never come close to critical theory. The task of critical theory is not and cannot be an easy, painless one. It is an effort which requires time and hard work.[16] If the teacher-therapist's over-arching goal is to help students to "feel good," not only will these students be manipulated as stimulus-response organisms governed by an overweening utilitarian calculus to maximize pleasure and to avoid pain, but coherent thinking about self and others will go by the board.

It is both bizarre and unfortunate that radical teachers, particularly those self-identified as Marxist and Marxist-feminist, whose thinking begins with a structural analysis, should fall for the lure of the therapeutic classroom. Neither students nor classrooms exist in some precious isolation abstracted from the totality within which they are lodged; neither can be severed from that reality through strategems, maneuvers, and "good vibes." Indeed, much of the explanatory force of Marx's thought lay in his insistence that no set of social relationships could repose in splendid isolation apart from the whole. The proponents of the therapeutic classroom are perpetuating the pipedream that a classroom is, or can be molded into, a community. As Jacoby puts it: "The endless talk about human relations and responses is Utopian; it assumes what is obsolete or yet to be realized: *human* relations. . . . To forget this is to indulge in the ideology of sensitivity groups that work to de-sensitize by cutting off human relationships from the social roots that have made them brutal."[17]

The pop-psych method, with its fetishization of form and its evisceration of content, conduces toward and legitimates a profoundly anti-intellectual and crude instrumentalism (pedagogy as a Hobbesian "reckoning consequences"). Indeed, the therapeutic classroom shares with capitalism a stress, not on the quality or content of the "goods" it produces, but on quantity and gross aggregates. Just as plastic models of GI-Joe and dialysis machines for persons with terminal kidney disease are all on a par as measured by the Gross National Product, student efforts in the pop-psych classroom, those who are careless and thoughtless together with those who are thoughtful and coherent, are flattened out and reduced to a single level. Capitalism ignores social goods and teacher-therapists repudiate critical judgment. This no doubt makes life simpler but it also infuses it with a monotonous, trivial, and ultimately demeaning imperative for it vitiates important distinctions. I concur with the insistence that "the only intelligence worth defending is critical, dialectical, skeptical, desimplifying."[18] That kind of intelligence does not emerge from fun and games.

It is perhaps best to begin with posing several straightforward and apparently simple hypotheticals in order to unravel further the murky mystifications of the therapeutic classroom. Assume a "traditional" teacher-scholar who gives (more or less) formal lectures with provision for discussion. The teacher stands in the front. The students sit lined up in rows. This teacher requires tests and written essays and even grades them with the criteria for what she or he considers coherent, rigorous intellectual work set forth as clearly as possible well in advance. If one were to pose the question as to whether or not the creation of critical consciousness could emerge within this traditional "form" the answer must, of course, be yes. Gramsci, for example, as a staunch defender of the classical curriculum and traditional pedagogy, maintained that leading a mass of people to think coherently and in some coherent fashion about the real present world is a "philosophic" event far more important and "original" than the discussion by some philosophical "genius" of a truth which remains the property of small groups of "intellectuals."[19] Now teaching coherent philosophy demanded sustained and focused effort, something Gramsci recognized clearly and defended consistently. The determination of the critical thrust of a course must be posed and answered with reference to content, not form.

Now assume for a moment the therapeutic teacher who is a disciple of "nonauthoritarian" teaching methods. He or she institutes the full panoply of pop-psych techniques to "facilitate" classroom interaction, trust, warmth, a sense of community and "good vibes" in order that students may, painlessly, absorb "content." He or she becomes a class participant not as a teacher, but as a "resource person" or "facilitator." If one were to consider the possibility that a simpleminded, noncritical, anti-intellectualism might emerge from all that warmth and facilitation, the answer must be that there is nothing in the technique per se to preclude this outcome. It may even be likely, for students within the therapeutic classroom, rather than confronting a difficult body of material directly, are paraded instead down the primrose path through fun and games. If the teacher were to challenge them, to make demands, to evaluate and to criticize, she would produce "pain and anxiety." Because teachers view students as helpless victims, an unhappy anomic grouping tossed about willy-nilly in their quest for painlessness, they obviously do their job best when they keep them comfortable, create surcease, and encourage learning only if it comes disguised as "fun."

I should now like to turn to the implicit philosophical and ideological presumptions, beyond or below that "bad subjectivity" Jacoby terms "not the negation of bourgeois society but its substance,"[20] which infuse the pop-psych classroom. First, the mechanistic model of the human mind adopted implicitly if not explicitly by pop-psych pedagogues (many of whom are steeped in behavioralist techniques) is part and parcel of a theory of human thought and action which is reductionistic and distorted. Human beings, within classical mechanistic psychology, are repositories of innate drives and tensions which propel them to pursue pleasure, to avoid pain, and to mistrust, if not seek actively to control, their fellows.[21] All mental dispositions follow in a simple one-to-one liaison from these physiological givens.

A mechanistic theory of mind is one of the complex dimensions of classical liberal-utilitarianism which features a hapless individual, prey to the twin forces of pleasure and pain, which are, on this view, simple unitary concepts—free-floating ideological abstractions which make no necessary reference to social relations.[22] It follows, in turn, that all moral concepts are reducible to mindless and rationally indefensible "opinion" or "feeling." Thus classical utilitarians, like Bentham, lose that human subject who is a self-reflective agent, who as the object of oppressive and exploitative social forms may be damaged, demeaned, and destroyed. Within liberal utilitarianism the fate of this human subject is inessential. What matters is that the quantity or yield of aggregate pleasure should be greater than the yield of unpleasure or pain. Utilitarianism "attaches value ultimately to states of affairs."[23]

That teachers, including radical teachers, should turn to this handy yardstick as a criterion of success or failure is further proof of the reification and objectification of human thought and praxis within an individualistic, capitalist society. Utilitarian instrumentalism, in theory and practice, constitutes such a "great simplemindedness" that it can neither criticize nor condemn manipulative practices if these practices lead toward an outwardly expressed (and "behavioristically" observable) satisfaction.[24] The theory cannot account for the fact that students may appear to be "happy" on some crude external calculus but that such "happiness" tells us little or nothing about their intrapsychic reality nor what their lives ought to be. For if one equates outward expressions of satisfaction with reality *simpliciter* the problem of false consciousness melts away. The liberal-utilitarian and behavioralist must take people at their word or make judgments based on some standard of what constitutes action in accord with happiness. The Marxist and the Freudian could take these external expressions and manifestations as indicative of false consciousness. Thus the "feel good" formulation can be and has been deployed to justify and to legitimate paternalistic and manipulative social practices and processes in schools, families, prisons, mental hospitals, and work-life.

That the advocates of pop-psych pedagogy belong, conceptually, in the same camp as liberal-utilitarians is clear. They, too, stress "immediate relevancy" and results. The "real" on this view is not the rational but the "felt." The

engineered search for warmth in the classroom, infused with
a regressive fantasy of placid, instant community, effortless
intimacy, and irresponsible ties to others, this totalizing ex-
ultation of the immediate, exemplifies a surrender in the
form of imitation of that which we do not have within any
genuinely oppressive and repressive social order, namely,
intimacy, friendship, and responsibility within a situated
human community.

Finally, why should the therapeutic classroom prove to be
a particularly seductive lure to feminists? (A discussion of
classroom "methods" and "techniques" emerged with boring
alacrity for years at nearly every conference billed "feminist.") Ironically, it is within the therapeutic classroom that
female students, as Jacoby points out in his critique of "bad
subjectivity," can simply do what presumably "comes
naturally," namely, eschew leadership and authority, revel in
the immediate, radiate an oozy warmth and good will which
is not to be confused with critical gentleness, and repudiate
all rules and leaders. The slogan "to get in touch with one's
feelings" is, as Jacoby points out, "to affirm an individual
existence already suspect. . . . That parts of the women's
movement made subjectivity programmatic, repudiating all
objective theoretical thought, indicates only the extent to
which the revolt recapitulates the oppression: women al-
legedly incapable of thought and systematic thinking but
superior in sentiments and feelings repeated this in their very
rebellion."[25] Pop-psych pedagogy legitimates further a
rejection of systematic thinking even as it encourages a celebration of the female student-as-victim, and this further
buttresses the infantization of women.[26] Enveloped within
the bosom of the therapeutic classroom the female student
can speak with the "authentic" voice of her "life experience."

There is a trap. If life experience, unmediated through a
critical conceptual medium, is given a privileged epistemologi-

cal status, and the "feelings" which attach to this experience are embraced without challenge or criticism, the analysis or conclusions which emerge will be riddled with the fatal flaws of a false, because uncritical, consciousness. If it is indeed true that women are oppressed, it follows, as Juliet Mitchell has pointed out insistently,[27] that this oppression must have psychic consequences. Women have internalized relations of dominance and submission—this is one of the potent "injuries" of class, sex, and race oppression. Thus to privilege "female experience" is to absolutize a distorted relativity, to ground oneself in the flux of repression, and to avoid the need to evaluate competing theoretical frameworks on the basis of their explanatory force—which comes closest to grasping coherently a complex totality which incorporates the human subject-object at its critical core.

The "life experiences" of students must and should be taken seriously as one dimension within the creation of radical and critical consciousness. But this experience must be mediated through conceptual categories if it is to support, to sustain, and to provide the prelude for critical theory.[28] There is no such thing as pure, unmediated receptivity: one comes to grasp the particulars of one's life within the prevailing epistemology, in this instance an ahistoric but relativistic instrumentalism that cannot recognize a dialectical logic that refuses to bifurcate reason and passion, the mental and the material, the "felt" and the "known."

The question that arises here is: if the pop-psych classroom is as mindless and potentially destructive as the critique asserts, what does that leave us? Teaching-as-usual? Without moving to create a "positive model," with all the reactionary pitfalls that implies, I shall delineate what I take to be the "critical classroom" with specific reference to teaching critical feminism. First, the feminist teacher who would defend rather than obliterate the critical mind must affirm the necessity for theory as the fundamental, irreducible grounding of any praxis of social liberation.[29] The critical feminist teacher rejects both manipulation and coercion as pedagogical modes—these are the methods of conceptual babyhood before we all grew up and became capable of forming intentions and purposes. Instead, a dialectical persuasion is pursued. Let me explain for, at first glance, the distinctions between coercion, manipulation, and persuasion may seem semantic niceties or self-justificatory labels which conjure forth division and distinction where none exists. The distinction turns on a presumption that the student is not a victim on the verge of a crack-up triggered by an adult capable of cracking through the self-contained world of bourgeois mystification. Persuasion gives "another reason to inform his choice. Neither the capacity for choice nor ability to act on that choice is impaired by persuasion."[30] Persuasion is the only pedagogical mode consistent with the articulation of radical, critical consciousness.

Because teachers of critical feminist theory often face the task of overcoming resistance to the enterprise of theory itself and opposition to any criticism of writings called "feminist," they may find themselves categorized as "traditional," "authoritarian," or "male-identified." Nevertheless, the insistence that student and teacher alike must fight all tendencies to flatten out important distinctions and to eliminate the imperatives for political and moral choice must never be allowed to succumb.[31] One of the first distinctions to draw is that between arbitrary force or power, between the capricious and careless manipulation of others, and between that authority which may devolve upon both teachers and students who work through complex bodies of material and who enter the classroom to criticize not to calm. There is, after all, nothing "radical" about distinction-erosion which makes students feel temporarily "happy" but does not assist them in the understanding and defense of a perspective critical of the prevailing order.

To those students who wish to "like" or to "agree with" every feminist analysis (because the writer's heart if not her head is in the right place, presumably), the answer can only be that there are feminists as well as nonfeminists who trade in simpleminded incoherence, the projection of destructive fantasies into political visions, who urge upon others a vague moral protest which demands as the price of a hollow solidarity the sacrifice of critical acuity. This surrender to unreason is never radical: it is now, as in the past, a seductive call to reaction whether this is its intent or not.

To move toward a critical stance, a way of looking at the world which can serve as the foundation of subsequent analysis and criticism, certain basic questions on the levels of ontology and epistemology must be posed. Such questions force students to confront their implicit and unexamined assumptions which are, almost invariably, grounded on some variant of positivism. (This holds true even for those who call themselves Marxists.) Thus we confront how it is we can grasp particulars and incorporate them within higher levels of conceptual complexity; what is the relationship between the knower and that which is known; are we implicated in or apart from knowledge? Do we absorb experience passively, as nonreactive spectators, or do we shape the material given to our sense actively?; what can we say about the nature of that "being," the human subject-object, who lies at the center of critical inquiry?

As previously held, unreflective positions are opened to scrutiny and to debate, students move in a manner not unlike that abstract and conceptual dialectic of the Platonic dialogues, from "received opinions" and conventional wisdom to a rethinking and resituating of concepts within a critical framework.[32] The gradual attainment of critical knowledge is neither a passive nor a pleasant experience. Indeed, the first step, as one moves to subject unreflective assumptions to critical scrutiny, may well be, not certainty and self-assurance, but perplexity, confusion, anxiety, and doubt. But this step cannot be bypassed nor short-circuited if the student is to break through a blur of inchoate beliefs and unorganized thought. Turmoil, self-doubt, and self-criticism are inescapable, essential components of the process.[33] Through conflict, questioning, and "trying out" ideas, the knowledge students gain will truly be their own: they will neither have absorbed it passively nor been tricked or cajoled into it. If the feminist teacher repudiates the demands of this process, she legitimates implicitly that very system which seeks to rob each and every one of us of our capacities for criticism, debate, and reconceptualization.[34]

The present "moment" is one which presents both perils and possibilities for the critical feminist teacher. The possibility is that critical consciousness will grow as the young, male and female, face the contradictions between proclaimed and experienced realities within their own lives. This can serve as the leak in the dike through which critical consciousness may finally burst into demands for social reconstruction. But the peril is there too, namely, that the student's recognition of contradiction, in the absence of a widespread and abiding commitment, even among radical teachers, to the articulation of critical consciousness, will simply lead to *ressentiment,* to feelings of impotence and rage and thus to the shortcut of donning one or more ready-made ideological "masks" as one's response to contradiction.[35] (On balance this seems the more likely, if pessimistic, outcome given the forces arrayed against critical thought and praxis.)

The adoption of "masks," to borrow Rosenthal's vivid phrase, seems to be a particularly acute peril for students who call themselves "feminists." They are confronted, on the one hand, with the ready-made "mask" of the self-sufficient, self-made male with his rights, his prerogatives, and his power. The other "apparent" alternative is the celebration of the sensitive, intuitive, spontaneous, warm, and kind woman (lesbian or straight, it doesn't matter as both may wear the "mask" of fetishized subjectivity) and the projection of a political future which will be an outgrowth of the "female principle" and within which that principle will reign supreme. If the former "face" or "mask" predominates, that of the assertive male-doer, women will simply take their places within the established system of stratification in increasing numbers. If the latter mode prevails, Jacoby's critique of "bad subjectivity" once more becomes apt for such fantasies of a femininity untouched by civilization issue "into the very prison that is the bourgeois world" as well,[36] an irrational and ultimately banal pastiche of unreflective ordinariness and precious warmheartedness.

Teachers and students in critical feminist theory are, for now, engaged first and foremost in critique—in a negation, a refusal not only to be what one has been before, but a refusal to capitulate to simplemindedness whether or not it comes with a feminist label attached. A critical consciousness which accepts the burdens of intentionality must reject all the easy dodges open to women to be "inept" and "nonabstract" and recognize them for what they are: features of the social construction of female reality. Finally, a critical feminism must insist that all the easy chatter about liberation is a vapor, a groundless metaphor, unless it forms part of a theory of human liberation, a social rather than exclusively women's liberation. For if the female individual can indeed "liberate" herself apart from changes in the social structure she will not emerge as the new woman but as a character familiar to us all: the old man.

Creating and clarifying a critical feminist theory will go forward, not within the cloying maneuvering of the therapeutic classroom, but among those teachers and students who go about what Wittgenstein called the "often downright nasty task" of thinking honestly rather than soaking up "good vibes." To me that means defending a critical feminist theory within which conceptual re-vision, transformative political praxis, and respect for the complexity and responsibility of persons form an irreducible whole which is neither identical to nor abstracted from but, rather, immanent within the situated reality which is my life and consciousness.

Notes

1. Roger Poole, *Towards Deep Subjectivity* (New York: Harper Torchbook, 1972), pp. 116, 131. Cf. Theodore Roszak, *The Making of the Counter Culture* (Garden City, N.Y.: Anchor Books, 1969), p. 97.
2. Shierry M. Weber and Bernard J. Somers, "Humanistic Education at the College Level: A New Strategy and Some Techniques," unpublished ms., 1973. Cf. Bruce Rappaport, "On Radical Teaching. Part Two: Marxist Teaching Practice," *Bulletin of the Union of Marxist Social Scientists* (April 1974), *passim*.
3. Weber and Somers, "Humanistic Education," p. 1.
4. Ibid., p. 3.
5. Ibid. Cf. Rappaport, "On Radical Teaching," p. 7.
6. Steven Lukes, "Alienation and Anomie," in William E. Connolly and Glen Gordon, *Social Structure and Political Theory* (Lexington, Mass.: D. C. Heath and Co., 1974), pp. 191–211. Lukes argues that the concepts of alienation and anomie are both constituent features of theories of human nature and social life—they are judgments made with reference to some standard. Durkheim, who was "haunted by the idea of man and society in disintegration," stressed the harmonic, the need to belong. The disharmonic leads to a state of anomie.
7. Weber and Somers, "Humanistic Education," pp. 2, 4. At this point in the article the authors deploy a little psych-ed strategy on the reader—presumably a teacher—who may be so devastated by their numbing prose describing benumbed students that she or he is likely to have fallen into a "blue funk." No need, adjure the authors, for they know she or he has "tried" to do the best to be interesting, relevant, and encouraging. A little balm (called positive reinforcement) for the perturbed spirit! Cf. Rappaport, "On Radical Teaching," p. 7.

8. Weber and Somers, "Humanistic Education," pp. 6-7.

9. Rappaport, "On Radical Teaching," p. 8. Emphasis mine. On the distinctions between coercion, manipulation and persuasion see William E. Connolly, *The Terms of Political Discourse* (Lexington, Mass.: D. C. Heath and Co., 1974), chapter 3, "Power and Responsibility," pp. 85-138. In a manipulative as opposed to a coercive situation it is "harder to grasp the role played by the manipulator" (p. 98). Coercion is morally preferable to manipulation. Although there is a moral presumption against *both* coercion and manipulation, in the case of coercion the coerced individual knows who to hold responsible.

10. What happens to "news and goods," say, on the day that the morning newspapers headline Kissinger's expressed desire to use B-52 bombers against Cambodia in retaliation for the seizure of the Mayaguez? Should "news and goods" be quashed by "bad things" that happen outside the classroom? To focus on these "bad things" would most certainly create some pain and distress.

11. Weber and Somers, "Humanistic Education," p. 15. The lonely, isolated hard labor of Marx at work on *Das Kapital* or Freud during his period of painful self-analysis which formed the basis of *Die Traumdeutung* perhaps? It is difficult to imagine Marx coming in with "news and goods" as a way to break the ice before he began to explore the social relations of capitalist oppression and exploitation. Both Marx and Freud saw their tasks, difficult and painful ones, as the creation of ways of looking at the world which were at odds with the dominant reality. The stress on "no pain" is reminiscent of B. F. Skinner's goal of a behavioralist-technologistic Utopia —the creation of a world of "automatic goodness" in which no one knows frustration nor pain. See B. F. Skinner, *Beyond Freedom and Dignity* (New York: Alfred Knopf, 1971), p. 66.

12. Ibid., p. 16.

13. Ibid., p. 18.

14. Weber and Somers, "Humanistic Education," p. 4. Cf. James Glass, "Epicurus and the Modern Culture of Withdrawal: The Therapy of Survival," *American Politics Quarterly* 2, no. 3 (July 1974), pp. 313-40. For the Epicurean, philosophy served a direct therapeutic purpose. "There is no profit in philosophy . . . if it does not expel the suffering of the mind" (p. 320).

15. Antonio Gramsci, *Selections from the Prison Notebooks*, ed. and trans. Quintin Hoare and Geoffrey Nowell-Smith (New York: International Publishers, 1971), p. 40. Glass, in the piece cited

above, writes: "The culture of withdrawal places great importance on reconstructing interpersonal communication . . . These concerns give to it a close affinity with psycho-therapeutic assumptions found in the humanist or 'third force' school of social psychology . . . hardly the creators of Marxian structures of perception. The emphasis lies on interpersonal transactions, on seeing the radical question as one of the discovery of 'self' in a situation unattached to conventional processes of socialization. To be with others in these arguments, is to be a 'person,' to find an 'authentic encounter,' to know a 'peak-experience,' has absolutely nothing to do with resisting unjust political regimes or organizing political struggle" (p. 319).

16. See Russell Jacoby, *Social Amnesia* (Boston: Beacon Press, 1975), particularly the chapters on "Revisionism: The Repression of a Theory" and "The Politics of Subjectivity." Cf. Glass, "Epicurus and the Modern Culture of Withdrawal," who notes that for Marx "the revolutionary task entailed the commitment to a radical social consciousness; it is in the space of 'species-being,' prepared by praxis, that radical self-awareness becomes possible" (p. 315). Marx's remarks on "instant revolution" are directly applicable to the quest for "instant community": "Easy come, easy go." From Karl Marx and Frederick Engels, *Basic Writings on Politics and Philosophy*, ed. Lewis S. Feuer (Garden City, N.Y.: Doubleday, 1959), "Excerpts from *The Eighteenth Brumaire of Louis Bonaparte*," pp. 318-48.
17. Jacoby, *Social Amnesia*, p. 105.
18. Susan Sontag, "Notes on Art, Sex, and Politics," *The New York Times*, February 8, 1976, Section D, p. 36.
19. Gramsci, *Prison Notebooks*, p. 325.
20. Jacoby, *Social Amnesia*, p. 103.
21. James M. Glass, "Schizophrenia and Perception: A Critique of the Liberal Theory of Externality," *Inquiry* 15 (1972), pp. 114-45. Pop-psych pedagogy's view of students is not unlike the Hobbesian characterization of the state of nature. In the words of Glass, Hobbes' state of nature depicts "a condition of disorganization and dissociation, anxiety imparts to life its reality, fear creates a perverse interpersonal nexus, and men dwell within a 'nasty' and 'brutish' existence."
22. The view critiqued above is not shared by Freud, although certain terms ("pleasure," "unpleasure") also figure within psychoanalytic theory. Freud's dialectical theory of mind, including the relation-

ship between reason and passion, the "inner" and the "outer," is directly at odds with the presumptions of utilitarianism.

23. J. J. C. Smart and Bernard Williams, *Utilitarianism For and Against* (Cambridge: Cambridge University Press, 1973). See especially Williams, "A critique of utilitarianism," which appears on pp. 77-150, and from which the above quote is drawn (p. 95).

24. Williams, "Utilitarianism," p. 149. Utilitarian simple-mindedness, according to Williams, "consists in having too few thoughts and feelings to match the world as it really is." Cf. Williams' interview with Bryan Magee in *Modern British Philosophy*, ed. Bryan Magee (New York: St. Martin's Press, 1971), pp. 150-65, in which he argues that the predominant notions of utilitarianism are currently "in a state of great conceptual confusion . . . people have the feeling that something shallow is being passed off as something deeper . . ." (p. 160).

25. Jacoby, *Social Amnesia*, p. 106.

26. This not only leads to political utopianism tied to a simple reversal of roles within a male-dominant order, but it negates moral agency or responsibility which demands that one not merely "behave" unthinkingly but be able to give reasons of a certain kind to explain and to interpret one's actions. If one abandons this distinction, the difference between people and machines is obliterated and one is left with a bland and mindless venting of spleen. Cf. Stuart Hampshire, *Thought and Action* (New York: Viking Press, 1959), p. 185. The self-reflexivity of which I speak is also the goal of Freudian therapy.

27. See her *Psychoanalysis and Feminism* (New York: Pantheon Books, 1974) and a shorter and more accessible essay "On Freud and the Distinction Between the Sexes" in *Women and Analysis*, ed. Jean Strouse (New York: Grossman Publishers, 1974), pp. 27-56.

28. It is often, quite disastrously, the case that oppressed groups have been seduced into believing that because they have been (or are) relatively powerless, they have somehow remained pure and untainted by the social order. Two essays which debunk this notion are Jean Bethke Elshtain, "Moral Woman and Immoral Man: The Public-Private Split and Its Political Ramifications," *Politics and Society* 4, no. 4 (1974), pp. 453-74, and Abigail L. Rosenthal, "Feminism Without Contradictions," *Monist* 57, no. 1 (January 1973), pp. 28-42.

29. See Jacoby, *Social Amnesia*, on the repression of theory and the

articulation of negative psychoanalysis and Marxism. I am not here advocating a collapse of theory and praxis such that praxis is to be viewed as some simple outgrowth of theory. I am insisting that without a critical theory one is incapable of deciphering bad praxis bound to the alternatives of present reality from that which seeks to break the boundaries of the present.

30. Connolly, *Terms of Political Discourse*, p. 94.
31. Cf. the Susan Sontag–Adrienne Rich exchange, "Feminism and Fascism: An Exchange," *New York Review of Books*, March 20, 1975, pp. 31–32, in which Sontag dissociates herself from "that wing of feminism that promotes the rancid and dangerous antithesis between mind ('intellectual exercise') and emotion ('felt reality')." This "banal disparagement of the normative virtues of the intellect," she notes, is "one of the roots of fascism . . ." (p. 32). It is also a central dimension of that bland optimism Freud so heartily despised as characteristic of Western civilization.
32. See G. W. F. Hegel, *The Phenomenology of Mind*, trans. J. B. Baillie (New York: Harper Torchbook, 1967), especially Section A on "Consciousness," pp. 147–214. Cf. Charles Taylor, *Hegel* (Cambridge: Cambridge University Press, 1975), the discussion of the *Phenomenology* in Part II, particularly the chapters on "The Dialectic of Consciousness" and "Self-consciousness."
33. See a fascinating two-part article by Bennett Simon, "Models of Mind and Mental Illness in Ancient Greece, II: The Platonic Model," Parts I and II, *Journal of the History of the Behavioral Sciences* 8, no. 4 (October 1972), pp. 398–404, and 9, no. 1 (January 1973), pp. 3–17.
34. The student who completes a course in critical feminist theory should understand and be able to criticize and to defend various feminist positions from the inside out. Because no easy recourse to "the facts" can ever prove or disprove a social theory, she or he must articulate the connections between assumptions, conceptual categories, appropriate "tests" of the theory as well as its normative implications. Facts move within theories and may be assimilated within a number of competing explanatory frameworks. For a lucid articulation of these connections see William E. Connolly, "Toward Theoretical Self-Consciousness," *Polity* 6, no. 1 (Fall 1973), pp. 5–35. Gramsci, too, insisted upon the centrality of language as the medium through which conceptions of "the world and of culture" are conveyed. Those with limited facility with language, including a dialect "which is fossilized and anachronistic

in relation to the major currents of thought which dominate world history," will possess a limited and provincial grasp of the totality of the world. See Gramsci, *Prison Notebooks*, p. 325.

35. Rosenthal, "Feminism Without Contradictions," *passim*. That Rosenthal refuses to exempt a particular type of narrow Marxism which wipes out or consigns to the wings the conscious human subject is important for the "mask" of a particular type of Marxism, as it is the "mask" of revolt, is often the most difficult to critique and to repudiate.

36. Jacoby, *Social Amnesia*, p. 117.

Beyond Student-Centered Teaching
....
Brent Harold

> Freedom is the consciousness of
> necessity.
>
> —Engels

During these last few years, in which capitalist America's barbarism has become clear to so many of its citizens, many teachers of literature have tried to make their courses into forces for social and political change. Some of us have transformed the content of traditional courses, both by assigning literature we consider progressive in point of view (Marxist, Third World, and women novelists, etc.), and by conducting discussions on the social class basis of standard works of our culture. But we have wanted to change the form of our courses as well, and many of us have embraced, as the natural pedagogical form of our progressive politics, some variety of what has come to be known as student-centered teaching.

Student-centered teaching means, usually, deemphasis on grades, exams, and lectures—traditional teacher-imposed phenomena—and emphasis on the freedom and independence of students. This new emphasis has appealed to many of us with developing political consciousness because it implies a breakup of entrenched academic forms, a mistrust of the received word, and—most important—a sensitivity to and advocacy of the needs of "the people," our "students as niggers" (to quote the title of an influential pamphlet). Most of us have found such student-centered manuals as Neil Postman and Charles Weingartner's *Teaching as a Sub-*

versive Activity helpful in working to overcome our own classroom highhandedness.

From what I can tell, however, student-centered education reform has not had spectacular results, for the politically conscious or anybody else. Certainly the flexible New Curriculum at Brown University, where I teach, is not living up to expectations.[1] The emphasis on freedom and independence, while it theoretically makes possible all things, in fact seems to encourage unhealthy introspection and aimlessness. The "identity problem" lays waste to more students than ever, and the campus doctors report that the ritual stimulants of Consciousness III are rapidly giving way to the consciousness killer, good old booze. Like the comfortable university bar, the sympathetic university headshrinkers are finding more work than ever, while campus reality is driving sophomores and juniors in significant numbers to drop out and rummage for "real reality" out in the world somewhere.

It is undoubtedly tempting to blame this state of affairs solely on conservative administrators and faculty who have failed to bring hiring and firing policies into line with the professed student-centered standards of the New Curriculum. (It's still professional and self-centered writing and publishing, and not teaching, that pays off at tenure time.) It has been particularly tempting for those of us with some political development to blame the failure of our educational innovations on the failure of our whole economic, social, and political system. We can't expect meaningful education, the argument runs, within an essentially inhumane and corrupt society (Ivan Illich would have us give up formal education altogether, a rather unhelpful bit of wishful thinking). Neither of these explanations is mere buck-passing; both contain considerable truth. Nevertheless, they tend to turn our attention from our own part in the failure. My own several years of experimentation in the student-centered mode have convinced me that the problem lies at least in part with our student-centered theory itself. Emphasis on the freedom and independence of the student, no matter how attractive an alternative this may seem to the drab educational authoritarianism we have had, simply cannot be counted on to create a consistently humane or valuable situation in the classroom, much less impart a politically progressive perspective.

The trouble is that student-centered teaching, while it eliminates authoritarian structures, leaves intact—and in some forms may even intensify—the dullest aspect of the traditional course, and the basis of its training in status quo values and attitudes: namely, its idealism. By idealism I mean the tendency to experience ideas as abstracted from the concrete, social experiences of the people holding them, as well as to abstract the people themselves from their actual classroom and other social situations.

To be as concrete as possible, I will give some examples of idealist procedures, habits, and assumptions. Some are more common in the traditional classroom, some are found only in the "reformed" classroom; many are common to both. Taken together, they constitute the still unreformed pedagogy of the present.

The Abstract Participants: Everyteacher and Everystudent. It is a rare discussion of literature that does not depend heavily on the universal "we" (meaning we human beings), on the "human condition," the "plight of modern man," "absurd man," and other convenient abstractions which obscure from their users the specific social basis of their own thought—both the privileged portion of the human spectrum occupied by the class as a whole (at least at a place like Brown) and the significant variations within the relatively homogeneous group.

As teachers and students we are trained to experience ourselves as the abstractions Everyteacher and Everystudent, our social reality (as husband or wife, citizen, son or daughter of rich man or not-so-rich man) muffled from each other, our ideas disembodied.

Education Without Advocacy. According to the charters they wrote, the founders of most established colleges and universities were emphatically not interested in the development of youthful intellect in the abstract, but in development of specific abilities and beliefs which would guarantee the continuity of the society of which the founders themselves were privileged participants. Now, however, more conservative teachers, subscribing to the sacred concepts of academic neutrality and professional purism, see education as a value-free transfer of information. And reformed teachers are encouraged by the student-centered literature to think of themselves as professional catalysts. (The Maxwell-Magaziner report, the student analysis of education at Brown University on which the New Curriculum was based, wants to see the teacher in the neutral-sounding business of "developing of intellect in the students and encouraging of their independence." Postman and Weingartner, and Carl Rogers in *On Becoming a Person*, relegate the teacher to the role of facilitator or "resource person.")

Both conservative and reformed conceptions of teachers are reductive and create a false dichotomy between education and advocacy. They hide the reality that no adult is interested in growth for its own sake, but rather in growth that, according to a value system derived from specific social circumstances, will make a positive contribution. They do a disservice in discouraging teachers from taking full responsibility for the effects of their advocacy.

Accumulation vs. Awareness. Every student is systematically trained to accumulate a repertoire of stances rather than to become aware of his or her own developing—but already well-formed—social and intellectual identity. Value judgments are crude, he or she is likely to feel (echoing academically neutral teachers), because all positions, intellectual and otherwise, when viewed sympathetically, are equally valid. (Thus the tendency of students to identify with the "weatherless" protagonists of the novels of John Barth.) This protean intellectual behavior, besides providing a workout for the mind, may serve the positive function of creating sympathy for the views of others. But it also has the effect of discouraging a student's responsibility for the part he or she actually plays in the world, in the class. Instead of substantial human beings, students become elusive shadows.

Abstract Subject Matter: Tyranny of Great Works. The books on the reading list are accorded a special existence as "great works," not to be related to as we relate to other human behavior or products but to be "taken on their own terms." Their structures are to be understood and appreciated (some more than others, of course; we are not indiscriminate). But their influence on us, for better or worse, the whole fascinating dynamic by which they help to create us and, through us and others, the world—this is usually not a part of literary criticism. The implications seem to be: (1) because the books that end up on the reading lists are usually of a high order of intelligence or talent, they must be good for us; (2) therefore, a student who does not appreciate a great work needs more education; (3) yet a work can be great and necessary without being influential or accountable.

Paper-Writing as an Abstract Exercise. The phenomenon of paper-writing in general enforces abstraction of the writer both from his or her experience of life and from the actual classroom situation. It is, of course, always and only his or her own personal relationship (both intellectual and emotional) with the literature that the student can communicate in a paper. But the implicit rules of the game, in discouraging reference to personal experience and the use of the first-person pronoun, discourage the student from making any thorough examination of his or her relationship to the literature. These rules encourage a prose of pseudo-objectivity, a persona of pure critical intelligence.

And instead of writing to all participants out of a desire to affect the course of things, the student writes as an exercise to the teacher, who is not an audience at all in the normal sense, but a kind of cosmic auditor. Abstracted thus from the conditions which usually impel and energize writing (involvement in a human situation which one sees as needing a corrective; a sense of an audience of peers), student writing is, not surprisingly, often stilted, limp, or dry—painful to write and to read.

The Class as Pseudo-Collective. Although teachers and students have all had the good experience of working with others toward a clear, common goal, most classes in literature do not provide such an experience. A student will not complain when other students cut class, fail to participate in discussions, or to hand in papers on time. Even in small classes there is likely to be little of the sense of mutual dependence and the other strong feelings (disappointment, pride, warmth, and so on) that usually result when people work together on something they care about.

Students are likely to see the class as something happening to them. They are not encouraged by the format or by previous training to take the responsibility for their part in creating what happens, although this is probably second nature to them in their other social activities. (Even the vaguely student-centered course evaluation questionnaires used to get feedback on teaching encourage students to think of the class as something outside of themselves. They can rate it a failure without feeling implicated.)

Divorce of Means from Ends. The concerned teacher, assuming all the responsibility for what goes on (he or she, of course, is getting paid for this), may try any or all of the following maneuvers to make the class work: (1) liberating the class from an ugly room in the bowels of the institution by moving it to a lounge or completely off campus; (2) escaping the taint of "business hours" by holding class in the evening; (3) relaxing the class by quasi-encounter group techniques; (4) breaking down into small groups; (5) "getting everyone involved" by substituting playreading for discussion; (6) spicing dull discussions of books with lively talk about current events; (7) catering to students' "creativity" by allowing them to submit stories or poems in place of papers. All these attempts to generate enthusiasm will fail to have any long-lasting effect because none of them creates any feeling of genuine purpose. In fact, such abstraction of feelings and atmosphere from goals, of means from ends, would seem to have the opposite effect of dramatizing the fact that nothing important is really happening. (Would we need to think so much about the trappings if the central activity were really important? If we had come together determined to build a house, would such incidentals as a cloudy day or lack of background music prevent us from hammering and sawing?)

In the pseudo-collective, not surprisingly, both sensitive teacher and sensitive student may well have—or repress—the uneasy feeling that they are participating in a mutual con-game.

This description of prevailing classroom behavior implies a rather specific prescription. Whether the instructor is interested merely in a more lively class or in a class which will encourage political awareness, whether he or she is "innovative," "progressive," "radical," or "Marxist," the antidote to stultifying idealism in the classroom is its opposite—dialectical materialism. By this I mean a method which systematically emphasizes and explores the complex interaction, interpenetration, and mutual creation of culture and society, of artwork and audience, of the social experiences of the teacher and those of the students, of students of differing economic and social origins.

Having rejected as outmoded much traditional academic discipline, we, as progressive teachers, need more than just freedom from such discipline. We need a new and useful discipline. In the age of encounter groups and the sexual revolution we don't need freer, more emotional relationships in the classroom, but we do need a compelling reason for relating in the classroom. We certainly do not need courses which "teach" by discouraging students' consciousness of the political implications of their own experiences. We do need the kind of education which has been effective for increasing numbers of people over the past few years (almost always, of course, outside established institutions): the education which has come to be known as consciousness-raising, in which one becomes aware both of the source of one's own alienation and dehumanization, of one's own contribution to the oppression of others, and of what can be done about it.

Progressive teachers in particular should realize what I hope I have sufficiently emphasized above: that the prevailing literature course is not just idealist in content, but in its procedures enforces on students an experience of, *an apprenticeship in*, idealism. It is not enough, then, for us to change the content of courses, to talk a politically conscious literary criticism. We must provide, within the limits of the classroom and our own miseducation, a *counter-apprenticeship.* As such, radicalism in the classroom ought to come not just as the laying on of yet another "ism," one more dry item in the marketplace of ideas, but as a refreshing new form.

There may be many effective versions of such a methodology. I suggest the following elements, which have been evolving in my fiction courses during the past year, as fundamentals (at least in my specific situation).

Purpose. The purpose of this course is, loosely speaking, the purpose of any course: to help ourselves to live in the world more effectively by improving our understanding of it. The specific part of the world on which we concentrate is literature. Our purpose, more strictly, is analysis of the part played by works of literature in our own lives, here and now, and in the lives of other people.

We start with the assumption that a work of literature always proposes, both in its form and its content, a model— usually implicit and usually highly seductive—of successful (that is, good, or valuable, or durable, depending on the terms of the work) human behavior. Our job is to describe as accurately as we can what the model is, how it works, and to assess its influence.

We do not have to make a friendly classroom atmosphere into a class goal. We will, if we pursue this intellectual work sincerely and energetically, come to know, respect, and like our coworkers.

General Method of Literary Criticism. Class study of any work breaks down into the following tasks:

1. A description of the model of the world and of the model of behavior proposed in the fiction, both by depiction of characters acting in various ways with varying degrees of success or attractiveness, and by the style itself (which can be helpfully thought of as the behavior of the writer in the work—the behavior of his or hers most directly accessible to us).

2. An analysis of the relationship between the author's social background and the literature into which he or she puts his or her energies.

3. An analysis of the relationship between the reader and the literature. The relationship, that is, between the individual's experience of the world, his or her implicit or explicit model of acting in the world, and the literary model.

4. A critique of the work based on items 1, 2, and 3—not just the strengths and weaknesses of a given work in its own terms, but the ways in which it strengthens and/or weakens us. The relative acceptability of the fictional model.

One effect of this program of work is to heal the split

found in the idealist classroom between the intellectual and the personal. It requires, first of all, accurate, intelligent description and analysis of the style and content of the work. (This is more, it should be pointed out, than has been managed by most published literary criticism—including Marxist criticism, which has been notably unresponsive or crudely responsive to the nuances of literary style.) It requires, too, a willingness and ability to assess the data of one's own life, to discover the structure of one's own experience and the relative importance of various influences (among which literature, of course, is just one). This is obviously an ambitious task. Literary "professionals" would no doubt scoff. But I doubt that anything less complete can serve as a meaningful purpose for a literature class.

When we do perform these operations, both in class discussion and in papers, there are certain general results. Once students are encouraged not merely to come to appreciate what is good about a novel but also to criticize it for what it does not say, perspectives it does not have (and the relationship of these omissions to what it does say), they are surprised to find what is missing. For instance, most students begin to become suspicious of Hemingway's *The Sun Also Rises* when they reflect that its model of correct behavior—the easily identifiable "code" that has so often been written about—is based on a model of humans in a world that omits almost all the elements on which the students themselves—and most other people—base their lives. These omissions include family relations, any male-female relationship that lasts more than a few days or ends in anything but disaster or ignominy for the man, any committed involvement in the social or political affairs of town or city or nation, or any permanent work done with or for others. (Jake's work is important to him, but the emphasis is on the discipline which he needs to give some structure to his otherwise free-floating existence, not on any social function it might serve, any significant connection it gives him to the world of people.) Its style (literary, sporting), which strikes most students as a neurotic defense against the risks of involvement, especially social involvement, also becomes an element in the class discussion.

In examining William Faulkner's *The Bear*, to take another example, students find a model which is likely to seem to them much more nearly complete and satisfying than that provided by the eviscerated characters and style of Hemingway. Still, we find a remarkable omission in Faulkner's dislike of people who actively try to change any social institution. Many students find that their own lives would be much more dismal if they did not have at least some hope of doing more than enduring the status quo, albeit with the style and soulful patience of a Faulkner black or woman. We get involved in discussing the connection between a certain abstract, strident, dry language—very unattractive in the context of typically lyrical, rhythmical, highly metaphorical Faulknerian language—and characters who have a vision of social change. The Faulkner model, while strengthening us in certain ways of being and working in the world, would seem to weaken us in its failure to suggest how individuals, by seeking to struggle against their own misery, participate in history.

John Barth's *The Sot-Weed Factor* asks the reader to accept as given a world in which the laws and experience of human relationships as most students know them in their everyday lives, and the meaning of history and change as many students are coming to understand them, arc made into a totally elusive, slippery, mystifying matter. Students have the choice of either allowing Barth's charm to seduce them into even greater confusion than they already experience, or seeing that there is, in fact, much more substantial and understandable reality in their social relations, even in the midst of their identity crises, than Barth's fiction suggests. We understand that any final judgment of Barth's value to middle-class America at present must see his immensely talented style and inspirational energy in the context of the bleak depiction of the human lot in the world—a lot which Barth himself seems actually to experience—to which the style and the energy are a rather desperate response.

But it would be presumptuous of me to speak any further for dozens of students about what "they" or even "we" have learned by following this method of analysis. My impression is that perhaps the most important consciousness-raising occurs before any analysis is attempted, in the mere statement and discussion of the purpose of the course. To students who have always been taught that a work of literature floats above our heads, an untouchable entity in the ethereal realm of art, it comes as a sometimes refreshing, sometimes upsetting, usually startling revelation that we can sit down in a classroom with a book and treat it like any other human product, that we can resent as well as admire it, enjoy and yet perhaps suspect it, and so on.

Whether a student initially accepts or rejects the notion that there is a politics of literature, to perform the operations listed above is to experience and to begin to understand such a politics. The only way a student can avoid this experience and understanding is to refuse to pursue the purpose of the course (and some students do this).

Organizational Meeting. The instructor calls a meeting well in advance of the official beginning of the course at which he or she explains, much more clearly than the course bulletin can: (1) the purpose and method of the course; (2) how and why it departs from what the students are probably expecting; (3) his or her own purpose in giving the course. The students, treated at this point as *prospective participants*, are charged with the responsibility of actively choosing, or rechoosing, if they have already registered, or unchoosing the course. (If it is not possible to have a meeting before the start

of the semester, the first listed meeting should be treated not
as part of the course but as prior to it.)

The emphasis of the meeting is neither on the instructor's
requirements nor on the students' independence and freedom, but rather on mutual expectations and responsibilities.
The course is teacher-structured in the sense that the instructor establishes the method; but the method becomes the
students' as well when they choose to make use of it. The instructor should expect there to be no griping halfway
through that the "course is not what *I* wanted"; only, perhaps, that "we are not doing what we said we wanted do to,"
along with suggestions for such and such a change.

Good discussions of the phenomenon of ideology can start
in the organizational meeting when a student complains of
having a method or point of view imposed, implying that this
does not happen in other courses. Or a student may ask: "If
this course method is consistent with your own social experience and political consciousness at this point, how is it logical
for us, who may have different experience and consciousness
now, to use it?" This can lead into a valuable discussion of a
teacher's dialectical relationship to his or her students. A
middle-class teacher can of course assume considerable
overlap between his or her experience of the world and that
of middle-class students; if there is potential for political
awareness in the contradictions of the former, so, too, with
the latter. A dialectical materialist method may, paradoxically, make a student aware of elements of his or her experience—the source of material comfort, status strength, and so
on—which have led to a suspicion of a Marxist view of
literature. And yet the same student may wonder what in his
or her experience makes the method an attractive alternative
to the traditional course.

Since we are not used to experiencing a class as a purposeful collective, it is a good idea to introduce analogies to
collectives with which students may have had experience—a

women's group, a camping trip, asking, for instance, "Is there any reason we should not feel as purposeful and mutually dependent in here as we would if we had come together to build a house?" It is good for the class to have such a clear example of collective purposefulness to check against when it feels itself beginning to drown in the unreality of classroom rhetoric.

The Instructor's Position. During the first two or three weeks, while students are becoming oriented to new concepts and procedures, and to help with the orientation, I take time to elaborate on the position I have already taken in the organizational meeting. Having announced myself as a variety of Marxist critic, I give a short course on Marxism and its relation to art—perhaps to one of the novels on the reading list. Using Marx's *Economic and Philosophical Manuscripts*, Engels' *Socialism: Utopian and Scientific*, and Plekhanov's *The Role of the Individual in History*, I discuss, in their interrelatedness, the definitive human act of work, alienated work, art as work, the material basis of thought, and the dialectic, the connection between freedom and necessity. In analytical (rather than confessional) form I suggest the connections between all of these and my own relationship to capitalism. This amounts to my version of the Fundamental Essay which the students will be writing (see discussion below).

To raise consciousness about the struggle of ideas—to exorcise the persistent ghost of Everyteacher—I go about this in a manner as emphatically unsocratic and unlike a Carl Rogers resource person or facilitator as possible. It is not enough just to advocate a position; one must emphasize that this is a position *I* am taking, since students trained in the "end of ideology" may have trouble recognizing a position as such. One must point out that one's views are not assumed merely for the sake of argument, but have an organic consistency with the whole of one's social existence; they are not the "truth," but truly (as one sees it now) representative of a life in struggle in the world.

The Fundamental Essay. Even though written assignments have become even less meaningful than classroom discussion, writing is important. For one thing, it is a fact of our situation that the existing dialogue about literature which partially explains how our culture and society are what they are is written as well as spoken. Any group or individual wishing to take part in and influence that dialogue must be able to write. Our task is to restore vitality to classroom writing by having it make sense in terms of the human situation of the course.

Having students choose one of several designated topics to write on encourages a fragmented as well as a pseudo-objective approach; leaving them free to write whatever they please (or not write at all) encourages them to experience themselves as free-floating individuals and noncontributors. Therefore, there is only one Fundamental Essay in this course: the disciplined attempt to account for one's literary taste by analyzing the relationship between one's own experience and background (economic, political, and so on) and the model of the world proposed in some literature. The student writes the Fundamental Essay not to the teacher alone, in a private relationship, but to all of the people concerned—all of the members of the class—in the form of an open letter. An effective Fundamental Essay will not only provide an analysis that will contribute to the collective task of consciousness-raising; it will communicate at the same time a sense of the author's responsibility (as well as natural inclination) to recommend to others what his or her own experience has taught him or her to be valid. It will, in fact, communicate the author's awareness of the whole situation in which he or she writes; of the purpose of the course, of his or her part in the proceedings, of comments made and positions taken by others.

The week's class time is divided equally between direct discussion of the books on the reading list and discussion of Fundamental Essays. It is the student's responsibility to make his or her essay a manageable length and to distribute copies for reading outside of class. It is part of class discipline and responsibility to respond to the essays honestly and discuss them thoroughly, touching on both style and content.

Collectives. Both the teacher's declaration of position and the Fundamental Essay should encourage students to begin to see learning not so much as a search for eternal varieties or the "key" to the novel, or as exposure to a variety of interesting critical views, as a coming to awareness of the consistency of one's responses to fiction with the "necessity" of one's social experience. This awareness should include both a sense of what one shares and does not share with others in the class.

I try whenever possible to puncture the popular, contradictory notions of individualism (uniqueness, solipsism) and Everystudent (universal identification) and get the class to face up to its middle- to upper-middle-class American homogeneity. A discussion of economic background (although one must exercise caution in encouraging individual students to talk candidly about this sacred subject) moves toward a useful definition of the collective-of-the-whole and an understanding of the need for such a comparatively privileged group to become aware of itself as a collective and to undertake the present project. (The definition of the collective should, of course, recognize and incorporate significant differences in background.)

As the collective-of-the-whole discusses books and student essays, individuals should slowly become aware of having natural allies and enemies in the dialogue—those with whom they tend to agree or disagree, with whose experiences they tend to sympathize or not to sympathize. (For instance, these days the women in the course tend to agree about a lot of things.) The second major writing assignment is a position paper or papers written by these smaller collectives of like-minded people. Meeting outside of class, these collectives work at articulating their views and at making their presence felt in class by writing anything from a one-paragraph proclamation to a long, intricate analysis.

Individuals who do not feel aligned with others serve the class by investigating either individually or in small groups matters pertinent to the class purpose. For instance, some students devised a questionnaire to find out how college graduates of ten years ago felt they were influenced by the fiction they read in college (Does the respondent now regard a given novel's picture of life as valid, mistaken, hurtful, insignificant? What experiences—job, marriage, national events, etc.—have caused him or her to admire a given novel more, or less?) Another group investigated the relationship in the experience of working-class people between what we call serious fiction and TV and other mass media. Another kept the class aware of significant biographical data of authors and suggested relationships between that data and the literature. Another read Cuban and Chinese literature and compared it with works of capitalist culture.

The important thing to remember about collectives is not to fake them. Do not have them just for the exercise in working together, but because the topics they investigate are important and require the energy, time, and judgment of more than one person, and because there are natural factions within the class which, in order to do justice to themselves, should write position papers.

Publishing. Since every class publishes its findings in the sense that class members go into other classes and other activities as carriers, for better or worse, of whatever has been picked up, conscious, responsible publishing in one form or another should be a class goal. The class (or individuals or collectives within the class) should try to get a written version of its findings published in a campus publication or at least reach other students and teachers by leafletting and stuffing mailboxes.

We should not be cynical about the value of encouraging students to publish in this fashion. Youthful writing, especially about controversial campus matters, has been influential in recent years (see, for instance, James Kunen's *The Strawberry Statement*), even though much of it has seemed self-indulgent, self-serving, and exploitative of its subject. The results of disciplined investigation and articulation of experiences to which only college-age people have access *should* be worth reading.

Most students appreciate the need for the disenfranchised, such as blacks, Chicanos, and women, to organize and make themselves heard as collectives. But many students, I have found, have difficulty understanding the logic of this activity for themselves, perhaps because, quite correctly, they instinctively feel favorably related to a ruling class which already speaks well for itself. Still, it is true that many of the deep contradictions of middle-class society are felt most strongly by students, and that expression of these contradictions—student outrage against the Vietnam war and other misdeeds committed by the very system from which they derive their economic security—turns out to be very much a *minority* expression. Since it is the nature of most jobs to force employees to assume the voice of the employer, it is important for students to grab every opportunity while still in college—even that presented by a class in literature—to make themselves heard.

Discipline and Self-Criticism. Part of the excitement of this kind of class is in the growing realization of the amount of self-discipline the activities described here require from each individual and from the class as a whole. There must be constant awareness of what the class has said it wants to accomplish and whether it is actually doing it. To help with this discipline, we set aside a few minutes at the end of the week's discussion for self-criticism. This is a session in which individuals, speaking not as outside observers but as committed participants, try to improve the class performance by criticizing procedures and suggesting improvements.

This is the time for the student to say: "I thought we said it was important for us to be explicit in describing the model implicit in a novel; as far as I can tell we are being pretty vague. At least if there is clarity, I need it explained." Or: "We are spending too much time talking about purely personal matters that come up when we discuss Fundamental Essays. We should try harder to relate personal experiences to the general purpose of the course." Or: "I sat here for half an hour on Tuesday and still can't figure out where that discussion was going. I think it was a waste of time." (To which another student might reply: "Then why did you sit there all that time? You should have said something then, because some of us thought it was a valuable discussion and we could have explained our interest in it.") Or: "I think people too often bounce their comments off the teacher, instead of directing them to the individual involved. For instance, X the other day addressed her comments about Y's essay to the teacher instead of to Y." It is not the responsibility of an individual to feel pleased with things 100 percent of the time; it is his or her responsibility to make his or her grievances known to the group and, if possible, to suggest improvements.

Grading. Although this course rejects much of student-centered learning theory, it is beholden to Brown University's education reform movement's abolition of letter grades. I have tried this course only on a basis of satisfactory/no credit (satisfactory being defined as full participation in the projects as described). I think there might be problems if individuals had to be graded in the traditional manner, since this would establish a conflict of motives between individual advancement and participation in group problem-solving. If grading is required, certainly the standards used should be those derived from the specific activities of the course and not extrinsic "academic" standards.

Expecting any departure from the dreary old academic routine to be relatively "easy," students have occasionally complained in amazement that it is hard to do all this. And it *is* hard—to speak out of one's own experience of the world when one has been trained to speak as an abstract Everyman. It is hard to focus on art as influencing human behavior when one has been taught to think of art as supramundane. It is hard to work collectively and write a position paper with others when one has been taught that education means writing one's own exam, getting one's own gold stars. It is very hard to believe that other students are going to care about whether one shows up in class or puts one's energy into a collective activity, when no one except the teacher— and he or she for suspicious motives—has ever cared about that before. It is hard to believe that mere students can discover something in a course worth publishing. It is hard to believe that a discussion in a humanities class can actually arrive at positions and results upon which one might—since decisions have to be made somewhere, sometime—base a decision. It is hard, in short, to take any of this, or one's part in it, seriously, since one has for so long taken education and oneself in the classroom with a grain of salt.

It is hard, not just for confused college students, but for their fellow victim of the education system, the teacher. I know that when I first introduced this course procedure I talked bravely enough about what I hoped would be the results (what I knew had better be the results if I was not to become totally cynical about teaching), but my enthusiasm was undermined by a sense of the bleakness of so many past moments in the classroom. I probably did not really believe,

myself, that a class could be anything but a relatively meaningless experience. Only as I noticed attendance running
high, people beginning to take real responsibility for what
they were doing and caring what others did (what a fine
thing to hear, for once, one student chastise another for
nonperformance!), students learning by struggling with new
concepts and activities, the class beginning to become conscious of its own strength—only then did I begin to be
strengthened in my original hopes.˙

Of course, I don't know how much of what I describe here
will apply to community colleges, large lectures, or other
humanities courses. I do feel, however, confident in recom-
mending that progressive teachers put student-centered
notions firmly behind them and do much more thinking
about the interaction of the relatively experienced and the
relatively inexperienced in the classroom. It is not as simple
as we may have thought.

Note

1. This article, it should be noted, was originally published in 1972. If
   I were writing about the New Curriculum now, I would refer to it in
   the past tense since there has been a retreat from its spirit, if not its
   letter, for several years. The specific innovations of the New Curriculum at Brown, as voted in by the faculty in 1969 under pressure
   from student demonstrations just outside the door, included the
   option for the student and teacher to take or give any or all courses
   without grades, and the elimination of "distribution requirements,"
   whose purpose had been to give the student at least some acquain-
   tance with several different fields of knowledge.

Facing Some Contradictions:
My Experiences as a White Professor
Teaching Minority Students
....
Alan Sable

Introduction

For the past three years I have taught a course which, although offered at an elite university, enrolls a majority of minority students. Specifically, I have been the faculty member principally responsible for a course called "Social Change in the Domestic Third World," offered at the Santa Cruz campus of the University of California. The majority of students enrolled in this first-year class are Asian-Americans, blacks, Chicanos, and Filipinos. Many of them have not had the same sort of academic preparation as the majority of Santa Cruz's white students; virtually all of them feel at least somewhat alien in this white-dominated elite institution.

All of those involved in this course (students as well as teachers) have had to deal with the contradictions inherent in this situation, contradictions heightened by the fact that the person formally in charge of the course (myself) is white. (I have used the word "contradictions" where others might prefer a simpler term such as "problems" because it better corresponds to the nature of the experiences I plan to discuss. To me a "contradiction" connotes dynamic tension between two opposing forces. Also, in dialectic thought, contradictions are never fully resolved; instead, they are continually being transformed into new situations of tension. Unlike problems, which may be "solved," contradictions require continual struggle. This has been the nature of my experience with this course.) This article shares my understanding of some of those contradictions. First, it presents a brief history of the course, relates how several initial contradictions were overcome, and describes how the course is structured. Then it analyzes the new contradictions that emerged as a result of what was done to resolve the old ones. Although the emergent contradictions are still unresolved, recognizing them is an important part of the continuing political-pedagogical struggle to make American colleges and universities serve *all* women and men, and not just the elite.

The Campus and the Course: Initial Contradictions

The Santa Cruz campus of the University of California is the very model of an elite educational institution. Built in 1965 as the newest campus in the system and conceived as a publicly funded "Oxford in the redwoods," it also drew upon private money to build a series of small (650 to 750 students) colleges clustered around extensive central library and science facilities—all situated in a magnificent park-like setting overlooking Monterey Bay and the quiet, pleasant town of Santa Cruz. Junior faculty were recruited almost exclusively from the "best" graduate schools, senior faculty from other "high quality" academic institutions. Innovative academic programs were fashioned in virtually all the liberal arts, and no practically oriented courses of study were established. Conventional grades were replaced by a pass/fail system and individually written instructor evaluations, and soon the new campus established itself as *the* place to obtain a high quality (if, in the minds of many, "far out") liberal arts education. In its first few years the campus attracted by far the highest number of applicants per admission place in the colleges of the UC system and hence became the most select campus of the already highly selective system.[1] Not surprisingly, Santa

Cruz students were overwhelmingly white and upper-middle-class, and had high College Board scores and the type of preparation provided by "good" suburban high schools. In response to the political struggles of Third World people and to legal and financial pressures applied by the federal government, in the late 1960s the University of California was forced to begin admitting more minority students. Between 1968, the first year records were kept on the ethnic origin of students, and 1969, the percentage of Third World students jumped by more than 80 percent (from 4.9 to 9.1 percent). By 1971, 16.1 percent of Santa Cruz students were nonwhite, a percentage that has remained roughly constant.[2] Although some of these students had what is traditionally called middle- and upper-middle-class origins and educational backgrounds similar to those of the predominant white student body, many did not, and many soon felt alienated by the white, elite nature of the institution in which they found themselves.

As ethnic students began to organize and articulate their grievances, the diverse elements of their alienation became clear. The central grievances were all connected to the elite nature of the institution: the strange combination of rigidly "high" academic standards in some courses and indulgently loose ones in others; the assumption of a high level of academic self-confidence based on prior training at "good" high schools; the dominance of white, male professors and administrators with *their* intellectual and interpersonal styles; the counter-cultural social atmosphere and countryclub-like physical setting; the social and academic "invisibility" of domestic Third World people—courses on American history that did not mention blacks, Chicanos, or Asians, on music that ignored black jazz, on literature that did not mention Chicano *corridos.*

Merrill College was one of the focal points of these struggles. Joined by the handful of ethnic faculty and staff at the college, students pointed to the bitter irony that this college, whose principal academic theme was social change in the Third World, offered many courses on the culture, politics, social systems, and economic conditions of peoples in Asia, Africa, and Latin America, but virtually none on domestic Third World peoples. (Each of Santa Cruz's eight colleges have an academic theme or set of themes. Students do most of their academic work in department courses, but they are expected also to take at least one first-year one-quarter "core course" examining the college's theme(s).) Particularly galling was the college's core course, "Social Change in the Third World," recommended for all first-year Merrill students, which analyzed everything from political struggles in Mozambique and Palestine to the culture of India and China, but which made no mention of our country's own Third World peoples. Providing a core course that would help both minority *and* nonminority students at Merrill understand the history, cultures, and struggles of domestic Third World peoples hence became an important demand. Fulfilling this demand entailed a long struggle that still continues.

The Struggle to Teach
"Social Change in the Domestic Third World"

Interestingly enough, there was little problem involved in getting a course entitled "Social Change in the Domestic Third World" accepted as the second quarter college core course, equal in status to the first quarter course focusing on the foreign Third World. But although none of the white faculty members (who made up over 90 percent of the staff) were opposed to the idea, almost all were apathetic about it. The exceptions were the faculty serving in administrative posts, who had more directly felt the political pressure exerted by the students.[3]

Diverse reasons were given by white professors for their

lack of interest in teaching Merrill 2, as the course was designated. Many confessed to be totally ignorant of the subject
matter. The few who had some competence were surprisingly
hostile: one explained to me that he had tried "to teach
those people about themselves and had gotten nothing but
trouble." The handful of ethnic faculty, impossibly over-
burdened by commitments to teach courses on ethnic themes
in their own departments, could not take on the additional
responsibility of the new core course. They did offer me
warm encouragement and support and virtually all offered to
serve as guest lecturers. In addition, several provided me with
syllabi, reading lists, lecture notes, and books used in their
ethnic study courses. Nevertheless, a crucial contradiction
presented itself: How was I, a white sociology professor,
assisted by a black South African lecturer in economics (the
only other Merrill faculty member who had agreed to participate), to teach a course that would do justice to its theme?

The problem was especially acute because my conversations
with Third World and white students interested in the course
had shown that to be successful it had to provide not only
many facts about the history, social and economic circumstances, and political struggles of domestic Third World
peoples, but had to meet a deeper need, the need for understanding—not just of the plight and accomplishments of
people of color in this country, but also of the meaning this
plight and these struggles have for us all. How could these
deep and sensitive goals be accomplished by a white American sociologist and a black African economist? Surely we
could provide important perspectives and meanings, but how
could we possibly speak validly for domestic Third World
peoples themselves? Clearly, given the goals of the course,
there was a deep contradiction in our responsibility for
teaching it.

The idea for resolving this contradiction came easily
enough, although its implementation took considerable time

and energy and led to later contradictions, which will be discussed below. It was decided to involve ethnic students themselves in teaching the course. We found Third World seniors to serve as assistant section leaders. Even more importantly, we decided to structure the course in such a way that the ethnic first-year students would participate in its teaching as well.

The Structure of Merrill 2

Merrill 2 is divided into two parts. During Part One (ranging from four to six weeks—its length has varied from year to year) the professors have the major teaching responsibility, lecturing on topics about which they are competent to teach. In my case, I lecture on such topics as institutional racism, racism and capitalism, and the sociology of ethnic groups. During this part of the course, students attend two lectures and two section meetings per week. Each section focuses on a particular ethnic group (e.g., Asian-Americans, blacks, Chicanos, Filipinos) and discussions center on the issues raised in the lectures. Reading assignments are made by the lecturing professors.

In Part Two (from four to six weeks), the structure of the course changes radically. Committees of interested minority group students, which have been formed during the second week, assume complete control. Each group usually assumes responsibility for a week's teaching about its own ethnic group, delivering lectures, assigning readings, bringing in outside speakers and cultural groups, and showing films. Considerable advice, support, and guidance is necessary from the professors and section leaders. Nevertheless, decisions as to the nature and content of what is presented, as well as of the structure of the class (e.g., lectures and/or discussions), has been entirely left up to the student-teachers. I have been extraordinarily impressed by the creativity, energy, and competence with which these groups of students have carried out their teaching. Indeed, somewhat to my chagrin (but also to my pleasure), student evaluations of the course invariably report that Part Two is far more interesting and instructive than Part One!

Not all the ethnic students participate in these teaching groups. Those who prefer do other sorts of term projects: research papers, written essays, photo essays, even original poems, plays, and slide shows—the medium and subject chosen for the term project is left to the students' own discretion, although they are urged to consult their section leaders before beginning a project. Collective term projects are encouraged. (Students who teach during Part Two fulfill their term project by their teaching.) In addition, for their final examination all students are required to write an answer to the question "What have you learned from this class?" The question is given the first day of class, and the final is written at home. Students are required to write individual answers, but are encouraged to discuss what they have learned with their peers and teachers.

The open nature of the examination and term projects encourages students to take control over their own learning. (Consider the difference between asking students what they have *learned* and what they have been *taught*—the usual final examination.) Further, it was felt—and this has been corroborated by experience—that much of the impact of the course would be highly personal and that many ethnic (as well as white) students would find conventional research papers inhibiting to the point of totally stifling their thoughts. Hence, giving students the power to determine both the subject and the medium of their term project was deemed essential to fulfilling the goals of the course. Finally, collective work is encouraged as a way to break down the assumption of most American students and teachers that intellectual work is by nature individual, when in fact few activities are more collective than intellectual ones.

Over the past three years the course has become quite successful. During the past two years it received special grants that provided funds for bringing community people and cultural groups to the campus to help analyze and celebrate the experiences of domestic Third World peoples. Several innovative features have been utilized by other teachers in their classes. The course receives very strong student evaluations, and virtually all students who have participated in teaching have reported this as an extraordinarily valuable learning experience. Finally, and most importantly in my judgment, the course has helped Third World students find a place and a voice in the college. Many of the ethnic first-year students involved in the course have gone on to be forceful leaders in the college and on the campus as a whole. Last year several of the Filipino students were instrumental in organizing the Caucus for Filipino Consciousness, the first organization at Santa Cruz representing the interests of Filipino students. Several of the teaching programs developed for the course are now permanent teaching materials on file with the campus Third World Teaching Resource Center, which provides teaching materials to California elementary and high schools.

Although the innovative features of the course are intimately connected with its effectiveness, they have also created new sets of contradictions. A consideration of these may help students and teachers facing the problems that arise in innovative teaching. But first it is important to comment very briefly on the resolution of the initial contradictions faced in setting up Merrill 2.

Brief Comments on Initial Contradictions

Mao Tse-tung's famous essay "On Contradiction" is an extremely useful analysis of the nature and functions of contradictions in social and political life. Among the most important points is Mao's distinction between principal and secondary contradictions. Mao also points out the possibility of achieving one's goals by using the contradictory features of a situation to one's own benefit by turning a contradiction around and, in his words, "turning a bad thing into a good thing." Both points are illustrated by our collective experience with this course.

Two features of the situation of Third World students at Santa Cruz that were originally seen as contrary to their interests were turned around and made to work on their behalf: the indifference of white faculty to Third World academic and intellectual needs, and the loose, experimental academic structure. In a more conventional academic setting many of the innovations in the structure of Merrill 2 could not have been instituted without a long struggle. Further, the very indifference of the controlling white faculty to the needs of Third World students gave space for them to step in and take considerable control over their own learning.

The notion of principal and secondary contradictions was helpful. It permitted us to identify the most critical shortcoming in the course: the inadequacies of the faculty. It also legitimated focusing our energy first on solving this critical problem—and allowing less significant difficulties to wait until there was the time, energy, and resources to solve them.

Unfortunately, Mao is correct in asserting that the successful resolution of one contradiction will lead to the emergence of new ones. It is to these emergent contradictions that we now turn.

The Emergent Contradictions

Three interrelated sets of contradictions have emerged out of our experiences in Merrill 2: (1) those that revolve around the partially reversed roles that teachers and students experience in the course; (2) those that reflect the dual purpose of the course, i.e., to provide *both* academic training *and* an arena for the discovery and expression of feeling and meaning; and (3) those that arise from the course's very distinctiveness. The first set of contradictions are those of power and authority; the second, of standards; and the third, of isolation and integration. Let us consider each in turn.

Power and Authority. Relying on ethnic students (both first-year students and senior section leaders)to help teach the course has inevitably meant sharing power and authority with them and this at times has led to contradictions.

In general, my approach has been to give student-teachers as much power and authority as possible. The seniors are free to structure their sections and lead discussions in whatever way they choose, although all section leaders meet with the course professor(s) each week to discuss their plans. Similarly, as explained above, the committees of first-year students who undertake to teach during the second portion of the course are free to make use of instructional support money in whatever way they wish—to schedule the speakers, films and cultural groups they choose, and to organize whatever number and kind of lectures, discussions, and section meetings they deem appropriate—although these things are also done in consultation with the section leaders and course professor(s). Similarly, the section leaders have the primary responsibility for approving and evaluating term projects and final examinations, although again discussion with the course professor(s) is encouraged. In general, this delegation of power and authority has worked well; students have been both responsible and creative about their teaching and evaluations, and I have found myself advising and helping rather than overseeing their efforts. Nevertheless, it has sometimes occurred that students delivering a lecture err badly or perhaps fail to present material effectively. At these times I wonder whether I am fully living up to my teaching responsibilities in placing so much responsibility on them, and the contradictions of having first-year students teach become painfully clear.

Difficulties have also arisen over those portions of the course for which I assume direct responsibility, particularly the presentation of lectures in the first half of the semester. The students have an exceptionally high level of sensitivity to both the politics and the content of what I say, especially about their particular ethnic groups, a sensitivity that often leads to extremely important discussions. This year, for example, a Chicano section leader publicly criticized my use of the term "illegal aliens," pointing out that this assumed the right of the United States government to legally control the migration of Chicanos within Aztlan. At other times I have found my students' sensitivities frustrating: during the first week of this year's course a student objected to my use of the term "Philippinos" on the syllabus, asserting that I should have used "Philippino-*American*"; a week later, another student objected to my writing "Philippino-*American*" on the board, saying his people were *not* "hyphenated Americans"; the next class, several students criticized my Anglicized spelling, arguing I should employ the Tagalog spelling, "Filipino." Although I have always tried to remain open and responsive, at times the challenge to my power and authority has been difficult to accept: in the middle of a lecture this quarter I remarked that one positive thing about white Americans was that, compared to people of most cultures, they were remarkably open about accepting foods of other nations. A Chinese student challenged me somewhat hostilely, saying that what I had said was "bullshit," and that Americans couldn't eat "real" Chinese food. Rather than hear the important issues that underlay his remark (the painful costs all Third World people experience as their culture is diluted and changed in this country), I defensively reasserted my position and we got into an unsatisfactory discussion of what was "real" Chinese food.

A further dimension of difficulty between myself and some ethnic students arises each year over our interpretations of the best political course of action for American ethnics to follow. As a Marxist, I argue the intimate connection of capitalism and racism and assert my belief that the liberation of domestic Third World people will only occur in the context of a socialist revolution participated in by *all* the peoples of our country. Many of the most politically conscious ethnic students are committed to nonsocialist, cultural-separatist positions, and these students consistently reject my analysis as a white telling blacks (or Chicanos or Asians) what to do. Compounding the problem, most first-year ethnic and white students simply have too little knowledge of either issue to formulate a reasoned judgment. Although confronting this disagreement is, for many students, one of the most valuable features of the class, it has often resulted in a gap between me and at least some of the students, who perceive me as subordinating their people's need for social and cultural freedom to the need for social revolution.

The heightened sensitivity and sometimes militant self-assertion of students is, of course, a sign of their engagement as well as their feeling of power. As such it is an extremely positive phenomenon. However, it sometimes challenges me (and other professors) and at times leaves us flustered, defensive, and revealed as partially ignorant and/or insensitive. The difficult task of maintaining leadership without arrogance, of admitting ignorance and yet inspiring confidence, and of being true to one's own political interpretations in the face of disagreements from those directly involved are all contradictory polarities I have experienced in this course.

Standards. "Academic standards" have also emerged as a central set of contradictions, as I assume they must wherever an attempt is made to encourage the emotional involvement of students. Frequently students may choose to express themselves in forms (for example, poetry, short stories, even murals) very difficult for me and other members of the teaching staff to evaluate competently. Further, students frequently use their term projects to awkwardly express deeply personal feelings, or to present ill-reasoned and poorly evidenced polemics. In such cases I have often found it difficult to affirm the validity of the feelings expressed while at the same time criticizing the method of expression. My personal tendency is to give more weight to the depth and sincerity of feeling than to the quality of expression. This is not because I do not recognize that skillful expression enhances what is being experienced. The problem lies in the fact that the course teaching staff are invariably social scientists rather than artists, creative writers, or skilled political polemicists and do not have the skills to respond to nonacademic projects. Consequently, students who choose more academic modes of expression (term papers or class lectures) tend to receive more careful and competent feedback on their work, and perhaps are also judged less leniently. One obvious solution to this problem—to involve creative writers, artists, etc., with the course—has not so far proven feasible, though I am seeking such involvement.

Because Merrill 2 is one of the few courses at Santa Cruz that unequivocally legitimates—and indeed encourages—emotional involvement on the part of students, only a small proportion (perhaps one-fourth) choose to write conventionally academic term papers. Not surprisingly, those who choose to do so tend to be those who feel most comfortable and competent with this medium. Few minority first-year students fall into this category. And this creates a further contradiction.

One of the greatest difficulties for minority students at Santa Cruz is their inability to write well, an inability that results both from the poor quality of primary and secondary schooling available to most Third World people and from the racist cultural biases of the content and processes of school-ing. By not insisting on term papers, this course frees such students from the oppression of being forced to express themselves in a way that is all too often impossibly difficult; at the same time, students who opt to complete the course requirement without doing a term paper miss the oppor-tunity to get instructive and supportive help with their writing.

To resolve this contradiction, this year, as an experiment, the students were required to write a brief (five-page) term paper applying to their own lives a psychological model developed by one of the professors teaching the course. This assignment met with strong resistance from the minority group seniors serving as section leaders. In a staff meeting one of the black section leaders spoke eloquently of his pain at enforcing such an assignment on his section and his worry that it would deeply alienate his students, forcing them to translate their lives into "the Man's" categories and language. In my judgment, such feelings are not to be taken lightly. On the other hand, there is the obvious consideration that ethnic college students *must* learn "the Man's" categories and lan-guage if they are to survive. As one Chicano politics professor said at a writing seminar attended by the course teaching staff, "Anyone who believes it isn't *crucial* to teach Chicano college students to write English well is my enemy and the enemy of my people."

Isolation and Integration. Merrill 2 has permitted still an-other set of contradictions to emerge. This course has been so successful in creating a place for ethnic students that few whites in the college take it, even though it is one of two recommended college core courses. Although approximately 80 percent of Merrill students are white, only about 25 percent of Merrill 2 is white. The white students who do enroll adjust extremely well and typically add exceptionally valuable contributions to the understanding of white racism.

But they are a self-selected group, obviously interested in and open to a class whose principal concern is confronting racism on the one hand and analyzing and celebrating the experiences of domestic Third World peoples on the other. (Because far too many whites come to perceive American minorities as people who not only *have* problems but who therefore *are* problems, one of the major themes of the course is to go beyond analyzing the plight of ethnic Americans to *celebrate* their extraordinary accomplishments in the face of adversity.)

Undoubtedly, it is precisely the predominance of Third World students in Merrill 2 that gives the course its special flavor and meaning. Many white students express the merits of experiencing, for the first time, a situation in which *they* are in the minority. Similarly, minority students clearly value and make excellent use of their predominance in the class and sections. But are not *most* white students badly in need of a course that focuses on racism, and on the problems and accomplishments of our country's Third World peoples? If such a course is to be dominated and controlled by minority students, how can the vastly greater number of whites at Merrill be involved in it?

Further, the special nature of Merrill 2 may undermine ethnic students' need for materials relevant to their groups in other university classes. I would like to believe that the experience of this class would only reinforce this need, and that the students will *demand* that advanced courses probe the issues raised in this first-year course. I fear, however, that the opposite also occurs. I have heard, for example, that certain professors respond to requests that their courses treat the domestic Third World: "We can't cover everything in this course. Take Merrill 2. That is a very good course that covers those things." In the absence of full-scale revolutionary change, all reforms face the contradiction that they may be counterproductive.

This last contradiction has important personal relevance. Over the past three years I have worked very hard to make Merrill 2 a meaningful and effective course. I fear that one of the consequences may have been to relieve pressure on the college to hire a domestic Third World professor to teach it. If I had not taught Merrill 2, no other white Merrill professor would have; given their overwork, no ethnic professor could have. Has my action therefore in part perpetuated the institutional racism the course is designed to expose, confront, and help overthrow?

There are many contradictions.

Notes

1. In the past three years Santa Cruz's attractiveness has declined and the campus has been superseded by Berkeley, UCLA, and Davis in selectivity. But as a member of the UC system, Santa Cruz remains a highly selective, and hence elite, educational institution.
2. These statistics were provided by Peggy Long, Assistant Registrar at Santa Cruz.
3. Note that this experience supports several observations made by Robert Blauner in his excellent essay, "Race and the White Professor," in *Racial Oppression in America* (New York: Harper and Row, 1972).

Part V
······
Letters from Socialist Teachers

The editors asked a number of socialist teachers how they teach Marxism and what materials they find most useful. The following are some of the replies.

From William Appleman Williams

I find the following sequence of operations to be the most satisfying and also the most effective in establishing the basis for a dialogue with students (at any level, including adult education):

1. Candor. Talk in terms of one's own coming to Marxism, and how it has informed one's understanding and comprehension of the world—past, present, and future. Admit that there are some real difficulties that remain unresolved, but that, overall, Marxism makes more sense than any other theory of knowledge and makes more sense of the world per se.

2. Discuss the theory itself, beginning with an exposition of the underlying theory of knowledge, and be open about the major differences of interpretation that have developed.

3. Give some examples of how the theory explains reality (from music to state capitalism), and be sure to give examples of analysis dealing with very long-range developments on down to specific examples of how decision-makers can

and do act against their own interests. Admit boners. Use "New Left" to show how, in Marx's classic phrase, the past weighs like an Alp on the living—how hard it is to be a Marxist in the basic sense of not applying nineteenth-century analyses to twentieth-century developments.

4. Define the era under discussion and review alternate analyses and interpretations—fairly and without direct or indirect putdowns. If you don't have enough confidence in a Marxist analysis to play it straight with other approaches, then Marx will spin in his grave.

5. Develop a Marxist analysis and interpretation of the era under consideration.

6. Explore the question of whether or not the present projections (or the present per se, if that is the subject) is a revolutionary situation. If not, then discuss what Marxism suggests as the relevant and consequential approach to it all.

Examples. Here one could go on forever. There *is*, after all, a great body of damn good work—either pre-Marxist or Marxist. But, for starters:

E. H. Carr	W. E. B. DuBois
L. R. Graham	M. Rogin
K. S. Karol	H. Cruse
J. T. Main	C. D. Darlington
C. A. Beard	S. Avineri
J. Weinstein	G. Lukács
L. Baritz	Frankfurt School
W. Sussman	C. B. MacPherson
D. F. Dowd	Yourselves

From Raya Dunayevskaya

Marxism, as the dialectics of liberation, does not allow for any separation between philosophy and revolution, subject and object, theory and practice, economics and politics, an analysis of capitalism and action against it. This does not mean that only those who are ready to "make" the revolution can "teach" it. Marx was much too firmly convinced of the spontaneity of revolution and the need for intellectuals to comprehend *its* dialectic to hold either that it can be "made," or that it can fully blossom without theory. It does mean, first, that teaching cannot be done "from above," on a platform separating educator from the one to be educated. As Marx put it in his *Theses on Feuerbach*: "The educators must themselves be educated." This requires that (1) some of the lectures be given "from below," not only to give the students "experience," but so that the teachers can learn; and (2) where possible, at least one of the lectures (say on the class struggle), be made "in the field" either by a tour of a factory or visit to a picket line. (There is sure to be one somewhere if eyes and ears are turned to the production line.) As for learning from students, it is not only a question of the dialectical principle Hegel articulated, that "Error is a dynamic of truth," but also a fact that even when a student commits errors, the teacher can discern where his or her presentation failed to communicate; failure to project an idea is every bit as wrong as failure to "know."

Second, distinct from the alleged neutrality claimed by non-Marxist interpretations of capitalism, Marxists openly state that their interpretations lead to a transformation of existing society, holding that their objectivity, far from excluding subjectivity, is proven by the subject, i.e., the proletariat, becoming the "gravedigger of capitalism" *because* that is both force and reason of the opposite to capitalist exploitation. That, at once, separates independent teaching of Marxism from teaching by the so-called orthodox (actually, statist professors in state-capitalist societies calling themselves communist), who attempt positivistic interpretations of "scientific" analysis of the functioning of the objective law of value irrespective of the will of humans, as if that applied to all societies instead of to capitalism only, as Marx never tired of emphasizing.

Third—and most important—is methodology. Here I must frankly admit that I was amazed that the announcement of your project on "how to teach Marxism" included not a single mention of dialectics. It isn't that those who constantly utter the word dialectic *practice* it. If that had been so—and that includes not only "us lowly teachers" but such great *practicing* revolutionaries as Lenin—it wouldn't have taken a world war and the collapse of the existing Socialist International to have made Lenin realize that none (himself included) had understood *Capital* (especially Chapter I), because no Marxist since Marx has understood the whole of Hegel's *Science of Logic*. But Lenin's *Abstract of the Science of Logic*, having finally appeared in English (by me in 1947 in mimeographed form, and in 1957 in publication of *Marxism and Freedom*, and in Moscow in 1961) contained more challenges to today's teachers of Marxism than those of the nineteenth and early twentieth century. I did not expect that Western teachers would help the Russian-Chinese et al. re-bury dialectics in such a mishmash as the official publication, including all that Lenin wrote from the 1890s on, as if there had been no Big Divide.

Methodology, then, must be a new beginning, that is, a projection of future study and action so that no one, teacher or student, should feel that teaching has "ended" when the last lecture of the course is delivered. Everyone must experience the lifeblood of the dialectic—continuity, a continuity that arises daily from the objective situation, both in the class struggles at the point of production, and through every layer of society.

From Kai Nielsen

To me the greatest obstacle to teaching Marx and Marxism is that to a large number of students Marxism is an unrealistic utopian ideology or faith that has been thoroughly undermined, so that what was sound in it has been incorporated into the main body of social thinking. For the many students who have been so oriented the problem is to get them to take Marx and Marxism seriously. There is another and much smaller group of students who profess to care about Marxism but don't get much beyond slogans. The problem in both cases is in some way to prod them into thinking with greater care about Marxism and to read Marxist texts carefully. I think with the former, larger group it is important to start with some concrete Marxist analysis of the contemporary capitalist society that they know. When they see that Marxism provides a perspicuous analysis about the society they know—an analysis not found in the usual liberal analyses— then I think we have made an important first move. (With philosophy students in North America, specialized as they are, the problem is different; it becomes methodological. One needs to square Marx off with the dominant analytical philosophy; to show that Marxism is not committed to a method that culminates in a plethora of utterances whose truth-value results only in confusion.)

From Stanley Aronowitz

I have been "teaching Marxism" for a number of years in many different contexts: alternative schools such as free universities, study groups of workers, students and persons with no particular group occupation, and within the college in which I am employed. I have found several approaches effective for making clear the importance of Marx's method as a mode of social and historical explanation. Among working-class students and employed persons who are not college educated, the only way to introduce Marx himself is to work with his own texts on a line-by-line basis, the so-called pedagogy of *explication de texte*. Many persons come to Marx with fear and trembling. Not only are they unfamiliar with his ideas, but they are intimidated by the style of writing and by the literary, philosophical, and other unfamiliar references. By demystifying both problems and extracting the ideas in their original form, students gain some psychological mastery over their own historic sense of intellectual failure. Moreover, the careful examination of Marx's own work yields immense insights that are simply not preponderant among his commentators.

On the whole, I do not favor teaching "Marxism." I find that students become interested in dialectical explanations when they illuminate burning questions and can be contrasted to other modes of explanation that are less rich and satisfying. Marx's answers to such questions as the motive force of history, the problem of the nature of human nature, the structure of political power within capitalism, the dynamics of capitalist development, the question of revolutionary consciousness, etc., are infinitely more interesting than the presentation of Marx's corpus as doctrine. "Marxism" becomes sterile, while Marx's own work is exciting. In this connection, I include a text by Marx, if possible, in any course I teach: mass media (the fetishism chapter of *Capital*), "Value, Price and Profit" or sections from *Capital* in a basic economic theory course, *Economic and Philosophical Manuscripts* and *German Ideology* in almost any general introduction to social theory whether I do it as sociology or urban studies, and *The 18th Brumaire* in any politics course. As someone who springs from the Marxist tradition, I have tried to stay away from course work on Marx himself because I believe this mode of discourse to be scholastic and not true to Marx's own theoretical intentions. In one course I teach frequently, Introduction to Social Theory, I contrast Marx, Freud, and Weber on types of social and historical explanation, the nature of human nature, the motive forces of history, and other specific concerns of theorizing in the social sciences. Even here, I always stress the nondogmatic character of Marx's own work.

Third, as a pedagogical technique I often play the role of Marx's adversary and ask the class to help refute my Freudian, Hegelian, Millsian, or Weberian objections. This manner of explication is particularly exciting because it asks the class to defend the position against classical attacks. Then I ask the class to critique Marx, both from traditional bourgeois perspectives and immanently. The latter, the method of immanent critique, helps preserve the students' independence of dogma because they are encouraged to view Marx in a Marxist way: from the point of view of historicity.

Finally, I try to show the open Marx by developing some interest in the epigones, showing that Marx lends himself to interpretations that are widely divergent. I never suggest "true" or "false" interpretations, but ask students to compare their own reading of Marx with that of Lenin, Gramsci, or Marcuse, etc. Often the comparative method reveals some important lessons about the problems associated with interpretation, as well as the dictum that changed circumstances change the text. Some students actually develop a "new" reading of some of Marx's texts, according to their own sense of his contemporary significance.

In answer to your second question, I am very reluctant to suggest any "simple" explanations because I firmly adhere to the idea that the best introduction to Marx's thought is Marx himself. When students are given the chance to encounter Marx, then it may be good to ask them to read other commentary and simplifications. My students at Staten Island Community College get a good laugh out of some of the textbook renditions after they have done a careful study of the *1844 Manuscripts* or the *German Ideology* or some of *Capital*. They become richer for their actual reading of Marx. This places a terrific burden on the teacher to find material from Marx on "class struggle" or any other topic. Good collections are *Karl Marx: Selected Writings in Sociology and Social Philosophy*, edited by T. B. Bottomore and M. Rubel, and *Writings of the Young Marx on Philosophy and Society*, edited by L. D. Easton and K. H. Guddat. Bottomore and Rubel arrange the material "topically," including good extracts on methodological foundations. This is particularly useful.

The problem of issues not dealt with by Marx to any significant extent—such as imperialism, the nature of the state, problems of consciousness, literature and art, and several other topics—requires a different list of authors and books. On the whole, I am opposed to a consideration of "Marxist" approaches to these questions without prior examination of Marx himself.

From Bertell Ollman

No book on pedagogy can hope to deliver all the strategies and techniques it seems to promise, but before the final cover comes down on the present effort there are still a few teaching experiences I would like to share with the reader.

Nonsense lecture. Everyone knows that people are very gullible, but few include themselves in this generalization. With the aim of showing students that they accept much more on authority than they think they do, I open my undergraduate course on the history of political theory with a nonsense lecture. I tell students I want to test how well they can understand a new and difficult subject by spending the first twenty minutes on an exciting new departure in political theory called "Proportional Political Theory." Afterward, I tell the class to write for fifteen minutes on the question, "What is proportional political theory and what do you think of it?" Without going into particulars, suffice it to say that, according to my lecture, "P.P.T." is based on the principle that "Politics is the logic of the political mind," that from this principle it follows that all political theory can be reduced to numbers, letters, and logical symbols, that—after giving appropriately complicated formulae for Marx, Rousseau, etc.—this permits us to add and subtract political theories, and so on.

When the papers are collected, I ask the students if any of them wrote that I was speaking nonsense. A few hands are raised, but from the rest, nothing. Most students, perhaps 95 percent, are quite shocked by my revelation; there is some nervous laughter, and a few people get angry. My response is to point out how important it is to think critically about what we hear (or read), because—well, look what can happen when you don't. And who is to say that this is the first time they have accepted as true some utter nonsense just because it came from an "authority"? Could it be, I ask, that this has also happened with other teachers, with newscasters and reporters, politicians, priests/ministers/rabbis, and even parents? At least in this case I have confessed to speaking nonsense, but what of the others? How can they know? The lively discussion that follows is devoted equally to hearing alibis and to looking for what, in the process of socialization, has so dampened students' critical spirit. I then promise that I will never knowingly speak nonsense to them again, but, as I point out, it is only they—by insisting that everything that is told to them make sense—who can judge whether I keep my promise.

I don't want to claim too much for this simple technique, but many students both during and after the term have thanked me for making them so directly and personally aware of their need for critical thinking. I believe I have said enough in my article, "On Teaching Marxism," to make it clear that I do not confuse becoming critical with becoming a socialist, but in our ideology-ridden society, acquiring a

critical consciousness is almost always a necessary first step
to acquiring a socialist one.

Log. The problem is how to get students to focus on the
more important and provocative questions arising out of
what they read and to try to answer them, not in some
hectic and distant final exam, but leisurely, while they are
doing the readings. In courses on socialist theory I have
recently begun to ask students to keep a critical log of what
they read, responding to what they consider the most significant arguments and generally giving their reasons for agreeing
or disagreeing with each author. I provide several study guide
questions for each work or school of thought in an attempt
to bring out their more striking political implications, both
for then and now. To encourage students to take their log
seriously, I've made it the only requirement for the course—
there are no exams or term papers. The result, I am convinced, is that students do more reading than they otherwise
would, and critically consider fundamental questions ranging
over the entire term's work. Marty Sklar, who first suggested
this technique to me, had an equally positive experience with
it in a course he taught on American History.

Newsmagazines. Many students who now subscribe to *Time*
or *Newsweek*, or feel guilty that they don't because it's the
"educated" thing to do, could become subscribers to some
radical newsmagazine if they knew of its existence. Rather
than participating in the conspiracy of silence which surrounds these magazines, it is our duty as teachers and socialists to make students aware of them as alternative sources of
information. I devote part of a lecture to introducing *Seven
Days, The Guardian*, and *In These Times* (along with a number of socialist journals), but I have come to feel that this is
not sufficient. To further encourage students to examine the
left press, I intend to ask them to compare its treatment of
some major story or problem area with that found in *Time*
and/or *Newsweek*. (It also doesn't hurt to leave old copies of
radical newspapers in the student lounge.)

Scrapbook. The advantage of asking students to keep a scrapbook on any subject is that by finding material and organizing it they are encouraged to pay special attention to its real content. There is an additional advantage in having students keep a scrapbook on social problems, which is what I have done in various introductory courses in political science. I have asked students to clip stories and articles from the daily newspaper which, in their opinion, discuss or illustrate the problems of our society, and to organize them by problem in a scrapbook to be handed in for extra credit at the end of the term. They can use any newspaper they like, though, because of its scope, I prefer *The New York Times.*

The chief difficulty students have in making the scrapbook is in deciding where to place such stories as: "Unemployed Man Robs Bank," or "Corporate Pollutor Fined $100." The lesson they generally draw from this experience is that the problems of our society are in some way related, and that therefore political solutions that treat one problem at a time are inadequate. The discovery and eventual reconstruction of the pattern of human suffering under capitalism is a major advance toward radical thinking (itself but a step toward Marxist thinking—see my article above). By keeping a scrapbook on social problems, students begin to see these patterns through the very difficulties posed in classifying stories from the liberal/conservative press.

Attitude survey. As socialist teachers we are acutely aware of the conservative biases and one-sided distortions associated with the attitude survey, the most widely used technique for acquiring knowledge in the social sciences today. The little known fact that on at least one occasion Marx himself used this technique and that a little later several Fabian researchers made widespread and progressive use of it should put us on guard that our initial negative reaction needs to be qualified.

In methodology courses I have had students collectively put together an attitude survey to help clarify its possibilities and limitations for acquiring information as well as for affecting the views of respondents. If the former is too well known to require any comment, the ways in which attitude surveys confirm people in their existing views or actually contribute to changing them is little understood. And since most surveys—generally in the misguided effort to be "objective"— take the status quo as given, the conservative implications of their practice is evident. In my class we tried to produce a questionnaire with just the opposite biases. Assuming a socialist analysis, our questions dealt with various forms of oppression and inequality, conveyed little known radical facts, and used concepts which brought out real emotions, including anger. Survey questions also produce conservative responses by the very comparisons respondents are urged, either explicitly or implicitly, to make. So where a typical question addressed to workers might be, "Given the poor financial health of your company (or the fact that you got a raise just last year, or that jobs are so hard to get, etc.), do you think you are being paid enough?", we would rephrase the question to read, "Given the high profits made by your boss (or that higher wages are made by people doing similar kinds of work, etc.), do you think you are being paid enough?" Depending on what one has the respondent focus on as an object of comparison (and most judgment and even belief statements are made in relation to some standard), the answers may vary enormously, and with them the need to change a given situation.

The survey we developed in class dealt with our lives in the university and included such questions as: "Do you believe that you as a student have adequate representation in a university senate dominated by administrative appointees?" "Do you see any reason why a university whose stated aim is the advancement of learning should have a board of trustees composed mainly of businessmen, bankers, and corporation lawyers?" "Should the university continue to play its part in keeping blacks and women out of the best jobs by training so few of them in its graduate and professional schools?" "Do you agree with having the president of New York University make 10-20 percent more than his City University counterpart, while all other workers at NYU—secretaries, professors, elevator operators, etc.—make 10-20 percent less than their City University counterparts?" Each student administered the questionnaire to ten other students, and at the following class we tabulated the results. More important even than the surprisingly progressive statistical results, or the consciousness-raising discussions which collecting them made possible, was the fact that these questions had become part of the mental framework in which many respondents now think about these problems. For if radical *answers* are too easily denied, ignored, isolated, or forgotten, radical *questions*, once accepted, refuse to disappear, and under favorable conditions can wreak unexpected socialist havoc on capitalist modes of thought and behavior.

Part VI
......
Teaching Materials

This section includes materials relevant to radical teaching and research, and the study of left political ideas and organizations. The section falls into three parts:

I. An annotated bibliography of radical professional and general journals and newsletters appearing in the English language. To make this bibliography manageable, we have omitted publications whose main thrust is countercultural rather than political, most single-issue newsletters, and student journals. This part of the bibliography is also divided according to country of publication (United States, Great Britain, other); and these works are further divided into those whose themes are mainly national and theoretical and those whose themes are mainly foreign and international (Third World in the case of "other").

II. A list of left newspapers, news agencies, and journals that are mainly (but not exclusively) affiliated with political organizations. This list does not include most single-issue newspapers, local radical newspapers, trade-union newspapers, and papers/journals of youth or subsidiary groups of the various political organizations.

III. An annotated bibliography of teaching and research materials and resources: books, pamphlets, bibliographies,

Special thanks for help in preparing this bibliography are due to Nigel Harris, Kai Nielsen, Robin Ridless, Martin Sklar, and Gail Sharman.

films, tapes, comics, games, songs, etc., and resource organizations in various areas. While there is some attempt to be comprehensive (at least as regards the United States) in the areas covered in Sections I and II, Section III offers—of necessity—a relatively select bibliography. Aside from exceptional items, only the most important of the many hundreds of radical groups which produce such materials has been listed.

The fairly rapid turnover of radical publications, presses, and parties, and the frequent changes of address, may quickly date some of our information. We would appreciate it, therefore, if readers who find this bibliography useful would help us keep it up to date by informing us as to needed corrections and additions. Finally, quoted material where it appears is taken from the publication's own advertisements.

I. JOURNALS AND NEWSLETTERS

A. United States

1. Mainly national and theoretical themes

Advocate, 2121 S. El Camino Real, San Mateo, Ca., 94403. Socialist gay lib.

Against the Wall, Box 444, Westfield, N.J., 07091. Anarchist.

Aims Newsletter, The American Institute for Marxist Studies, 20 E. 30th St., New York, N.Y., 10016. Contains extensive bibliographies of current books, periodical literature, and dissertations on Marxism (broadly defined) and related issues.

Akwesasne Notes, Mohawk Nation, Via Rooseveltown, N.Y., 13683. Sometimes radical Indian news and analysis.

ALA/SRRT Newsletter, 60 Remsen St. (10E), Brooklyn, N.Y., 11201. Newsletter of the Social Responsibility Round Table. Radical librarians.

Alternate View Newsletter, P.O. Box 70, Gracie Station, New York, N.Y., 10028. Publication of the Radical Alliance of Social Service Workers (RASSW).

Alternative Media, Box 775, Madison Square Station, New York, N.Y., 10010. Alternative and establishment media coverage of major issues.

Alternative Press Revue, Alternative Press Syndicate, P.O. Box 777, Cooper Station, New York, N.Y., 10003.

Alternatives, Oberlin Political Caucus, Box 32, Wilder Hall, Oberlin, Ohio, 44074. "A forum for activism in the '70s."

Alternatives in Health Care, c/o Claire Douglas, P.O. Box 56, Deadwood, Oregon, 97430.

Anarcho-Feminist Notes, c/o Karen Johnson, 1821-8th St., Des Moines, Iowa, 50314. Recently merged with *Emma*, another anarcho-feminist journal.

ANG Bulletin, 1901 Q St., N.W., Washington, D.C., 20009. Newsletter of the Alliance for Neighborhood Governments.

Antipode: A Radical Journal of Geography, P.O. Box 225, West Side Station, Worcester, Mass., 01602. Emphasis on urban and cultural geography, political economy.

Appeal to Reason: A Social Democratic Monthly, 1733 Madera, Berkeley, Ca., 94707.

Arsenal/Surrealist Subversion, c/o Franklin Rosemont, 2257 N. Jansen Ave., Chicago, Ill., 60614.

Association for Economic Democracy Newsletter, Box 802, Ithaca, N.Y., 14850. Self-management.

Benjamin Rush Society Newsletter, P.O. Box 371, Planetarium Station, New York, N.Y., 10024. Marxist news and analysis of psychology.

Berkeley Journal of Sociology, 410 Barrows Hall, University of Calif., Berkeley, Ca., 94720. Radical Sociology.

Black Circles, Box 405, W. Somerville, Mass., 02144. Anarchist.

The Black Scholar. P.O. Box 908, Sausalito, Ca., 94965. Frequently radical material in the whole range of black studies.

Black Star, Box 92246, Milwaukee, Wis., 53202. Anarchist.

Blind Justice, National Lawyers Guild, 853 Broadway, New York, N.Y., 10003. Radical lawyers.

Booklegger, 555 29th St., San Francisco, Ca., 94131. Radical library journal.

Bulletin of the Institute for Workers Control, c/o Paul Booth, 817 W. George St., Chicago, Ill., 60657.

Camera Obscura, P.O. Box 4517, Berkeley, Ca., 94704. Socialist and feminist film theory.

Catalyst, Institute for Social Service Alternatives, Dept. A, P.O. Box 1144, Cathedral Station, New York, N.Y., 10025. "A socialist journal of the social services."

Catholic Agitator, 605 N. Cummings St., Los Angeles, Ca., 90033. Radical Catholics.

Cataloging Bulletin, c/o Sanford Berman, Hennepin County Library, Edina, Minn., 55345. Information on social change resources for librarians.

Center for Radical Studies and Education Newsletter, Box 211, Teachers College, New York, N.Y., 10027.

Children's Cultural Newsletter of the Marxist Literary Group, c/o Tom Moylan, Dept. of English, University of Wisconsin-Waukesha, Waukesha, Wis., 53186.

Chutzpah, P.O. Box 60142, Chicago, Ill., 60660. Independent Jewish socialist.

Cineaste, 333 Sixth Ave., New York, N.Y., 10014. Offers a "social and political perspective on the cinema."

Collector's Network News, State Historical Society, 816 State St., Madison, Wis., 53706. Newsletter of resource information on left periodicals.

The College Teacher Worker Newsletter, 235 W. 23rd St., New York, N.Y. Publication of the CPUSA.

Common Ground, 2314 Elliot Ave. South, Minneapolis, Minn., 55404. Self-reliance and community control.

Communities, Box 426, Twin Oaks, Louisa, Va., 23093. Focus on communes, coops, and collectives.

Concerned Demography, c/o R. T. Reynolds, Sociology Dept., Ithaca College, Ithaca, N.Y., 14850.

Conference on Critical Studies Newsletter, c/o School of Law, University of Wisconsin, Madison, Wis., 53706.

Conference on Language Attitudes and Composition Newsletter, Dept. of English, Portland State University, P.O. Box 751, Portland, Oregon, 97207. Against the class bias in using a single standard for "good English."

Counter Spy, Fifth Estate, P.O. Box 647, Ben Franklin Station, Washington, D.C., 20044. Your move.

Crime and Social Justice: A Journal of Radical Criminology, P.O. Box 4373, Berkeley, Ca., 94704. Devotes an entire section in each issue to problems of socialist pedagogy.

CSC News Letter, Childhood Sensuality Circle, P.O. Box 20163, El Cajon, Ca., 92021. "News and views of the Children's Liberation Movement."

Cultural Correspondence, Dorrwar Bookstore, 224 Thayer Ave., Providence, R.I. Focus on popular culture.

The Cultural Reporter, GPO Box 1760, New York, N.Y., 10001. Socialist culture.

Cultural Worker, Box 302, N. Amherst, Mass., 01059. Socialist culture.

Dandelion, Outreach Collective, 4722 Baltimore Ave., Philadelphia, Pa., 19043. Newsletter of Movement for New Society. Social change through nonviolent means.

Dialectical Anthropology (U.S. and International), Elsevier Scientific Publishing Co., P.O. Box 211, Amsterdam, The Netherlands. Marxist and critical approaches to anthropology.

Dialectical Psychology Newsletter, c/o H. Gadlin, Dept. of Psychology, University of Massachusetts, Amherst, Mass., 01002.

Dissent, 505 Fifth Ave., New York, N.Y., 10017. General political and cultural journal. Democratic socialist orientation.

Dollars and Sense, 324 Somerville Ave., Somerville, Mass., 02143. Union for Radical Political Economics' economic newsjournal. Popular format.

Dragon, Bay Area Research Collective, Box 4344, Berkeley, Ca., 94704. News and analysis of American underground movements.

East Coast Socialist Sociologists Newsletter, Dept. of Sociology, State University College, 1300 Elmwood Ave., Buffalo, N.Y., 14222.

Economics Notes, Labor Research Assoc., 80 E. 11th St., New York, N.Y., 10003.

Edcentric: A Journal of Educational Change, P.O. Box 10083, Eugene, Oregon, 94701. Educational analysis, resources, bibliographies.

Ekistics, Page Farm Rd., Lincoln, Mass., 01773. Technical aspects of large-scale community planning.

Endarch, Dept. of Political Science, Atlanta University, Atlanta, Ga., 30311. Black radical political theory journal.

Equality, Box 2418, Evansville, Ind., 47714. Newsletter of the Kropotkin Society.

Faculty Action, M.C.C.-C.U.N.Y., 1633 Broadway (Rm. 368), New York, N.Y., 10019. Publication of the New York-based Faculty Action Committee. Radical professors.

Feminist Studies, 417 Riverside Dr., New York, N.Y., 10025. Contains frequent discussions of socialist feminism.

Fifth Estate, 4403 2nd Ave., Detroit, Mich., 48201. Anarchist news.

Foolkiller, 818½ E. 31st St., Kansas City, Mo., 64109. "A journal of popular and people's culture."

FPS: A Magazine of Young People's Liberation, 2007 Washtenaw, Ann Arbor, Mich., 48104. Radical news and analysis together with tips on organizing for high schoolers.

Freedomways, Freedomways Associates, Inc., 799 Broadway, New York, N.Y., 10003. Radical black studies in the U.S. and abroad.

Freespace, 339 Lafayette St., New York, N.Y., 10012. Anarchist newsletter.

Green Mountain Quarterly, 462 N. Main St., Oshkosh, Wis., 54901. Devotes whole issues to the radical history of different communities—Oshkosh, Dallas, etc.

Guild Notes, National Lawyers Guild, 853 Broadway, New York, N.Y., 10003. Radical lawyers.

Guild Practitioner, National Lawyers Guild, 1715 Francisco St., Berkeley, Ca., 94703. Radical lawyers.

Harvest Quarterly, 907 Santa Barbara St., Santa Barbara, Ca., 93101. Concerned with "historical materialism."

Haymarket News, Haymarket Peoples' Fund, 2 Holyoke St., Cambridge, Ma., 02139. Radical philanthropy.

Health Activists' Digest, 19920 Lichfield, Detroit, Mich., 48221. Publication of the New American Movement (NAM).

Health/PAC Bulletin, Health Policy Advisory Center, 17 Murray St., New York, N.Y., 10007. Radical analyses of the health sector.

Health Rights News, Medical Committee for Human Rights, 203 Oakland Ave., Pittsburgh, Pa., 15213.

Heresies, P.O. Box 766, Canal Street Station, New York, N.Y., 10013. Predominantly socialist feminist studies of art and politics.

Heretics Journal, 2202 N.W. 60th St., Seattle, Wash., 98107. Politics as well as religion.

Historians Committee on Alternative Resources Newsletter, P.O. Box 1516, New Brunswick, N.J., 08903.

The Human Factor, Dept. of Sociology, Columbia University (Rm. 203), 605 W. 115th St., New York, N.Y., 10025. Radical sociology.

Independent Publishing Fund of the Americas News, P.O. Box 3080, Grand Central Station, New York, N.Y., 10017. Hoping to help finance the publication of socialist books.

Indigena, P.O. Box 4073, Berkeley, Ca., 94704. Native Americans.

Insurgent Sociologist, Dept. of Sociology, University of Oregon, Eugene, Oregon, 94703. Premier radical sociology journal.

Interface Journal, Box 970, Utica, N.Y., 13503. "Alternatives in higher education."

Issues in Radical Therapy, P.O. Box 23544, Oakland, Ca., 94623.

Jewish Affairs, 235 W. 23rd. St., New York, N.Y., 10011. Publication of the Communist Party (CPUSA).

Jewish Currents, 22 E. 17th St. (Rm. 601), New York, N.Y., 10003. Socialist information and analysis of special interest to Jews.

Jump Cut, P.O. Box 865, Berkeley, Ca., 94701. Radical film criticism.

Just Economics, Movement for Economic Justice, 1611 Connecticut Ave. N.W., Washington, D.C., 20009. Organizing the community around utilities, taxes, public services.

Kapitalistate, c/o J. O'Connor, Dept. of Sociology, University of Calif.-Santa Cruz, Santa Cruz, Ca., 95064. Major Marxist theoretical journal focusing on the state in capitalist society.

Labor History, Bobst Library, Tamiment Institute, New York University, Washington Square, New York, N.Y., 10012. American labor history.

Labor Today, 343 S. Dearborn (Rm. 600), Chicago, Ill., 60604. Good left source of labor news.

Left Curve, 1230 Grant Ave., Box 302, San Francisco, Ca., 94133. Ranges over all the arts. Published by artists.

Left Open, Box 211, Teachers College, Columbia University, New York, N.Y., 10027. Newsletter of the Emancipatory Education Collective.

Liberation, 186 Hampshire St., Cambridge, Mass., 02139. Wide coverage of current political, social, and cultural issues.

The Longest Revolution, P.O. Box 350, San Diego, Ca., 92101. "Progressive feminism."

Madness Network News, 2150 Market St., San Francisco, Ca., 94114.

Magnus, P.O. Box 40568, San Francisco, Ca., 94140. Socialist gay lib.

Majority Report, 74 Grove St., New York, N.Y., 10014. Often contains radical articles on issues related to women's liberation.

Marxist Perspectives, 420 West End Ave., New York, N.Y., 10024. Scholarly Marxist history journal.

The Match, P.O. Box 3488, Tucson, Arizona, 85722. Anarchist.

Matter Over Mind, 333 Central Park West (Apt. 14, Rm. 314), New York, N.Y., 10025. Newsletter of the New York Institute of Social Therapy.

Mediations, c/o Sonia Michel, 18 Middlesex St., Cambridge, Mass., 02140. Newsletter of the Marxist Literary Group of the Modern Languages Association.

Minnesota Review, Box 5416, Milwaukee, Wis., 53211. Frequently includes Marxist literary theory and criticism.

Modern Times, P.O. Box 11208, Moiliili Station, Honolulu, Hi., 96828. Seeks out dialogue between different kinds of socialists.

Monthly Review, 62 West 14th St., New York, N.Y., 10011. Most widely read American Marxist journal. Focuses on the American economy, imperialism, liberation movements, and the socialist world.

Mother Jones, 1255 Portland Place, Boulder, Col., 80302. Radical generalist, an attempt to start up where *Ramparts* left off.

Mountain Life and Work, Drawer N, Clintwood, Virginia, 24223. Publication of the Citizens for Social and Economic Justice in the Appalachians.

The National Conference on Alternative State and Local Public Policies Newsletter, c/o I.P.S., 1901 Q Street, N.W., Washington, D.C., 20009. News of/by progressives in government.

The Network Project Newsletter, 101 Earl Hall, Columbia University, New York, N.Y., 10025. The communications media.

New German Critique, German Dept., Box 413, University of Wisconsin-Milwaukee, Milwaukee, Wisc., 53201. Radical and Marxist approaches to German studies. Many important translations.

The New Harbinger: A Journal of the Cooperative Movement, Dept. P, Box 1301, Ann Arbor, Mich., 48106.

The New International Review, P.O. Box 26020, Tempe, Ariz., 85282. Political and theoretical journal of social democratic orientation.

New Politics, 507 Fifth Ave., New York, N.Y., 10017. General political and theoretical journal of social democratic orientation.

A New Political Science, c/o Vanden, Dept. of Political Science, University of South Florida, Tampa, Fla., 33620. Newsjournal of the Caucus for a New Political Science.

New Schools Exchange Newsletter, NSE, Pettigrew, Ark., 72752. "Educational liberation."

News from the Federation for Economic Democracy, 2100 M St., N.W. (Rm. 607), Washington, D.C., 20063. Self-management.

New York Review of Books, P.O. Box 940, Farmingdale, N.Y., 11735. Review essays from generally progressive standpoints.

No More Teachers Dirty Looks, 88 Sanchez, San Francisco, Ca., 94114. Journal of the Bay Area Radical Teachers Organizing Committee (BARTOC).

Notes on Health Politics, Health Professionals for Political Action, Box 386, Kenmore Station, Boston, Mass., 02215.

NRAG Papers, 9 Placer St., Helena, Mont., 59601. Journal of the Northern Rockies Action Group.

October, c/o Jaap Rietman, 167 Spring St., New York, N.Y., 10012. Radical film criticism.

Off Our Backs, 1724 20th St., N.W., Washington, D.C., 20009. "Feminist . . . socialist, anarchist, communist" news journal.

Oral History of the American Left Newsletter, Tamiment Institute, Bobst Library, New York University, Washington Square, New York, N.Y., 10012.

Outlaw, Prisoner's Union, 1315 18th St., San Francisco, Ca., 94107. Radical prison news and analysis.

Partisan Review, 1 Richardson St., New Brunswick, N.J., 08903. Frequently contains radical criticism of culture, politics, and philosophy.

Pass-Age, 3617 Powelton Ave., Philadelphia, Pa., 19104. "Humane investigation of future possibilities."

Paunch, 123 Woodward Ave., Buffalo, N.Y., 14214. From literature to Marxist theory.

Philosophers Committee on Alternative Resources Newsletter, c/o Dr. C. Ake, Dept. of Philosophy, Rutgers University, New Brunswick, N.J., 08903.

PIE Newsletter, 1714 Massachusetts Ave., N.W., Washington, D.C., 20036. Newsletter of Public Interest Economic Foundation.

Planners Network Newsletter, 360 Elizabeth St., San Francisco, Ca., 94114. Radical planners.

Point of Production, 168 St. Johns Pl., Brooklyn, N.Y., 11217. Marxist economics. A lot of useful statistics.

Political Economy of the World System Newsletter, c/o Fred Block, Dept. of Sociology, University of Pennsylvania, Philadelphia, Pa., 19074. Especially interested in the effects of the international division of labor on the origins and development of capitalist society. (See also *Review.*)

Politics and Education, Wesleyan Station, Fisk Hall, Middletown, Conn., 06457. Radical news and analysis of higher education.

Politics and Society, Geron-X Inc., Box 1108, Los Altos, Ca., 94022. Radical theory and research in political science and related social sciences.

Politiks and Other Human Interests, 271 Madison Ave., New York, N.Y., 10016. Mildly left news and analysis with many interesting columnists.

Poverty Law Report, 1001 S. Hull St., Montgomery, Al., 36101. Focus on civil rights issues affecting the poor, particularly in southeastern U.S.

Praxis, P.O. Box 207, Golita, Ca., 93017. Wide range of articles on aesthetics and the arts.

Prison Newsletter, Voices from Within, P.O. Box 5548, Berkeley, Ca., 94705. "Analysis of prison, revolutionary prisoners' movement, community struggles."

Progressive, 408 W. Gorham St., Madison, Wis., 53703. A long-time liberal magazine has moved a few notches left with a new editor.

Psych-Agitator, Dept. of Psychology, SUNY, Stony Brook, N.Y., 11794. Marxist-oriented psychology newsletter.

Quest: A Feminist Quarterly, P.O. Box 8843, Washington, D.C., 20003. Issues on special topics. Marxist and feminist theory.

Radical Alliance of Social Service Workers Newsletter, P.O. Box 70, New York, N.Y., 10028.

Radical America, P.O. Box B, North Cambridge, Mass., 02140. Emphasis on workers and worker history.

Radical History Review, P.O. Box 946, New York, N.Y., 10025. Journal of the Mid-Atlantic Radical Historians' Organization (MARHO).

Radical Philosophers' Newsjournal, 12 Dartmouth St., Somerville, Mass., 02145. Radical and Marxist philosophy. Becoming less of a newsletter and more of a journal with each issue.

Radical Religion, P.O. Box 9164, Berkeley, Ca., 94709. Radical approaches to theology.

Radical Teacher, P.O. Box 102, Kendal Square Post Office, Cambridge, Mass., 02142. Journal of the Radical Caucus in English and the Modern Languages Association. Focus on the theory and practice of radical teaching in all disciplines, though most pieces so far have dealt with cultural subjects.

Recon, P.O. Box 14602, Philadelphia, Pa., 19134. "Keeping an eye on the Pentagon."

Red Herring, P.O. Box 557, Canal Street Station, New York, N.Y., 10013. Successor of *The Fox*. Chiefly cultural workers analyzing and commenting on culture.

Redlining Reporter, 1516 Westwood Blvd., Suite 202, Los Angeles, Ca., 90024. Against unfair banking practices.

Reliable Source, Fenwick Publishing Co., 36 W. 22nd St., New York, N.Y., 10010. Sometimes radical humor magazine.

Resist, 720 Massachusetts Ave., R.4, Cambridge, Mass., 02139. Newsletter focusing on resisting illegitimate authority.

Review, Fernand Braudel Center, SUNY-Binghamton, Binghamton, N.Y., 13901. "Economics, historical systems, and civilizations" from generally Marxist perspectives. (See also *Political Economy of the World System Newsletter*.)

The Review of Radical Political Economics, c/o Union for Radical Political Economics (URPE), 41 Union Square West (Rm. 901), New York, N.Y., 10003. Wide range of topics in political economy. Frequent special issues, including one on teaching and some devoted to bibliography.

Revolutionary World (U.S. & International), B. R. Grunner, P.O. Box 70020, Amsterdam, Holland. "Marxist philosophy."

Rights, National Emergency Civil Liberties Committee, 25 E. 26th St., New York, N.Y., 10010.

Roots, Box 344, Cooper Station, New York, N.Y., Publication of Ecology Action East (EAE). Radical ecology.

Science Fiction Studies, Dept. of English, Indiana State University, Terre Haute, Ind., 42809. Frequently contains radical criticism of science fiction.

Semiotexte, 522 Philosophy Hall, Columbia University, New York, N.Y., 10027. Analyzes "the power mechanisms which produce and maintain the present division of knowledge." The latest from France.

Science and Society, John Jay College (Rm. 4331), CUNY, 445 W. 59th St., New York, N.Y., 10019. Oldest of the extant scholarly Marxist journals published in the U.S. Important contributions in many fields.

Science for the People, 897 Main St., Cambridge, Mass., 02139. Popular articles on science and the politics of science and technology.

The Second Wave, Box 344, Cambridge A, Cambridge, Mass., 02139. Multifaceted feminist journal. Mixed politics.

Shelterforce, 380 Main St., East Orange, N.J., 07018. "A national housing newspaper."

Sing Out!, 270 Lafayette St., New York, N.Y., 10012. Radical folk songs.

Sipapu, Route 1, Box 216, Winters, Ca., 95616. Newsletter on alternate press and Third World studies mainly for editors and librarians.

Social Policy, Suite 500, 184 Fifth Ave., New York, N.Y., 10010. Often radical treatment of social services and public policy.

Social Research, New School for Social Research, 66 W. 12th St., New York, N.Y., 10011. Academic journal frequently devoted to articles by socialists on topics of interest to the Left.

Social Text, c/o John Brinkman, 944 Van Hise Hall, University of Wisconsin, Madison, Wis., 53706. Marxist theoretical journal. Focus on bourgeois ideology and culture.

Socialist Review, 396 Sanchez St., San Francisco, Ca., 94114. Formerly *Socialist Revolution*. Major Marxist theoretical journal.

Social Theory and Practice, Dept. of Philosophy, University of Florida, Tallahassee, Fla., 32306. Academic, but frequently contains articles on socialist theory.

Society, Box A, Rutgers University, New Brunswick, N.J., 08903. Left social science, popular slant.

Society for Social Responsibility in Science Review, 86 Lenox Hill Station, New York, N.Y., 10021.

Sociologists' Committee on Alternative Resources Newsletter, c/o Dr. Francine Moulder, Dept. of Sociology, Livingston College, Rutgers University, New Brunswick, N.J., 08903.

Soil of Liberty, Box 7056, Powderhorn Station, Minneapolis, Minn., 55407. Anarchist.

Southern Exposure, Box 230, Chapel Hill, N.C., 27514. Radical and left liberal articles on the South, old and new.

Southern Struggle, 3210 W. Broadway, Louisville, Ky., 40211. Publication of the Southern Conference Education Fund (SCEF).

South West Economy and Society, Box 4482, Albuquerque, N.M., 87106. Critical studies of regional development in the Southwest.

Spark, C.S.R.E., 475 Riverside Dr., New York, N.Y., 10027. Radical engineering journal.

Spirit of the People, P.O. Box 3426, St. Paul, Minn., 55165. Newsletter of the Native American Solidarity Committee.

State of Mind, P.O. Box 89, W. Somerville, Mass., 02144. Formerly *RT: A Journal of Radical Therapy* (before that *Rough Times* and *The Radical Therapist*). What does Freud say about changing names so often?

The Storm, 227 Columbus Ave., Apt. 2E, New York, N.Y., 10023. Anarchist.

Studies in Marxism, Marxist Education Press, c/o Dept. of Anthropology, University of Minnesota, 224 Church St., S.E., Minneapolis, Minn., 55455. Each issue focuses on a different problem in Marxist theory.

Synthesis, Box 1858, San Pedro, Ca., 90733. Newsletter of League for Economic Democracy. Self-management.

Synthesis, Box 1858, San Pedro, Ca., 90733. Newsletter of League for Economic Democracy. Self-management.

Talking Back, c/o Workers Studies/A.S., College of Old Westbury, Old Westbury, N.Y., 11568. In the voices of real workers.

Televisions, Washington Community Video Center, P.O. Box 21068, Washington, D.C., 20009. Moderately left reportage of what is happening in/on TV.

Telos, Dept. of Sociology, Washington University, St. Louis, Mo., 63130. Social theory and philosophy. Translates many important articles. Recent issues contain short, annotated reviews of many left theoretical journals.

Theory and Society (U.S. and International), 52 Vanderbilt Ave., New York, N.Y., 10017; Elsevier Scientific Pub. Co., Box 211, Amsterdam, The Netherlands. Academic journal, frequently contains articles by socialists on various aspects of social theory.

Toward Revolutionary Art, P.O. Box 40909, San Francisco, Ca., 94140.

Transnational Link Newsletter, Institute for Policy Studies, 1901 Q St., N.W., Washington, D.C., 20009. On the activities of I.P.S. and its affiliate, The Transnational Institute.

Union of Concerned Scientists Newsletter, 1208 Massachusetts Ave., Cambridge, Mass., 02138.

Union of Marxist Social Scientists Newsletter, Dept. of Sociology, 410 Barrows Hall, University of California, Berkeley, Ca., 94720.

Union for Radical Political Economics' Newsletter, 41 Union Square West (Rm. 901), New York, N.Y., 10003.

Urban and Social Change Review, McGuin Hall, Boston College, Chestnut Hill, Mass., 02162.

U.S. Farm News, Box 496, Hampton, Iowa, 50441. Radical farm news and analysis.

The Veteran (formerly *Winter Soldier*), Vietnam Veterans Against the War/Winter Soldier Org., P.O. Box 20184, Chicago, Ill., 60620.

Washington Watch, Dept. GUI, 3308 Cedar, Lansing, Michigan, 48910. "Inside report to and from grassroots America."

The Welfare Fighter, 1424 16th St., N.W., Washington, D.C., 20036. Publication of the National Welfare Rights Organization (NWRO).

Win, Box 547, Rifton, N.Y., 12471. Pacifist-socialist journal.

Woman and Film, P.O. Box 4501, Berkeley Ca., 94704. "A journal of Sex-Media-Art in transition."

Women: A Journal of Liberation, 3028 Greenmount Ave., Baltimore, Md., 21218. "A Socialist/Feminist magazine."

Women and Revolution, Box 1377, GPO, New York, N.Y., 10001. Publication of the Sparticist League (SL).

Working Papers for a New Society, Dept. 538, 123 Mt. Auburn St., Cambridge, Mass., 02138. Socialist and left liberal articles emphasizing alternatives to the present order.

Workforce, 5951 Canning St., Oakland, Ca., 94609. Publication of Vocations for Social Change.

2. Mainly foreign and international themes

Africa Today, G.S.I.S., University of Denver, Denver, Col., 80208. Emphasis on liberation struggles.

Amnesty Update, National Council for Universal Unconditional Amnesty (NCUUA), 339 Lafayette St., New York, N.Y., 10012.

The Asia Mail, P.O. Box 1044, Alexandria, Va., 22313. Socialist analysis of Asian affairs.

Bulletin of Concerned Asian Scholars, Bay Area Institute, 604 Mission St. (Rm. 1001), San Francisco, Ca., 94105. What it says.

Brazil Information Bulletin, P.O. Box 2279, Station A, Berkeley, Ca., 94702.

Canto Libre, Center for Cuban Studies, 220 E. 23rd St., New York, N.Y., 10010. Cuban culture.

Center for Cuban Studies Newsletter, 220 E. 23rd St., New York, N.Y., 10010. Cuban culture.

Chile Newsletter, Non-Intervention in Chile (NICH), P.O. Box 800, Berkeley, Ca., 94701.

Chinese Scientific Journals, Plenum Publishing Co., 227 W. 17th St., New York, N. Y., 10011. Translations from Chinese periodicals.

Chinese Economic Studies, M.E. Sharpe, Inc., 901 N. Broadway, White Plains, N.Y., 10603. Translations from Chinese periodicals.

Chinese Education, ibid.

Chinese Law and Government, ibid.

Chinese Sociology and Anthropology, ibid.

Chinese Studies in History, ibid.

Chinese Studies in Philosophy, ibid.

Coalition for a New Foreign and Military Policy Newsletter, 120 Maryland Ave., N.E., Washington, D.C., 20002. Radical foreign policy information and analysis.

Community Action on Latin America Newsletter, 731 State St., Madison, Wis., 53703.

Cuba Review, Cuban Resource Center, P.O. Box 206, Cathedral Station, New York, N.Y., 10025.

Demokratia, P.O. Box 678, New York, N.Y. 10009. Struggles for Greek liberation.

European Labor and Working Class History Newsletter, Dept. of History, University of Southern California, Los Angeles, Ca., 70007. Stresses reviews and bibliographies.

Far East Reporter, P.O. Box 1536, New York, N.Y., 10017. China news.

First World, 1580 Avon Ave., S.W., Atlanta, Ga., 30311. International journal of black thought.

Gulf Solidarity, Box 40155, San Francisco, Ca., 94140. Radical politics in the Gulf.

Haiti Report, The Friends of Haiti, P.O. Box 348, New City, N.Y., 10956. News and analysis of imperialism in Haiti and the struggle for liberation.

Indochina Chronicle, P.O. Box 4000 E, Berkeley, Ca., 94704.

Indochina Solidarity Committee Newsletter, Box C, Old Chelsea Station, New York, N.Y., 10011.

Info: West Germany, New York Committee for Civil Liberties in West Germany, P.O. Box 483, Village Station, New York, N.Y., 10014.

Iran Report, P.O. Box 2310, Berkeley, Ca., 94702. Publication of the Confederation of Iranian Students National Union (CISNU).

Iranian People's Struggle, SCIPS, P.O. Box 671, New York, N.Y., 10011.

Israel Horizon, 150 5th Avenue, New York, N.Y. Publication of Americans for a Progressive Israel (Israeli MAPAM).

Journal of the Hellenic Diaspora, Hellenic American Society, P.O. Box 22334, Indianapolis, Ind., 37820. Critical views on modern Greece.

Korea Bulletin, P.O. Box 1952, San Francisco, Ca., 94101. Publication of the Committee for Solidarity with the Korean People (CSKP).

Korea Link, 665 Lytton Ave., Palo Alto, Ca., 94301. Radical analysis of South Korea.

Latin America and Empire Report, P.O. Box 57, Cathedral Station, New York, N.Y., 10025. Journal of the North American Congress on Latin America (NACLA). Focus on imperialism.

Latin American Perspectives, C.M.S.I., P.O. Box 792, Riverside, Ca., 92502. Radical L.A. political, social, and cultural analyses. Frequently special issues.

Liberation, P.O. Box 1247, New York, N.Y., 10027. Publication of Eritreans for Liberation in North America (EFLNA).

Liberation Support Movement News, LSM Press, P.O. Box 2077, Oakland, Ca., 94604.

Merip Reports, P.O. Box 48, Cambridge, Mass., 02138. Publication of the Middle East Research and Information Project, focusing on the politics and political economy of the Middle East.

Monthly Review (see Part 1).

NATO Analysis, Norfolk Action Research on the Military (NARM), Box 11324, Norfolk, Va., 23517.

New China Magazine, 41 Union Square (Rm. 1228), New York, N.Y., 10003. Publication of the U.S.–China People's Friendship Association.

New Internationalist, 113 Atlantic Ave., Brooklyn, N.Y., 11201. Mildly radical, popular treatment of key issues in international affairs.

News from Libertarian Spain, Libertarian Press Service, Freespace Alternate U., 339 Lafayette St., New York, N.Y. 10012.

Newsfront International, People's Translation Service, 4216 Telegraph Ave., Oakland, Ca., 94609. Translations of news and analysis from the progressive foreign press.

Pacific Imperialism Notebook, Pacific Rim Project, Box 26415, San Francisco, Ca., 94126.

Pacific Research and World Empire Telegram, Pacific Studies Center, 1963 University Ave., East Palo Alto, Ca., 94303. Articles on multinationals, the political economy of S.E. Asia, and on U.S. foreign policy.

Pakistan Progressive, P.O. Box 8, Cathedral Station, New York, N.Y., 10025. Publication of the Organization of Progressive Pakistanis (OPP).

Palestine, Palestine Solidarity Committee, Box 1757, Manhattanville Station, New York, N.Y., 10027.

Philippines Information Bulletin, Box 409, W. Somerville, Mass., 02144.

Philippine Liberation Courier, P.O. Box 24737, Oakland, Ca., 94623. Publication of International Association of Philippine Patriots.

Point of Contact, 110 Bleecker St. (16B), New York, N.Y., 10012.

Latin American themes in literature and politics. Some articles in Spanish.

Puerto Rico Libre, Puerto Rico Solidarity Committee, P.O. Box 319, Cooper Station, New York, N.Y., 10003.

Resistance, Box 4002, Berkeley, Ca., 94701. Newsletter of the Iranian Student Association. Emphasis on repression in Iran and the role of U.S. imperialism.

Resistance Courier, Box 116, Oakland, Ca., 94604. News of the Chilean resistance.

Soviet Anthropology and Archeology, M.E. Sharpe, Inc., 901 N. Broadway, White Plains, N.Y., 10603. Translations from Soviet academic journals.

Soviet Education, ibid.

Soviet Law and Government, ibid.

Soviet Neurology and Psychiatry, ibid.

Soviet Psychology, ibid.

Soviet Sociology, ibid.

The Soviet Review, ibid. Various fields.

Soviet Studies in History, ibid.

Soviet Studies in Literature, ibid.

Soviet Studies in Philosophy, ibid. Write to M.E. Sharpe, Inc., for the full list of such publications.

Southern Africa, 156 5th Ave. (Rm. 707A), New York, N.Y., 10011. Radical news and analysis of Southern Africa.

The Struggle, United in Struggle Press, 175 5th Ave., New York, N.Y., 10010. Focus on struggles against poverty around the world.

Third World Women's Research Newsletter, c/o Harriet G. McCombs, Dept. of Psychology, University of Nebraska, Lincoln, Neb., 68588.

Thoi-Bao-Ga, Vietnam Resource Center, 76a Pleasant St., Cambridge, Ma., 02139. Newsletter on Indochina.

Union of Radical Latin Americanists Newsletter, c/o LAPAG, 2205 San Antonio St., Austin, Texas, 78705.

U.S./Indochina Report, 1322 18th St., N.W., Washington, D.C., 20036.

Vietnam Quarterly, 108 N. Mole St., Philadelphia, Pa., 19102.

Zimbabwe Bulletin, ZANU Solidarity Committee, Box 181, Bronx, N.Y., 19453.

B. Great Britain

1. Mainly national and theoretical themes

Alternative Press Digest, 22 Dane Rd., Margate, Kent.

Artery, c/o Jeff Sawtell, 2 S. Villas, London NW1. Left culture.

Black Flag, Publications Distribution Coop., 27 Clerkenwell Close, London EC1R 0AT. Anarchist.

Black Liberator, Publications Distribution Coop., 27 Clerkenwell Close, London EC1R 0AT. Theory and practice of black liberation.

Bulletin of the Institute for Workers Control, Bertrand Russell House, Gamble St., Nottingham N67 4ET.

Bulletin of the Society of Labour History, 111 Kings Rd., Old Trafford, Manchester. A lot of bibliographies.

Bulletin of the Workers' Music Association, 236 Westbourne Park Rd., London W11.

Calgacus, The Schoolhouse, Dornie, by Kyle of Lochalsh, Ross-shire, Scotland. Scottish socialist journal.

Camerawork, c/o Half-Moon Gallery, 27 Allie St., London E1. Radical critique of photography.

Cambridge Journal of Economics, 111 Fifth Ave., New York, N.Y. Journal of the Cambridge Political Economy Society. Articles from critical perspectives, including Marxism.

Capital and Class, C.S.E., c/o Economics Dept., Birkbeck College, 7-15 Gresse St., London W1P 1PA. Formerly the *Bulletin of the Conference of Socialist Economists*. Theoretical journal of the C.S.E., Britain's U.R.P.E. Contains some of the best articles on Marxist economics.

Case Con, Basement Flat, 110 Lansdowne Way, London SW8. Radical social work.

The Christian Socialist, Kingsway Hall, Kingsway, London WC2.

Cienfuegos Review of Anarchist Literature, Publications Distribution Coop., 27 Clerkenwell Close, London EC1R 0AT.

Community Action, 27 Clerkenwell Close, London EC1. Focus on local struggles.

Crisis, Counter Information Service, 9 Poland St., London W1. Left journalists report on what's behind the news.

Critique of Anthropology, P.O. Box 178, London WCLE 6BU. Chiefly Marxist anthropology.

Education Today and Tomorrow, 16 King St., London WC2. Education journal of the Communist Party of Great Britain. (CPGB).

Economy and Society, Broadway House, Reading Rd., Henley-on-Thames, Oxon RG9 1EN. "Concentrates on fundamental theoretical and philosophical work, and on structural and holistic analysis."

Falling Wall Review, 79 Richmond Rd., Monpelier, Bristol BS6 5EP. Wages for housework perspective.

Fireweed, 107 Bowerham Rd., Lancaster. Focus on socialist and working class arts.

Gay Left, 36a Craven Rd., London W2.

History Today, 16 King St., London. History journal of the CPGB.

History Workshop, P.O. Box 69, Oxford OX2 7XA. Excellent Marxist history journal making use of film, museum, literary, and oral as well as written sources.

Humpty Dumpty, 28 Redbourne Ave., London N3. Radical psychology, therapy.

Ideology and Consciousness, Woburn Mansions, Torrington Place, London WC1. "Marxist journal in psychology, psychoanalysis, education, linguistics, semiology."

In the Making, Publications Distribution Coop., 27 Clerkenwell Close, London EC1R 0AT. "Forum for the feasibility of self-management both now and in the future."

Labour Monthly, 16 King St., London WC2. Labor publication of the CPGB.

Labour Research, 68 Blackfriars Rd., London SE1. Industrial notes and statistics.

The Leveller, 155a Drummond St., London NW1. News of what is happening on the British left.

Libertarian Communism, Publications Distribution Coop., 27 Clerkenwell Close, London EC1R 0AT. Formerly *Anarchist Worker*.

Libertarian Education, 6 Beaconfield Rd., Leicester.

Librarians for Social Change, c/o J.L. Noyce, P.O. Box 450, Brighton BN1 8GR.

Literature and History, The Library, Thomas Polytechnic, Woolwich, London SE18. Where the two meet.

Medicine in Society, 74 Bookdale Rd., London E17. Marxists journal of health studies.

Musics, 48 Hillsborough Ct., Mortimer Crescent, London NW6. Radical music criticism.

National Deviancy Conference Newsletter, c/o Mike Fitzgerald, Faculty of Social Science, Open University, Milton Keynes.

New Dance, 103 Delaware Rd., London W9. Radical dance criticism.

New Left Review, 7 Carlisle St., London W1V 6NL. Major Marxist theoretical journal. Also translates important contributions from France, Germany, etc.

New Statesman, 10 Great Turnstile St., London WC1. Political news and analysis, culture.

Newsletter of the Marx Memorial Library, 37a Clerkenwell Green, London EC1. Book notes and brief reviews of works on Marxism.

Oral History, Dept. of Sociology, University of Essex, Colchester. Emphasis on working class and socialist history.

Past and Present, P.O. Box 28, Oxford OX2 7BN. Established journal of socialist historians.

Power of Women, Falling Wall Book Service, 79 Richmond Rd., Montpelier, Bristol. Magazine of the International Wages for Housework Campaign.

Private Eye, 34 Greek St., London W1. Sometimes radical humor mag.

Race Today, 74 Shakespeare Rd., London SE24 0PT. Problems of race and class, particularly as they are developing in England.

Radical Education, 86 Eleanor Rd., London E8. Socialist criticism of contemporary education; also explores radical education in England and abroad.

Radical Philosophy, 40 Langdon Park Rd., London N6 5QG. Offers admirably clear critiques of establishment philosophy along with radical, usually Marxist, alternatives. Great cartoons and humor for those who know some philosophy.

Radical Science Journal, 9 Poland St., London W1 3DG. Scholarly Marxist approach to history, current practice, philosophy, and ideology of science and technology.

Radical Statistics, c/o John Irvine, 14 Upper Wellington Rd., Brighton, Sussex.

Red Letters, 16 King St., London WC2. Literary journal of the CPGB.

Red Rag, 22 Murray Mews, London NW1. Marxist feminist journal.

Review of International Cooperation, 11 Upper Grosvenor St., London W1X 9PA. Journal of the International Coop. Alliance.

Revolutionary Socialism, Publications Distribution Coop., 27 Clerkenwell Close, London EC1R OAT. News of the left in Britain and abroad.

Rights, 186 King's Cross Rd., London WC1. Civil liberties.

Science Bulletin, 16 King St., London WC2. Science and technical journal of the CPGB.

Science for the People, British Society for Social Responsibility in Science, 9 Poland St., London W1V 3DG.

Searchlight, AF & R Pubs., 21 Great Western Bldgs., 6 Livery St., Birmingham 3. On the struggle against racism and fascism.

Social Studies of Science, Sage Publications Ltd., 44 Hatton Garden, London EC1 N8ER. Many articles have a critical slant.

Socialist Register, Merlin Press, 2/4 West Ferry Rd., London E14. Annual collection of some of the best in socialist scholarship on a wide range of topics.

Socialist Teacher, 24 St. Agnes Close, London E9. Focus on teacher struggles and unions.

Sparerib, 9 Newburgh St., London WC1. Socialist feminism.

The Spokesman Journal, Bertrand Russell House, Gamble St., Nottingham NG7 4ET. Wide-ranging socialist journal of analysis.

Studies in Labour History, J. L. Noyce, P.O. Box 450, Brighton BN1 8GR.

Teachers Action, 2 Turguand St., London SE 17. Teachers as workers.

Teaching City Kids, 79 Ronalds Rd., London N5. Radical teaching strategies.

Time Out, 374 Grays Inn Rd., London WC1.

Undercurrents, 213 Archway Rd., London N6. "Radical science and people's technology."

Voice of the Unions, 73 Ridgeway Pl., London SW19. Especially news relating to workers' control of industry.

Wedge, Publications Distribution Coop., 27 Clerkenwell Close, London EC1R OAT. Revolutionary cultural theory and practice.

Wildcat, Box 999, 197 Kings Cross Rd., London WC1.

Women's Voice, 6 Cottons Gardens, London E2.

The Workers Control Bulletin, Bertrand Russell House, Gamble St., Nottingham NG7 4ET.

Working Papers in Cultural Studies, Center for Cultural Studies, University of Birmingham, Birmingham. Includes important theoretical as well as empirical studies of culture, especially of popular culture. Also some general Marxist theoretical pieces.

Zero, Rising Free, 182 Upper St., London N1. Anarcho-feminist.

Zoo, Dept. of Town and Country Planning, Heriot-Watt University, Edinburgh College of Art, Lauriston Pl., Edinburgh, Scotland. Radical planning mag.

2. Mainly foreign and international themes

African Communist, Inkululeko Publications, 39 Goodge St., London W1. Publication of the South African Communist Party (CPSA).

China Now, 152 Camden High St., London NW1 ONR.

China Policy Study Group Broadsheet, 62 Parliament Hill, London NW3 2TJ.

Critique, 31 Clevedon Rd., Glasgow G12 OPH, Scotland. Independent, scholarly Marxist journal offering critical analyses of the USSR and East Europe. Includes relevant theoretical pieces.

Ikwezi, 8–11 Victoria Centre, Nottingham. Analysis of politics in South Africa.

Labour Focus on Eastern Europe, Publication Distribution Coop., 27 Clerkenwell Close, London EC1R OAT. Focus on working-class developments.

Namibia News, SWAPO, 21/25 Tabernacle St., London EC2.

On Target, Publications Distribution Coop., 27 Clerkenwell Close, London EC1R OAT. Libertarian socialist analysis of the Middle East.

Problems of Communism, c/o BICO Printers, 9 Denmark St., London WC2, England. Publication of the British and Irish Communist Organization focusing on problems in the communist countries.

Race and Class, 247–9 Pentonville Rd., London N1. Journal of the Institute of Race Relations and the Transnational Institute. Emphasizes labor movement and workers' struggles in former British colonies, and conditions of immigrant labor in Britain and Europe.

Review of African Political Economy, Merlin Press, 2–4 West Ferry Rd., London E14. Mainly Marxist analysis of African affairs.

Sechaba, African National Congress, 49 Rathbone St., London W1A 4NL.

South Asian Marxist Review, 182 Pentonville Rd., London N1.

Verboten, Publications Distribution Coop., 27 Clerkenwell Close, London EC1R OAT. News on the repression of the Left in West Germany.

C. Other (selected)

1. Mainly first and second world, and theoretical themes

AA News, AA Verlag, Postfach 3, Unt. Haupstr. 9, Austria-7100, Neusiedl/See. Theory and practice of Actions-Analytical Organization for Conscious Life Praxis, a libertarian commune.

Albania Report, P.O. Box 912, New York, N.Y., 10008. Albanian journal of political news and analysis.

Albania Today, P.O. Box 912, New York, N.Y., 10008. Albanian journal on politics and life in Albania.

Alive Magazine, Box 1331, Guelph, Ontario, Canada. Marxist literary mag.

Alternatives: Perspectives on Society and Environment, Trent University, Peterborough, Ontario, Canada.

AMEX Canada, P.O. Box 189, Station P, Toronto, Ontario, Canada. Published by American war resisters in exile.

Arena, Box 36, Greensborough, Victoria 3088, Australia. General radical journal treating politics, history, and culture.

Australia Left Review, Box A247, Sydney, South P.O. 2000, Australia. Marxist analysis and information.

Body Politic, Dept. OW Box 7289, Station A, Toronto, Canada MSW 1X9. Left gay liberation journal.

Canadian Dimension, P.O. Box 1413, Winnipeg, Manitoba, Canada R3C 2Z1. Left politics and culture.

Canadian Revolution, P.O. Box 164, Station G, Toronto, Ontario, Canada.

Cine-Tracts, 4227 Esplanade Ave., Montreal, Quebec, Canada H2W 1T1. "Current issues of social theory and cultural practice."

Class Struggle, Lutte Ouvrière: Spark, BP 233, 75865 Paris, Cedex 18, France. In French and English.

The Critical List, 32 Sullivan St., Toronto, Ontario, Canada. Socialist health journal.

Dialectics and Humanism, Studia Filozoficzne, Nowy Swiat 49, 00-042 Warszawa, Poland. Polish philosophical journal.

Economics and Law, Imported Publications, Inc., 320 W. Ohio St., Chicago, Ill., 60610. Abstracts published by the Bulgarian Academy of Sciences. (Write to Imported Publications, Inc., for their full list of Eastern European English-language publications.)

Etudes de Marxologie, 76 rue des Plantes, Paris 14, France. Leading scholarly journal on Marxism. Frequently publishes articles and reviews in English.

European Group for the Study of Deviance and Social Control Newsletter, c/o Mario Simondi, Dept. of Stat., via Curtatone, 1-50123 Firenze, Italy.

Hecate, G.P.O. Box 99, St. Lucia, Queensland 4067, Australia. Socialist feminism.

International Affairs, Four Continent Book Corp., 149 5th Ave., New York, N.Y., 10010. Soviet journal of international affairs.

International Review of Social History, International Institute Voor Sociale Geschiedenis, Herengracht 262-6, Amsterdam, The Netherlands. Scholarly, generally Marxist, articles.

The Journal of Australian Political Economy, APEM, C-Box 76, Wentworth Bldg., University of Sydney, N.S.W., 2006, Australia. Radical academic economists.

Labour/Le Travailleur, Committee on Canadian Labour History, c/o G. Kealy, Dept. of History, Dalhousie University, Halifax, Nova Scotia, Canada. Canadian labor history.

Labour History, P.O. Box 1577, Canberra City, ACT 2601, Australia. Journal of the Australian Society for the Study of Labor History.

Last Post, Canadian Journalism Foundation Inc., 454 King St. (Rm. 302), Toronto, Ontario, Canada MV5 126. Left politics.

Leftward, P.O. Box 429, Station E, Toronto, Ontario, Canada. Anarchist.

May Day, P.O. Box 69403, Station K, Vancouver, British Columbia, Canada. Socialist criticism of the arts.

New Albania, P.O. Box 912, New York, N.Y., 10008. Pictorial magazine on Albania's domestic and international affairs.

New Canada, N.C. Press Ltd., Box 6106, Station A, Toronto 1, Ontario, Canada. Radical look at Canadian affairs.

New Times, Four Continent Book Corp., 149 5th Ave., New York, N.Y., 10010. Soviet journal on "current international events."

Next Year's Country, Box 3446, Regina, Saskatchewan, Canada. Left politics.

Organizing, Commonact, Box 333, Cobalt, Ontario, Canada.

Our Generation, 3934 rue St. Urbain, Montreal 131, Canada. Canadian and international questions.

Peace and the Sciences, The International Institute for Peace, Mollwaldplatz 5, A-1040 Vienna, Austria.

Radical Biologist, P.O. Box 87, Carlton South, Victoria 3053, Australia.

Radical Education, 10 Reuss St., Glebe 2037, Sydney, Australia. Focus on schools as reproducers of inequality.

Social Praxis (Canadian), published by Mouton, Box 462, The Hague, The Netherlands. "International and interdisciplinary quarterly of social sciences." Frequently contains socialist material.

Social Sciences, Four Continents Book Corp., 149 5th Ave., New York, N.Y., 10010. Soviet journal on the theory and practice of social science.

Socialism: Theory and Practice, ibid. Soviet "digest of the political and theoretical press."

Soviet Film, ibid. Soviet journal on Soviet and foreign films.

Soviet Union, ibid. Glossy Soviet journal on all aspects of Soviet life.

Soviet Woman, ibid. Soviet journal on women in the USSR.

Twentieth Century and Peace, ibid. Soviet journal on Soviet views of peace and disarmament. (Write to Four Continents Book Corp. for the full list of Soviet English-language publications.)

This Magazine, 56 Esplanade St. E (4th Fl.), Toronto, Ontario, Canada. Radical politics.

Working Teacher, Box 46534, Postal Station G, 3760 W. 10th Ave., Vancouver, British Columbia, Canada V6R 2GO.

2. Mainly Third World themes

AMPO Japan-Asia Quarterly Review, P.O. Box 5250, Tokyo International, Japan.

ANCHA, B.P. 59, Cedex 13, 75623 Paris, France. Publication of the Chilean Anti-Fascist News Agency.

Asia and Africa Today, Four Continent Book Corp., 149 5th Ave., New York, N.Y., 10010. Soviet journal on politics and culture of Africa and Asia.

Brazilian Studies, Box 673, Adelaide Station, Toronto 1, Ontario, Canada.

The Call, 780 Ballimaran, Delhi-6, India.

Caribbean Dialogue, Box 442, Station J, Toronto, Ontario, Canada. Publication of the New Beginning Movement of Trinidad.

Chinese Medical Journal, China Books and Periodicals, 125 5th Ave., New York, N.Y., 10003. Chinese journal reporting on the achievements of Chinese medicine.

China Reconstructs, ibid. Glossy Chinese journal on life in China. (For a full list of Chinese English-language publications, write China Books and Periodicals.)

Eastern Horizon, 472 Hennessy Rd. (3rd fl.), Hong Kong. News on China.

Economics and Political Weekly, Skylark, 284 Frere Rd., Bombay, India.

The Eritrean Review, Eritrean Liberation Front, P.O. Box 9029, Beirut, Lebanon.

Facts and Reports, Angola Committee, Da Costastraat 88, Amsterdam, The Netherlands.

Far Eastern Affairs, Four Continents Book Corp., 149 5th Ave., New York, N.Y., 10010. Soviet journal of politics and culture of the Far East.

The Forward, P.O. Box 562, Times Square Station, New York, N.Y., 10036. Publication of the Revolutionary Marxist League of Jamaica.

Frontier, 61 Mott Lane, Calcutta-13, India.

Israeleft, P.O. Box 9013, Jerusalem, Israel. News and views of the left opposition.

Israel and Palestine, B.P. 130-110, 75463 Paris, Cedex 10, France. Socialist anti-Zionist.

Journal of Contemporary Asia, P.O. Box 49010, Stockholm 49, Sweden. Radical analyses of Asian affairs.

Latin America Working Group Letter, Box 6300, Station A, Toronto 1, Ontario, Canada.

Libero International, C.P.O. Box 1065, Kobe, Japan G50-91. Asian anarchism in English.

The Marxist Review, Ajit Roy, Mudranee 131 B, BB Gangaly St., Calcutta, India.

Minus 8, 180 Lockhart Rd. (1st fl.), Wanchai, Hong Kong.

New India Bulletin, P.O. Box 37, Westmount, Montreal, Quebec,

Canada. Publication of the Indian People's Association of North America (IPANA).

New Outlook, 8 Rechov Karl Netter, Tel Aviv, Israel. Progressive articles on Arab-Israeli *rapprochement.*

Peking Review, China Books and Periodicals, 125 5th Ave., New York, N.Y., 10003. Chinese journal analyzing national and international affairs.

Proletarian Correspondence, Datah-Sha, Shriashi Bldg., 2-11-2 Ikebukuro, Toshima-ku, Tokyo, Japan.

Shdemot, 10 Dubnov St., Tel Aviv, Israel. Journal of the Kibbutz movement.

Social Scientist, Indian School of Social Sciences, Trivandrum 695 001, India. Marxist social science journal.

Third World Forum, Box 685, Station C, Montreal, Quebec, Canada. Focuses on imperialism and liberation movements in the Third World.

Vietnam Courier, 46 Tran Hung Dao St., Hanoi, Vietnam. News on Vietnam.

Zimbabwe News, Dept. of Publicity and Information, Caixa Postal 743, Maputo, Mozambique. Publication of the Zimbabwe African National Union (ZANU).

II. LEFT NATIONAL NEWSPAPERS, NEWS AGENCIES (BOTH U.S. ONLY) AND JOURNALS (U.S., BRITAIN, AND CANADA) MAINLY ASSOCIATED WITH POLITICAL ORGANIZATIONS

(Major independent papers and newsjournals are preceded by an asterisk.)

Against the Grain, P.O. Box 692, Old Chelsea Station, New York, N.Y., 10011. Independent libertarian socialist newspaper focusing on rank-and-file struggles, particularly in New York.

The Black Panther, 8501 E. 14th St., Oakland, Ca., 94621. Publication of the Black Panther Party (BPP).

Blast Newspaper, P.O. Box 672, Spokane, Wash., 99219. Paper of the Youth International Party (YIP).

Bolshevik, P.O. Box 351, Bronx, N.Y., 10452. Publication of the Revolutionary Wing. (RW).

The Bond, World View Publishers, 46 W. 21st St., New York, N.Y., 10010. G.I. newspaper associated with the Workers' World Party (WWP).

Breakthrough, P.F.O.C., Box 40614, Station C, San Francisco, Ca., 94110. Journal of the Prairie Fire Organizing Committee (PFOC).

Burning Spear Newspaper, P.O. Box 12903, University Station, Gainesville, Fla., 32604. Publication of the African People's Socialist Party (APSP).

The Call, Box 5597, Chicago, Ill., 60680. Journal of the Communist Party–Marxist-Leninist (CP–ML), formerly October League (OL).

The Campaigner, 231 W. 29th St., New York, N.Y., 10001. Journal of the National Caucus of Labor Committees (U.S. Labor Party) (NCLC) (USLP).

The Catholic Worker, 36 E. 1st St., New York, N.Y., 10003. Catholic anarchist paper.

Challenge, Box 808, Brooklyn, N.Y., 11201. Progressive Labor Party newspaper (PLP).

Class Struggle, Box 4899, Baltimore, Md., 21211. Journal of the Lutte Ouvrière Group (LUG).

Common Sense, San Francisco Socialist Coalition, 2811 Mission St., San Francisco, Ca., 94111. Paper of the Northern California Alliance (NCA).

The Communist, P.O. Box 1297, Chicago, Ill. Publication of the Workers' Congress–Marxist-Leninist (WC–ML).

The Communist, P.O. Box 3486, Merchandise Mart, Chicago, Ill., 60654. Theoretical publication of the Revolutionary Communist Party (RCP).

Communist Viewpoint, 487 Adelaide St. West, Toronto, Ontario, Canada, M5V 1T4. Theoretical publication of the Canadian Communist Party (CPC).

Community Press Features, 2 Park Sq., Boston, Mass., 02116. Alternative news service specializing in graphics.

Critical Practice, 125 W. 17th St., New York, N.Y., 10011. Publication of the International Workers Party (IWP).

Cyffro: Change, A. Wilson, 4 Tudor St., Cardiff, Wales. Journal of the Welsh Committee of the Communist Party of Great Britain (CPGB).

Daily World, Long View Publishers, P.O. Box 544, New York, N.Y., 10011. Newspaper of the Communist Party (CPUSA).

The Elements, 1901 Q St., N.W., Washington, D.C., 20009. Independent socialist newspaper emphasizing environmental issues.

Getting Together, P.O. Box 26229, San Francisco, Ca., 94126. Paper of I Wor Kuen (IWK).

Grass Roots, 1065 31st St., N.W., Washington, D.C., 20007. People's Party newspaper (PP).

*The Guardian, 33 W. 17th St., New York, N.Y., 10011. Independent radical newsweekly with Marxist-Leninist orientation. Particularly good coverage of Third World struggles.

Hammer and Sickle, Workers and Oppressed Unite, 156 5th Ave. (Rm. 416), New York, N.Y., 10010. Publication of the Communist Cadre (CC).

Imprecor, Red Books, 97 Caledonian Rd., London N1, England. Information organ of the United Secretariat of the Fourth International (USFI).

In These Times, 1509 N. Milwaukee Ave., Chicago, Ill., 60622. Independent socialist weekly. Multi-tendency; contains many excellent columns.

Industrial Worker, 752 W. Webster, Chicago, Ill., 60614. Newspaper of the Industrial Workers of the World (IWW).

Intercontinental Press, P.O. Box 116, Village Station, New York, N.Y., 10014. International newsjournal of the Socialist Workers' Party (SWP).

International, 97 Caledonian Rd., London N1. Quarterly journal of the British International Marxist Group (IMG).

International Bulletin, P.O. Box 4400, Berkeley, Ca., 94704. Alternative news service.

International Socialism, 6 Cotton Gardens, London E2 8DN, England. Journal of the Socialist Workers' Party of Great Britain (SWPGB), formerly International Socialists (IS).

International Socialist Review, 14 Charles Lane, New York, N.Y., 10014. Journal of the Socialist Workers' Party (SWP).

International Worker, 125 W. 17th St., New York, N.Y. Paper of the International Workers Party (IWP).

Internationalism, P.O. Box 961, New York, N.Y., 10027. Publication of the International Communist Current (ICC) in the U.S.

Keep Strong, 1222 W. Wilson Ave., Chicago, Ill., 60640. Publication of the Intercommunal Survival Committee (ISC).

Liberation News Service (LNS), 17 W. 17th St., New York, N.Y., 10011. Alternative news service.

Marxism Today, Central Books Ltd., 37 Gray's Inn Rd., London WC1, England. Theoretical journal of the Communist Party of Great Britain (CPGB).

The Militant, 14 Charles Lane, New York, N.Y., 10014. Socialist Workers' Party newspaper (SWP).

Moving On, 1643 N. Milwaukee, Chicago, Ill., 60647. Publication of the New American Movement (NAM).

New America, 275 7th Ave., New York, N.Y. Social Democrats--U.S.A. newspaper (SD-USA).

News and Letters, 1900 E. Jefferson, Detroit, Mich., 48207. News and Letters (Marxist humanist) newspaper.

Newsletter of the Democratic Left, 125 W. 77th St., New York, N.Y., 10024. Democratic Socialist Organizing Committee (DSOC).

October, C.P. 364, Station Place d'Armes, Montreal, Quebec, Canada. Publication of the Canadian Communist League–Marxist-Leninist (CCL–ML).

The Open Road, Box 6135, Station G. Vancouver, British Columbia, Canada, V6R 465. Impressive anarchist paper.

The Organizer, Box 11768, Philadelphia, Pa., 19101. Newspaper of the Philadelphia Workers' Organizing Committee (PWOC).

Osawatomie, no address. Organ of the Weather Underground.

Pacific News Service, 604 Mission St. (Rm. 1001), San Francisco, Ca., 94105. Alternative news service.

People's Tribune, Box 170, Brooklyn, N.Y. Communist Labor Party (CLP).

People's World, 1819 10th St., Berkeley, Ca., 94710. Newspaper oriented to the Communist Party (CPUSA).

Political Affairs, 23 W. 26th St., New York, N.Y., 10010. Theoretical journal of the Communist Party (CPUSA).

PL Magazine, Box 808, Brooklyn, N.Y., 11201. Journal of the Progressive Labor Party (PLP).

Prairie Fire, P.O. Box 5246, San Francisco, Ca., 94101. Journal of the Prairie Fire Organizing Committee (PFOC).

Proletarian Unity, 4933 de Grand Pre, Montreal, Quebec, Canada. Publication of "the Marxist-Leninist group, In Struggle (IS)."

Proletariat, Workers Press, P.O. Box 3774, Chicago, Ill., 60654. Journal of the Communist Labor Party (CLP).

The Real World, P.O. Box 21093, Washington, D.C., 20009. Publication of the Marathon Group.

The Rebel Worker, 625 Post St., (869), San Francisco, Ca., 94109. Publication of the League for Proletarian Socialism (LPS).

Red Banner, P.O. Box 32026, Los Angeles, Ca., 90032. Journal of the August Twenty-Ninth Movement–Marxist-Leninist (ATM–ML).

Red Flag, Box 3503, Hollywood, Ca., 90028. Newspaper of the Red Flag Union (RFU).

Resistance, Box 513, Triboro Station, New York, N.Y., 10035. Paper of the League for Proletarian Revolution–Marxist-Leninist (LPR–ML).

Revolution, P.O. Box 3486, Merchandise Mart, Chicago, Ill., 60654. Theoretical journal of the Revolutionary Communist Party (RCP), formerly Revolutionary Union (RU).

Revolutionary Cause, P.O. Box 32026, Los Angeles, Ca., 90032. Paper of the August Twenty-Ninth Movement–Marxist-Leninist (ATM–ML).

Revolutionary Communist Papers, Publications Distribution Coop., 27

Clerkenwell Close, London EC1R 0AT, England. Journal of the Revolutionary Communist Tendency (RCT) of Great Britain.

*Seven Days, 206 5th Ave., New York, N.Y., 10011. Independent socialist newsweekly. Glossy attempt to become the *Time/Newsweek* of the left.

Socialist Action, 170 Broadway (Rm. 201), New York, N.Y., 10038. Newspaper of the League for the Revolutionary Party (LRP).

Socialist Appeal, P.O. Box 831, New York, N.Y., 10008. Publication of the Trotskyist Organizing Committee (TOC).

The Socialist Republic, P.O. Box 825, Madison Square Station, New York, N.Y., 10010. Newspaper of the League for Socialist Reconstruction (LSR).

Socialist Standard, Publications Distribution Coop., 27 Clerkenwell Close, London EC1R 0AT, England. Journal of the Socialist Party of Great Britain (SPGB).

Socialist Tribune, 1012 N. 3rd St. (Suite 217), Milwaukee, Wisc., 53203. Newspaper of the Socialist Party (SP).

Socialist Voice, 170 Broadway (Rm. 201), New York, N.Y., 10038. Journal of the League for the Revolutionary Party (LRP).

Socialist Worker, P.O. Box 18037, Cleveland, Ohio, 44118. Paper of the International Socialist Organization (ISO).

Spark, P.O. Box 1336, Boston, Mass., 02104. Newspaper of the Party for Workers' Power (PWP).

The Spark, Box 4899, Baltimore, Md., 21211. Newspaper of the Lutte Ouvriere Group (LUG).

SRA Federation Bulletin for Anarchist Agitators, Box 4091, Mt. View, Ca., 94040. Organ of the Socialist Revolutionary Anarchist Federation (SRAF).

Stand Up, P.O. Box 10272, Eugene, Oregon, 97401. "Workers newspaper."

Strategy, Box 419, Audubon Station, New York, N.Y., 10032. Journal of the Committee for Socialist Organizing (CSO).

Synthesis, 625 Post St. (869), San Francisco, Ca., 94109. Journal of the League for Proletarian Socialism (LPS).

The Torch, 13755 Woodward Ave. (Rm. 200), Highland Park, Mich., 48203. Publication of the Revolutionary Socialist League (RSL).

Tribune, 24 St. John St., London EC1, England. Unofficial paper of the British Labour Party's Left.

Tricontinental News Service, 30 E. 20th St., New York, N.Y. Radical Third World news service.

Union W.A.G.E. (Women's Alliance to Gain Equality), P.O. Box 462, Berkeley, Ca., 94701. Independent socialist newspaper about working women and their fight to organize.

Unite, Box 8041, Chicago, Ill., 60680. Newspaper of the Marxist-Leninist Organizing Committee (MLOC).

United Labor Action, 167 W. 21st St., New York, N.Y., 10010. Independent socialist newspaper focusing on workers' struggles.

Unity and Struggle, P.O. Box 1181, Newark, N.J. Newspaper of the Revolutionary Communist League–Marxist-Leninist (RCL–ML).

The Urban Guerrilla, P1R-1, 423 Oak St., San Francisco, Ca., 94102. Publication of the World Liberation Front (WLF).

The Weekly People, Dept. 3C, 914 Industrial Ave., Palo Alto, Ca., 94303. Newspaper of the Socialist Labor Party (SLP).

Western Socialist, 295 Huntington Ave., Boston, Mass., 02115. Organ of the World Socialist Party (WSP).

Workers' Advocate, Box 11942 Ft. Dearborn Station, Chicago, Ill., 60611. Publication of the Central Organization of U.S. Marxists-Leninists (COUSM-L).

Workers' Power, 14131 Woodward Ave., Highland Park, Mich., 48203. Newspaper of the International Socialists (IS).

Workers' Vanguard, G.P.O. Box 1377, New York, N.Y., 10001. Newspaper of the Spartacist League (SL).

Workers' Viewpoint, 43 W. 28th St., New York, N.Y., 10001. Publication of Workers' Viewpoint (WV).

Workers' World, World View Publishers Inc., 46 W. 21st St., New York, N.Y., 10010. Newspaper of the Workers' World Party (WWP).

World Marxist Review, 487 Adelaide St. W., Toronto, Ontario, Canada M5V IT4. Publication of the Canadian Communist Party.

The Yipster Times, 9 Bleecker St., New York, N.Y., 10012. Anarchist.

Zodiac News Service, 950 Howard St., San Francisco, Ca., 94103. Alternate news service.

Besides newspapers and journals, most of the political organizations listed above also publish pamphlets and occasionally books. There are also many left political groups, of course, which only publish pamphlets and are not included in this list.

To the comrade who supplies the sorely needed guide to and through these left groups, this section of our bibliography is humbly dedicated.

III. RESOURCES: PAMPHLETS, BOOKS, FILMS, TAPES, COMICS, BIBLIOGRAPHIES, GAMES, SONGS, ETC.—CHIEFLY U.S.

Africa Information Service, 244 W. 27th St., New York, N.Y., 10001. Slide shows, tapes, publications on African liberation movements and independent Africa.

Alternative America, Box 134, Harvard Sq., Cambridge, Mass., 02138. Alternative resources and organizations listed by community.

Alternative Press Directory, Alternative Press Syndicate, Box 777, New York, N.Y., 10003. Good source for local underground papers.

Alternative Press Index, P.O. Box 7229, Baltimore, Md., 21218. Indexes articles from about a third of the publications listed in this bibliography.

Alternatives in Print, 1977-78, Glide Publishers, 330 Ellis St., San Francisco, Ca., 94102. Somewhat weak in the areas covered by this bibliography, but still impressive.

American Women: Our Lives and Labor, Feminist Theory Collective, University of Oregon, Eugene, Oregon, 97403. Annotated bibliography.

Americans for a Working Economy, Box 19530, Washington, D.C., 20036. Moderately left information materials on our malfunctioning economy.

Appalachian Press, P.O. Box 8074, Huntington, W. Va., 25705. Pamphlets on Appalachian struggles.

Black and Red, Box 9546, Detroit, Mich., 48202. Pamphlets and books on workers' struggle and Marxist theory.

Bread and Roses Mail Order Catalogue, 1724 20th St., N.W., Washington, D.C., 20009. Selection of political records.

Carrier Pigeon, 88 Fisher Ave., Boston, Mass., 02120. Distribution network for small radical publications.

Center for Cuban Studies, 220 E. 23rd St., New York, N.Y., 10010. Library of books, slides, films on Cuban affairs.

China Books and Periodicals, 125 5th Ave., New York, N.Y., 10003. Wide range of materials on China and good selection of American and foreign Marxist-Leninist publications.

Class Struggle: A Socialist Board Game for Kids from Eight to Eighty, c/o B. Ollman, Dept. of Politics, N.Y.U., Washington Square, N.Y., 10003. A fun way of introducing young people to the workings of capitalism and the importance of thinking in terms of class.

Class War Comix, Epic Productions, 76 Peckham Rd., London SE5, England.

Communist Manifesto Comic Book, by Marx, Engels, and Rius (Mexican cartoonist), c/o Quixote Magazine, 153 E. Gilman, Madison, Wisc., 53703. Brilliantly done. Provides an excellent introduction to Marxism for high schoolers and college undergraduates. Don't miss this one.

Counter Course: A Handbook for Course Criticism, ed. by Trevor

Pateman (Penguin Books, 1972). Contains useful radical bibliographies on a wide range of topics.

Cut Cane Associates, P.O. Box 98, Mineral Bluffs, Georgia, 30559. Pamphlets on practical problems of organizing.

Edcentric, P.O. Box 10085, Eugene, Oregon, 97401. Issue no. 38 is an educational resource guide.

Education Exploration Center, 3104-16th Ave. S., Minneapolis, Minn., 55407. Newsletter, pamphlets, and directories on alternate education.

Exploratory Project for Economic Alternatives, 2000 P St., N.W. (Suite 515), Washington, D.C., 20036. Publishes studies offering concrete socialist alternatives to current government policy in various areas.

Films for Social Change, 22 W. 83rd St., New York, N.Y., 10024. As it says.

Film Programmer's Guide to 16mm Rentals, Reel Research, Box 6037, Albany, Ca. Second edition lists over 10,000 titles.

Freespace Alternate U., 339 Lafayette St., New York, N.Y., 10002. Included among its resources and services are a bibliography of anarchist periodicals and a "walking tour of radical N.Y."

Friends of Malatesta, Bidwell Station, Buffalo, N.Y., 14222. Anarchist pamphlets.

Frog in the Well, 669 Lytton St., Palo Alto, Ca., 94301. Pamphlets, mostly anarchist.

From Radical Left to Extreme Right, by R.H. Muller et al. (Ann Arbor, 1970). Annotated bibliography. Somewhat out of date, but meaty for those periodicals covered.

FUD: Free University Directory and *Directory of Free Universities and Experimental Colleges*, Edcentric, P.O. Box 10085, Eugene, Oregon, 97401. The Marxist Education Collective (one of four free universities in the Greenwich Village area of New York) also keeps a list of such institutions. Write P.O. Box 560, Old Chelsea Station, New York, N.Y., 10011.

Gilman Street Books, 420 W. Gilman St., Madison, Wisc. Perhaps the best radical book store in the country, with the biggest selection of radical journals and papers. Offers consulting services to other radical bookstores on problems of organization and distribution.

Grasping Revolutionary Theory: A Guide for Marxist-Leninist Study Groups (pamphlet), by Irwin Silber, *The Guardian*, 33 W. 17th St., New York, N.Y., 10011. What it says.

The Great Atlantic Radio Conspiracy, 2743 Maryland Ave., Baltimore, Md., 21218. Large catalogue of radical radio tapes.

Guide for Alternate Periodicals, Sunspark Press, P.O. Box 6341, St. Petersburg, Fla., 33736. Rather better on the counterculture than on the political left.

Guide to the American Left, U.S. Directory Service, P.O. Box 1832, Kansas City, Missouri, 64141.

Guide to Marxist Philosophy: An Introductory Bibliography, ed. J.M. Bochenski et al. (Chicago: Swallow Press, 1972). Very introductory and strongest on works by anti-Marxists.

Haymarket Revisited, Illinois Labor History Society, Box 914, Chicago, Ill., 60690. A walk and drive tour of sights associated with the Haymarket affair of 1886, and a model of how to bring radical local history to life.

The History Book, c/o Tri-Continental Film Center, 333 Sixth Ave., New York, N.Y., 10014. A three-and-a-half-hour cartoon history of capitalism as told by a rat, in color. Excellent.

Human Rights Organizations and Periodicals Directory, ed. D. Christiano (Berkeley, Ca.: Meiklejohn Civil Liberties Institute, 1977).

Imported Publications, Inc., 320 W. Ohio St., Chicago, Ill., 60610. English-language books and pamphlets published in the Soviet Union and Eastern Europe.

Indochina Solidarity Committee, Box C, Old Chelsea Station, New York, N.Y., 10011. Publishes magazines, newsletters, and pamphlets dealing with Indochina.

Institute for Workers' Control, 45 Gamble St., Forest Rd. West, Nottingham, England. Books and pamphlets.

Insurgent Sociologist, Dept. of Sociology, University of Oregon, Eugene, Oregon, 97403. Spring 1978 issue is supposed to be devoted to bibliographies in the social sciences.

Interaction Center, 1500 Farragut St., N.W., Washington, D.C., 20011. Bibliography and alternative resources on Third World.

International Publishers, 381 Park Ave. South, New York, N.Y., 10016. Publishes the largest selection of works by Marx and Engels.

Karl Marx: Selected Writings, ed. by David McLellan (Oxford University Press, 1977). Contains annotated bibliography of the more important commentaries on Marxism in English, as well as of the various English-language editions of Marx's writings.

League for Economic Democracy, P.O. Box 1858, San Pedro, Ca., 90733. Pamphlets on socialism, especially workers' control.

Liberation Support Movement Information Center, P.O. Box 2077, Oakland, Ca., 94604. Provides various materials on liberation movements, particularly in Africa.

Living Library Corporation, P.O. Box 5405, London Hill Station, Flushing, N.Y., 11354. Wide selection of radical tapes.

The Little Red School Book, by S. Hansen and J. Jensen (New York: Pocket Books, 1971). What every adolescent should know about self and society clearly and cogently laid out.

Madison Area Committee on Southern Africa (MACSA), 731 State St., Madison, Wis., 53703. Radical pamphlets and other materials.

Marx for Beginners, by Rius, Writers and Readers Cooperative, 233a Kentish Town Rd., London NW5, England. Cartoon book on Marx's life and concepts.

Marxism and Aesthetics, by Lee Baxandall (New York: Humanities Press, 1968). Book-length annotated bibliography.

Marxism and History, by L.M. Manly and E. Wangerman (London: Lawrence and Wishart, 1967). Bibliography.

Marxism and the Mass Media, Research Project of the International Mass Media Research Center (IMMRC), P.O. Box 350, New York, N.Y., 10013. A bibliography of Marxist writings on the media in several languages.

Marxism and the Study of Antiquity, by Robert Padgug, *Arethusa* (Spring 1975). Annotated bibliography.

Marxism Versus Sociology, by Martin Shaw (London: Pluto Press, 1974). Annotated bibliography.

Marxist Philosophy: A Bibliographical Guide, by John Lacks (North Carolina Press, 1967).

Marxist Readings, Critique Livres, 173 avenue de la Dhuys, 93170 Bagnolet, France. Bibliography of Marxist works in English, German, and Italian.

Midwest Academy, 600 W. Fullerton Ave., Chicago, Ill. Pamphlets on organizing.

Monthly Review Press, 62 W. 14th St., New York, N.Y., 10011. America's premier publisher of Marxist books.

National Action Research on the Military Industrial Complex (NARMIC), 112 S. 16th St., Philadelphia, Pa., 19102. Pamphlets and other materials.

National Labor Federation, 200 W. 20th St., New York, N.Y., 10011. Pamphlets on organizing.

National Lawyers Guild, 853 Broadway, New York, N.Y., 10003. Radical pamphlets, newsletters, and other materials related to the law.

New England Free Press, 60 Union Square, Somerville, Mass., 02143. Publishers of one of the largest and most diversified collections of radical pamphlets.

New Hogtown Press, 12 Hart House Circle, University of Toronto, Toronto, Ontario, Canada. Big selection of pamphlets on socialism, emphasizing Canadian and Chinese themes.

New Left Books (subsidiary of *New Left Review*), c/o Humanities Press, Inc., 171 First Ave., Atlantic Highlands, N.J., 07716. Socialist publisher and book club noted for important theoretical works.

New Outlook, 205 W. 19th St. (9th fl.), New York, N.Y., 10011. Large variety of CPUSA pamphlets.

New World Coalition, 419 Boylston St. (Rm. 209), Boston, Mass., 02116. Radical tapes and transparencies, including one on Paulo Freire's teaching methods.

New World Resource Center, 2546 N. Halstead, Chicago, Ill., 60614. Radical pamphlets and other materials on Africa.

New York Labor News, 116 Wassau St., Brooklyn, N.Y., 11201. Variety of Socialist Labor Party pamphlets on Marxism and socialism.

News from Neasden, 22 Fleet Rd., London NW3 2QS, England. A catalogue of new radical publications.

Non-Intervention in Chile (NICH), P.O. Box 800, Berkeley, Ca., 94701. Newsletter, slide shows, and other information on Chile.

North American Committee on Latin America (NACLA), Box 57, Cathedral Station, New York, N.Y., 10025. Publishes wide assortment of radical materials, including a journal, on Latin America and imperialism generally.

Ohio Newsreel, P.O. Box 19241, Cincinnati, Ohio, 45219. Big selection of radical films.

Organizers Book Center, P.O. Box 21066, Washington, D.C., 20009. Books and pamphlets on organizing.

Other Voices: Black, Chicano, and American Indian Press, by Sharon Murphy, from Pflaum/Standard, 38 W. 5th St., Dayton, Ohio, 45402. Annotated Bibliography.

Paladin Press, Box 1307, Boulder, Colorado, 80302. Books and pamphlets on guerrilla warfare.

Paredon Records, Box 889, Brooklyn, N.Y., 11202. Radical records, songs, talks.

The Partisan Press, Bertrand Russell House, Gamble St., Nottingham N67 4ET, England. Pamphlets on socialism, emphasizing workers' control issues.

Pathfinder Press, 410 West St., New York, N.Y., 10014. Socialist Workers Party books and pamphlets. Largest selection of works by Trotsky.

Peaceful Alternatives Information Services, Box 841-N, Winon, Montana, 55987. Anarchist materials.

People Power, 7325 Humbolt Ave. S., Minneapolis, Minn., 55423. Bibliography of government and private agencies, international groups and other organizations, listing the services of each.

People's Business Commission (formerly People's Bicentennial Commission), 1346 Conn. Ave., N.W. (Rm. 1025), Washington, D.C., 20036. Pamphlets emphasizing a radical interpretation of American history.

People's Press, 2680 21st St., San Francisco, Ca., 94110. Radical pamphlets and other materials.

Periodicals on the Socialist Countries and on Marxism: A New Annotated Index of English Language Publications, by H.G. Shaffer (New York: Praeger, 1977). Particularly good on the numerous English-language publications of the Soviet bloc countries.

Political Change: A Film Guide, Audio Visual Library Service, University of Minnesota, 3300 University Ave., S.E., Minneapolis, Minn., 55414. Contains reviews of films on economic and political issues.

Popular Economics Press, 5A Putnam St., Somerville, Mass., 02143. Good introductory pamphlets on radical economics.

Public Citizen, P.O. Box 19404, Washington, D.C., 20036. For bibliography of Nader study-group reports and other Nader-influenced investigations.

Publications Distribution Cooperative, 27 Clerkenwell Close, London EC1R 0AT, England. Just what it says for numerous socialist journals and newspapers.

Radical Africana: Bibliography, c/o Chris Allen, Centre of African Studies, 40 George Square, Edinburgh, Scotland.

Radical Women, 3815 Fifth Ave., N.E., Seattle, Wash., 98105. Radical women's liberation pamphlets.

Radio Free People, 133 Mercer St., New York, N.Y., 10012. Radical tapes.

Red Shadow: The Economics Rock and Roll Band, The Physical World, P.O. Box 125, Cambridge, Mass., 02140. Marxist lyrics to a rock and roll beat—literate and fun.

Research Group One, 2743 Maryland Ave., Baltimore, Md., 21218. Wide range of radical pamphlets. Excellent bibliography on anarchism.

Resource Manual for a Living Revolution, by V. Coover et al. (New York: New Society Press, 1977). Collection of "specific skills that can facilitate the transition to a new society."

Resources for Community Change, Box 21066, Washington, D.C., 20009. Pamphlets, especially on organizing.

The Review of Radical Political Economics, c/o URPE, 41 Union Square West (Rm. 901), New York, N.Y., 10003. The December

1971 issue consists of two volumes of "Reading Lists in Radical Political Economics," as do the Summer 1974 and Winter 1977 issues. The Spring 1974 issue is devoted to a bibliography of works relevant to a socialist reconstruction of America. The Summer 1974 issue contains more reading lists in radical political economics. The Winter 1975 issue is a special issue devoted to radical teaching. In short, URPE offers a model of what a radical publication can do to help its teacher-readers.

Rising Free, 197 Kings Cross Rd., London WC1, England. Wide variety of radical pamphlets, including some of the early Marxist works of Wilhelm Reich.

Science for the People Study Group, c/o Progressive Technology Co., P.O. Box 20049, Tallahassee, Fla., 32304. For a radical bibliography of journals on science and technology.

Sojourner Truth Organization, P.O. Box 8493, Chicago, Ill., 60680. Pamphlets, particularly on racism.

South End Press, P.O. Box 68, Astor Station, Boston, Mass., 02123. Publishes a wide range of radical books of particular interest to movement groups, and a newsletter dialoguing with readers of these books.

Taking Off, Center for Alternatives in/to Higher Education, 1118 S. Harrison Rd., East Lansing, Mich., 48823. Organizational and resource guide for nontraditional higher education.

Third World Newsreel, 26 W. 20th St., New York, N.Y., 10011.

Times Change Press, 62 W. 14th St., New York, N.Y., 10011. Radical books and pamphlets.

Tricontinental Film Center (See *The History Book* above). Big selection of radical films.

Underhanded History of the U.S.A. Comic Book, by Nick Thorkelson and Jim O'Brien (Boston: New England Free Press). Excellent.

Union Maids, New Day Films, P.O. Box 315, Franklin Lakes, N.J., 07417. Brilliantly made film on the union struggles of three socialist heroines.

United Front Press, P.O. Box 40099, San Francisco, Ca. Radical pamphlets and other materials.

The University-Military-Police Complex, NACLA (see above). Somewhat out of date but still very useful.

Urban Planning Aid, Inc., 639 Massachusetts Ave., Cambridge, Mass., 02139. Pamphlets on urban questions.

Voices of the Third World, 853 Broadway (Rm. 1422), New York, N.Y., 10003. Speakers' bureau for Third World and U.S. national movements.

War Resisters League, 339 Lafayette St., New York, N.Y., 10012. Newsletter, books, pamphlets.

West End Press, P.O. Box 697, Cambridge, Ma., 02139. Marxist press focusing on literary works, old and new.

The Woman's Press, 280 Bloor St. W. (Suite 305), Toronto, Ontario, Canada. Pamphlets.

Women's History Research Center, Inc., 2325 Oak St., Berkeley, Ca., 94708. Useful archives on various aspects of socialism and the women's movement.

Women's Liberation and Revolution: A Bibliography, by Sheila Rowbotham (Old Westbury, N.Y.: Feminist Press).

The Women's Work Project, Box 462, Silver Spring, Md., 20907. Pamphlets on organizing.

World View Publishers, 46 W. 21st St., New York, N.Y., 10010. Wide assortment of pamphlets by the Workers World Party.

Who Rules the Universities?, by David N. Smith (New York: Monthly Review Press, 1974). Other useful studies on this subject include, *Who Rules Columbia?* (New York: NACLA, 1968); *Newt's Guide to C.U.N.Y.*, Newt Davidson Collective, P.O. Box 1034, Manhattanville Station, New York, N.Y., 10027; *N.Y.U. INC.*, c/o B. Ollman, Dept. of Politics, New York University, Washington Square, New York, N.Y., 10003.

Young Socialist, c/o Edith Findlay, 50 Dunglass Sq., East Mains, East Kilbride, Glasgow, Scotland G74 4EN. A magazine for children aged five to eleven.

Youth Liberation Press, 2007 Washtenaw Ave., Ann Arbor, Mich., 48104. Pamphlets and other materials relating to young people's liberation, including an excellent manual on how to organize in high schools.